THE ARTIST'S TAX WORKBOOK FOR 1990

For Visual, Performing, and Literary Artists,
and Other Self-Employed Professionals

Carla Messman

Lyons & Burford, Publishers

Printed in the United States of America

10 9 8 7 6 5 4 3 2 1

Library of Congress Cataloging-in-Publication Data

Messman, Carla.
  The artist's tax workbook.
  Includes bibliographical references.
    1. Artists—Taxation—Law and legislation—
United States. 2. Self-employed—Taxation—Law and
legislation—United States. 3. Income tax—Law and
legislation—United States. I. Title.
KF6369.8.A7M47   1990   343.7305′26   89-13932
ISBN 1-55821-053-9   347.303526

About the Sponsors— Resources & Counseling/United Arts

The Artists' Tax Workbook by Carla Messman was published from 1985 to 1989 by Resources & Counseling/United Arts under the title *The Art of Filing.* Those editions were also written by Messman, a St. Paul tax preparer who specializes in working with artists and arts organizations.

Resources & Counseling, itself a nonprofit organization, conducts workshops and provides counseling and information to artists and nonprofit arts managers on business and management topics. The Twin Cities-based agency took on publishing a tax book for artists and other independent professionals for two reasons: to fill the gap left when the Volunteer Lawyers for the Arts stopped publishing a similar book, *Fear of Filing,* and as a project to generate earned income.

Messman had published her own tax workbook in 1984, which led to her teaching workshops on taxes and recordkeeping for Resources & Counseling, which finally led to the publishing collaboration with R&C. Mariann Johnson was instrumental to the entire publication process of *The Art of Filing* during her tenure as Artists' Services Manager at Resources & Counseling from 1985–89. R&C, as sponsor of *The Artists' Tax Workbook,* still promotes and markets the books to nonprofit organizations and individual artists.

Contents

PART I
The Business of Being an Artist

PART II
Your 1989 Tax Return

PART III
Appendices

List of Figures

List of Forms and Schedules

Preface to the 1990 Edition

Six years have passed since this book was first published as *The 1984 Tax Workbook for Artists and Other Self-Employed Persons*. In those six years, two major tax reforms have occurred, accompanied by numerous pieces of new legislation fine-tuning existing legislation and an avalanche of regulations interpreting what all that legislation—old and new—means when it comes down to the individual taxpayer.

Keeping up with these tax-law changes has stretched the workload of tax accountants, strained the Internal Revenue Service's ability to provide professional collection services, and left taxpayers exhausted, bewildered, and sometimes downright ornery. Paying taxes is never fun, and many of the changes appeared, at first blush, to be more harmful than helpful.

The most recent reform, the Tax Reform Act (TRA) of 1986, represents the coming of age of computer reporting and tracking and the automated collection of tax revenues. The IRS now knows so much about the average taxpayer, it's legitimate to ask why many people even need to go to the bother of filing a tax return.

Then there are the "nonaverage" taxpayers, consisting these days primarily of small-business operators and sole proprietors. The IRS knows next to nothing about them, although it's eager to learn more. Most artists fall into this "nonaverage" category in more ways than one.

Be that as it may, it's become more important than ever for artists to understand what the IRS is about, and what can and can't be deducted, and what kinds of records you're expected to keep as a small-businessperson. The purpose of this book is to take your activities and document them via an evolutionary path through books and recordkeeping to a finished tax return that can stand up to IRS audit. Another purpose of this book is to educate you about business by demystifying some of the terms businesspeople throw around, by identifying in plain terms some of the options you have for reducing your tax load, and by empowering you to use your art to support yourself.

You have to promise some things in return. First, you must be prepared to spend some time with this book. It's not a book you pick up and read from cover to cover. Rather, it's a book with parts that will come in handy at one time or another throughout the year, and in years to come. If it's March 20, 1990, and you're desperate to file your 1989 tax return, go directly to Part II and the explanation of how to file your 1989 tax return. It's too late to do your books for 1989. Resolve, instead, to do your books for 1990 as soon as you finish the 1989 tax return. Or if it's the end of 1990 and you still don't have books set up, turn to Part I for some guidance and examples. Get yourself ready for the tax-preparation session coming up in a few months.

Let's assume you have books on your business and you know what your tax liability is likely to be for 1989—ugh! What can you do about it? Use the "Answers to Frequently-Asked Tax Questions" section to investigate IRA, SEP Plan, and Keogh Plan options to reduce your tax bill in a sensible way.

Second, be prepared to spend more time on the business aspects of your art activities. It's no longer enough for an accountant to bail you out of trouble at tax time. You must pursue your art as a business and run it as a business or revert to the status of hobbyist. The IRS won't show you any special consideration because you're an artist. You're not showing your art much consideration if you don't give yourself a chance to be (financially) good at it.

Third, reporting requirements are being stringently enforced, with penalties automatically levied for late filing. This fact pertains not only to tax returns but also to information returns you are required to file if you hire independent contractors or pay rent to an individual on your studio.

Finally, completing a tax return takes time. The forms are more condensed and more complicated. For 1989, one of them (Form 8582, for rental property losses) has four attached worksheets. Taxes have become more just and more complicated. Do not leave tax preparation to the last moment.

On the positive side, income taxes are generally lower than they were six years ago. For self-employed people, the overall decrease in the tax rates has been offset by an increase in the Social Security tax. This increase will continue until the distinction between the self-employment rate (13.02 percent in 1989) is equivalent to the combined employer-employee share (15.30 percent in 1990). Expect relief on the 1990 Schedule C when sole proprietors can deduct part of their Social Security tax directly on Schedule C. Also, if you have children, you will feel the special advantages given to families in the 1986 tax reform. Within six years, the personal exemption has doubled, and the earned income credit expanded by 150 percent. Whatever aggravations you face in preparing yourself to complete the 1989 tax forms, rest assured you're dealing with a system that, in the aggregate, is the fairest tax system seen in the past forty years.

You likely were drawn to this book because you needed help in sorting out your tax problems. But as you become familiar with it, begin to turn what all Americans dread as the great spring exorcism into something positive for you—a chronicling, a documentation of your year in the arts community. You owe it to yourself to give your art every chance to support you. That's what this book is all about.

Introduction: A Note on How To Use this Workbook

The *Artist's Tax Workbook for 1990* has been totally revised and updated to make it easier to use as a tax-return preparation guide and as an ongoing source of tax and recordkeeping advice.

Part I considers the various aspects of recordkeeping. It describes several ways to set up and keep books. For more established businesses, the use of books as business tools is explained in detail. A separate section on the reporting requirements for self-employed individuals reflects the importance now placed on timely reporting by the Internal Revenue Service.

Part II describes most of the forms you will need to complete your 1989 tax return. Background and explanatory material is relegated to the Glossary or to the Quick Guide to Deductibility for a cleaner description of how each form is completed. Also, in response to reader feedback, there are more examples of completed forms, along with several examples of how finished returns might look. To the extent possible, given the many conflicting regulations at the state level, some guidelines on preparation of state income tax returns are also included.

Use the Glossary of Terms for definitions of words and phrases frequently used in the tax and finance area. The glossary also provides information on some tax strategies and options. Answers to Frequently Asked Tax Questions is expanded from the previous year. The Quick Guide to Deductibility is updated with further information about automobiles and depreciation, two of the most complicated facets of the 1989 tax return.

The Guide to Further Reading suggests where to go from here as you educate yourself about the business aspects of your art activities. The Index provides easy access to the topics discussed throughout the book.

As before, I welcome your comments and inquiries. Please write to me in care of Lyons & Burford, Publishers, 31 West 21 Street, New York, New York 10010.

PART I
The Business of Being an Artist

1
Receipts and Recordkeeping

The key to managing your business well is keeping good records. Keeping good records means keeping track of income and expenses so you know reliably what you earned and what you spent during the year.

Anyone who runs a business needs to distinguish clearly between business and personal items. Business items include:

1. Income from the sale of a product or a service on which no tax has been withheld. Examples: sale of a painting at a sidewalk art fair; commission you receive from a gallery; honorarium for a talk at a professional meeting; payment for typesetting a theatre program; fee for a professional installation.

2. Expenditures you incurred while making that income that generate paper receipts. Examples: purchase of art supplies from a local dealer; fee paid for parking at a ramp.

3. Expenditures you incurred while making that income that do not generate paper receipts. Examples: coins put in a parking meter; cash payments (stay away from these!); rental payments; payments for services.

4. Payments made to other individuals in the course of generating income.

The bulk of your records relate to your personal life. They are payments for health care, payments on charge accounts and installment loans, rent or mortgage payments, a paycheck from your regular job, telephone bills, and so on. Some of these items may have a bearing on your business (your rent or mortgage payment, for example, if you have an office in the home), but they are primarily personal. Good recordkeeping starts with a clear distinction between the business and personal facets of your life.

Every month you receive bills. One may be a telephone bill, another a credit card statement or a renewal notice on your health or auto insurance. You tear off part of the form and mail it with your check by a certain date. At certain times every month (usually around the first) you make payments previously scheduled by virtue of leases or mortgages or installment plans. Usually you have a coupon to send with the payment, but no other bill is sent. If you are employed, you receive one or more paychecks every month. You tear off the check stub and cash the check. The expenditures and income described here are personal. They are necessary to run your life but are not directly related to being in business for yourself. As a person who has a personal life in addition to a business life, you need to track income and expenses for both.

For both personal and business items, start the tracking the same way: Pick a central location where you can store receipts and records temporarily. Pay a credit card bill; put the "customer's receipt" in a manila folder or an envelope or a drawer along with the rest of your personal receipts. Pick up your paycheck; put the check stub in the same folder or envelope or drawer. The key is to have a record repository in a convenient and consistent place so records are stored there as soon as payment is made or received—that is, as soon as the transaction is complete.

Use the same system, but a separate repository, for your business expenses and income. Go to an art store and buy four brushes and some canvas; put the receipt in a separate manila folder or envelope or drawer along with the rest of your business receipts. Receive a check for seventy-five dollars for moderating a panel of judges; tear off the stub (or make a separate note if there is no stub), cash the check, and put the stub or note in that same folder or envelope or drawer.

You now have separate locations for personal and business records. What do you do then? Leave the personal records alone until the end of the year. Personal records are easier to manage. While they may outdo business records in sheer volume, most of them are summarized annually. For a credit card, the first statement of the year tells you what you paid in interest for the previous year. Homeowners receive before January 31 a statement from their mortgage companies summarizing mortgage interest, property taxes, insurance payments, and payments to principal for the previous year. Income from a regular job is summarized on a W-2 form. If you are part of a limited partnership, you receive a Form K-1 early in the year summarizing last year's tax consequences of the partnership for you. Bank interest on checking and savings accounts is reported to you via Form 1099-INT; earnings from mutual funds are reported on Form 1099-DIV. If you sell stock during the year, you receive a Form 1099-B early the following year to remind you to report the proceeds of that sale. Other information, while not summarized for you, is readily accessible. Checks you wrote for insurance premiums are entered in your check register and the canceled check is filed in numerical order in a box of checks written that year. Your telephone and utility bills are not summarized, but there are only twelve of them to add up at the end of the year. Your medical expenses are easily totaled in one sitting.

Beyond the ease and convenience factor, however, it's all right to leave your personal income and expenditure records alone the entire year because the bulk of these items are not discretionary. You do not, in the main, control your salary, nor can you stipulate what you would like to pay for rent or utilities. Someone else controls what you receive and what you pay.

A major exception is rental property. If you own rental property, you should follow the rules presented subsequently for business recordkeeping. Rental property ownership resembles self-employment activity in both the level of control and the need for contemporaneous recordkeeping.

As a self-employed person owning your own business, you are in control both of what you earn and of what you spend. For this reason you need to pay closer attention to your business records than to your personal records. Closer attention means setting up and keeping books to track both income and expenses in your business.

How often you work with your business records depends on the age and complexity of your business. If you are just starting out, setting aside four hours a month to update and analyze your records is probably sufficient. If you have a mature business or if your business requires frequent expenditures or generates a multiplicity of payments to you, you may need to keep books weekly or even daily.

Lest your eyes glaze over at the thought of bookkeeping, consider this. Business owners keep books to tell them about their business, not to be compulsive about recordkeeping or to complete their tax returns. If your books do not tell you about your business, you probably will not keep them. Good records tell you how you are doing in the real world. They measure your success in terms that a materialistic society can understand and that you, as part of that materialistic world, need to address. They tell you where you spend your money and how much your art generates for you in spendable income. They help you pinpoint your resources for maximum effect so that the "starving artist" syndrome does not become your permanent lifestyle. What's more, the IRS is placing increased emphasis on the presence of financial records as a factor in determining whether an activity is being carried on as a business or as a hobby. The absence of such records, kept on a contemporaneous basis, may lead to a categorization of your art activities as "hobby" activities and to the disallowance of any loss you show from those activities.

2

Setting up Your Books

The key to keeping good books is setting them up so they make sense to you. Do not go to a stationery store and buy a preprinted ledger. Usually anything preprinted is appropriate for external salespeople or store owners. Most of them will not make sense to the individual artist. What you should buy are blank ledger sheets—usually six (numbered) columns wide with a small left-hand column to use for the transaction date and a wider column next to it to annotate your entries. Label the six numbered columns according to how you earn or spend money in your business.

The other things you will need to do your bookkeeping include:

1. Black-ink pen or black ballpoint pen (pencil looks unprofessional, tends to smudge, is difficult to duplicate, and can be erased, which makes the IRS nervous).

2. Records from your file/envelope/drawer and your check register for the period being entered (to catch expenditures or income for which there is no receipt).

3. Your date book or appointment book for the period.

4. A calculator.

5. Uninterrupted time and a clock to keep track of that time (usually four hours). Do not take telephone calls during this period. If you have children, find a time when they are away or when someone else is caring for them. Use any excess time to catch up on business correspondence or to plan your marketing strategy for the next week.

Never let so many records accumulate in your file or envelope or drawer that you dread the prospect of sitting down to enter the items. Limit the number of items you need to enter at one sitting so you have time to reflect on what you're doing.

Begin by dividing the records into income and expenses. Check each record for completeness. Each should bear information as to who, what, when, where, and why, as follows:

Who . . . is the payer (income) or vendor (expense)?

What . . . is the item for? A lecture? A sketchbook? A leotard?

When . . . was the income received or expenditure made?

Where . . . (if not obvious from above information).

Why . . . business purpose, project name or number.

Use your date book or appointment book to refresh your memory. Identifying your records in this way will save time later in case you are audited or need to review your records.

If you are setting up books for the first time, look at receipts for completeness, getting a sense of what categories they fall into. Using these categories, separate the receipts into piles. You may have up to six piles of receipts. Three of them can consist of receipts for supplies that went into the product you sell. A fourth will be for dues, publications, and books; a fifth, for office supplies and postage; the last, the ubiquitous "miscellaneous" pile. When you first divide your receipts, you may not have receipts in all the piles.

Enter these six categories in the six numbered columns of the ledger sheets. Record each receipt on a separate line, entering date, perhaps a note of identity, and the amount paid under the appropriate column heading. Do this for each receipt until you have worked through all of them. Complete the record by adding entries from your check register for which you do not have receipts.

Use the same six categories for three months before you make any changes. Do not include automobile or office in the home expenses in your books since the rules on deductibility of each vary from year to year. For recordkeeping on automobile use and office in the home expense, see Appendix C: A Quick Guide to Deductibility, for "Automobiles" and for "Home Office."

Keep track of travel expenses separately. When you go out of town on a business trip, take along an envelope in which to put receipts related to that trip. At the end of the trip, total the expenses by category (lodging, transportation, local transportation, cleaning, supplies) on the front of the envelope. If the trip is 100 percent business, enter this total in the miscellaneous category of your expense journal when you do your books. If the trip was part business and part personal, review the guidelines on deductible travel expense in Appendix C, under "Travel," and allocate the expenses accordingly. Enter only the deductible portion in the miscellaneous column of your expense journal.

On business travel, keep track of your meals separately. They are only 80 percent deductible. Make sure you make a clear record of the total amount spent on meals so that you have the correct data for your 1989 tax return.

From month to month, you should find no more than 10 percent of the entries popping up in the miscellaneous category. Any item in the miscellaneous category requires an explanatory note and separate treatment when it comes time to prepare your tax return, so it behooves you to fine-tune your expense categories to hold down the number of special cases.

If you find excessive entries in the miscellaneous column, change your six expense categories to reflect a truer picture of your expenditure habits. As your business matures and your sense for distinctions among expenses develops, you will find it preferable to use two six-column expense sheets, each facing the other. Do not start out with twelve columns, however; you probably will not be able to keep them from overlapping and your books will soon be jumbled and you will be confused.

Once you have completed the expense receipts for the period, turn to the income. Again, divide the income receipts into like categories; from these like categories establish your column headings. For income you may choose fewer columns if you want to keep track only of gross income. If you wish to distinguish among your sources of income, use the six-column format. Most income entries will require an explanatory note.

When you have entered all income items for which you have a stub or written record, look at your check register and review all deposits for self-employment income made that month that you have not already recorded. Remember to include in your income journal only those items of income from which no tax has been withheld. If you have a part-time job that pays $4.50 an hour and Social Security or income taxes are withheld by your employer, that income should not appear in your books. It is not self-employment income. Remember—your books are for your business only, not for your personal income or expenses.

When you have finished entering income and expenses for the month, total each column so you know how much you spent in a particular category or received from a particular activity. Then add the totals across the page to arrive at total expense and total income for that month. Subtracting your expenses from your income gives you your net profit for that month.

The last step in doing your books is to store permanently the records you've just entered in your books. A large envelope or box will do. It's not absolutely necessary to store your receipts by category, but it is recommended. If you are audited you will need to break them out by category to substantiate the total entered on your tax return for each expense item. Do not store them by month.

When you are all through, the folder/envelope/drawer in which you temporarily store individual receipts is empty; your books reflect your expenditures and income for the period; the receipts have been permanently transferred to a storage envelope or box. Preferably, the receipts are stored in individual envelopes corresponding to the categories listed in your income and expense journals.

As you do your books month after month, always add the total for the current month to the total for the previous months so you have a cumulative expense total by category and for the entire year through the current month. Carrying the totals forward makes life easier when the time comes to prepare your income tax return and allows you to see your net profit at any given point. Also, when you calculate your estimated tax payment, you need to know your net profit.

Because your books do not include automobile expense or home office expense, they probably overstate your net profit. That's okay. That overstatement provides you with a little cushion in calculating your estimated tax payments. It also reflects reality, in that you pay for an automobile, whether or not you use it for business, and you pay for a home, whether or not you deduct part of those payments for your business. They are basically nonessential parts of your business operation that can provide some tax relief.

3

Examples

The following pages show sample income and expense records for artists. The examples are not exhaustive but are intended to provide some suggestions for categorizing expenses by medium. The example of the graphic designer represents a record kept by an artist who wants "audit-proof" books—that is, books requiring little additional preparation in case of an audit. The audit-proof level of detail should be undertaken only by those with established businesses who already find bookkeeping a valuable tool in operating their businesses.

Sample Expense Record for a Photographer

Figure 1.a is a facsimile of the first page of an expense record kept by a novice photographer. Because the business is new, the six-column format is appropriate. Cumulative expenses are the same as May expenses since this is the first month of recordkeeping.

Sample Expense Record for an Actor, Dancer, or Choreographer

Figure 1.b reproduces a page from an expense record for an actor or a dancer/choreographer. Expense categories for each are similar so this example suffices for these professions.

Items to note include: Separate listing for business meals and entertainment (since these are only 80 percent deductible); Sufficient identification of independent contractor payments to allow for issuing 1099-MISC forms at the end of the year, if necessary; Column 1 includes purchases; rentals are entered under Supplies; Line 3 has two entries on the same line. This means one receipt was issued for two different categories of expenses; Line 22 is the price of a round-trip airplane ticket to New York. If the trip turns out to be less than 100 percent business, the Travel column will need to be adjusted in subsequent months, with an appropriate explanation in the Notes column; Column 10 (Small Equipment) includes expenditures of less than $400. Any piece of equipment costing more than $400 should appear on the depreciation form (Form 4562) as an expensed item or a depreciated item.

It's also obvious from this expense sheet that the bulk of the year-to-date expenditures were made in May, which coincides with the opening of a show.

Sample Expense Record for a Painter

The expense record in Figure 1.c shows how the Notes section of an expense record can be used to keep track of supplies purchased.

Sample Expense Record for a Writer

Figures 1.d and 1.e constitute an expense record for a writer and show how subtotals can be carried from one page to another without losing track of some figures.

Notice that the cost of large equipment (the computer and peripherals) are entered in the Miscellaneous column. At the end of the year, the taxpayer can decide whether to expense the equipment (that is, write it off in its entirety) or depreciate it (take a part of its value

EXPENSES
MAY 1989

DATE	NOTES	FILM + DEV.	FRAMING	SUPPLIES	DUES/PUBS/BOOKS	OFFICE + POSTAGE	MISC.
4	No. SHORE TRIP	47¹²					
5				116²⁰			
7	No. SHORE - SLIDES	48⁷⁴					
8						22⁰⁰	
14	PORTFOLIO DEV'MT						500⁰⁰
15	J. REYNOLDS		60⁰⁰				
19		102⁵⁶					
26				18³⁹			
27	BUSI. CARDS					47⁴⁰	
29		66¹²					
30		47⁴⁴					
	TOTAL EXPENSES: 1075⁹⁷	311⁹⁸	60⁰⁰	134⁵⁹	—	69⁴⁰	500⁰⁰
	CUMULATIVE EXPENSES: 1075⁹⁷	311⁹⁸	60⁰⁰	134⁵⁹	—	69⁴⁰	500⁰⁰

Figure 1.a. Sample Expense Record for a Photographer

EXPENSES
MAY 1989

	NOTES	1 MAKE-UP + COSTUMES	2 PROPS	3 TRAINING/ CONT ED	4 COMMISSIONS TO AGENT/MGR.	5 DUES/FEES/ RESEARCH	6 TRAVEL	7 BUSINESS MEALS + ENTERTAINMENT	8 OFFICE + POSTAGE	9 SUPPLIES	10 SMALL EQUIPMENT	11 REHEARSAL SPACE RENTAL	12 BUSINESS GIFTS	13 MISC.
8	PRINTING (PETER + WOLF)	97°°												
8	"PETER + WOLF"	42¹⁷	7²¹											
8	"PETER + WOLF"													
12	VOICE WORK			30°°					14⁷⁵					
14	OPENING NITE: CAST GIFTS												80°°	
14	" " : CAST PARTY							126¹⁰						
17	LONNIE				100°°									
17	NIGEL				100°°									
17	MARTIN				100°°									
18	SALLY				100°°									
18	BRIAN				100°°									
22	LIGHTING RENTAL									174⁴⁴				
22	WOLF COSTUME RENTAL									65¹⁹				85°°
24	ROYALTY					18¹								
26	STAMPS								22°°					
26	"TWELFTH NIGHT"	6°°												
26	GARAGE SALE		20°°											
28	1000 BUSINESS CARDS								47⁶⁴					
30	12TH ST. LOCATION											35°°		
30	TAPE DECK										178⁴⁰			
30	BILL SULLIVAN / MARTY'S							22°°						
31	NYC TICKET						198°°							
25	TOTAL EXPENSES: 1682.09	57¹³	27²¹	30°°	500°°	18¹	198°°	148¹⁰	84³⁴	239⁵³	178⁴⁰	35°°	80°°	85°°
28	CUMULATIVE EXPENSES:	91⁴³	66¹²	30°°	500°°	48⁵⁰	198°°	166¹²	106³⁴	297³⁴	217⁴⁰	140°°	80°°	111¹
30	CUMULATIVE TOTAL = 2118.16													

Figure 1.b. Sample Expense Record for an Actor or a Dancer/Choreographer

EXPENSES

MAY 1987

NOTES	1 Brushes + Paints	2 Canvas/Paper	3 Other Supplies	4 Freight	5 Tools + Small Equipment	6 Dues, Pubs + Books	7 Travel	8 Busi. Meals + Entertainment	9 Office + Postage	10 Pmts to Wkrp Contractors	11 Confs/Cont Ed	12	13 Misc
5/6 Jansen	16.80												
6 Magenta, Sienna, Zephyria	18.43												
6 4 Nat. Bristle - Var.													
7 Turp.			3.16										
7 H. Mkts?/Serigos								9.00					
9 H.F.M Art Ship.										320.00	8.00		
11 Framing - (Jimbo Questo)													
14 Mat		86.42		142.20									
22 NYC Exhibit													16.60
22 Insurance for Same	42.77												
24 Basestock/Re-order					7.82	22.00							
25 Artpaper Svp													
27 Kasto Frames													
Total Expenses: 792.44	78.19	86.42	3.16	142.20	7.82	71.95	—	8.60	1	320.00	8.00		16.60
Cumulative Expenses	416.77	792.18	64.20	142.20	116.98	111.95	327.10	109.21	26.11	408.00	38.00		201.30
Cumulative Totals 2713.30													

Figure 1.c. Sample Expense Record for a Painter

Figure 1.d. Sample Expense Record for a Writer (1st page)

EXPENSES
MAY 1989

Prepared By _____ Initials ____ Date ____
Approved By _____

NOTES	RESEARCH	TRAVEL	BUSINESS MEALS + ENTERTAINMENT	DUES + PUBS	BOOKS	OFFICE + POSTAGE	CONFS / CONF ED	SUPPLIES	SMALL EQUIPMENT	COMMISSIONS TO INDEP CONTRACTORS	BUSINESS GIFTS		MISC.
3 Sally Kresimind / J+J	496.00												
3 Hornby, Bent., Boca													
3 Basta Tickets	52.00												
3 Travel Docs			14.00		67.14								
4 Doug Flisel / Grunwald's			19.40										
4 Stamps						44.00							
4 Pads + Pens						27.70							
6 NYC Ticket		198.00											
7 Refs									165.00				
7 Dictaphone													
7 Typing - Proposals		313.20											
9 NYC Conf - Lodging		64.84					195.00						
9 " " - L.D.													
11 " " - Meals			62.00										
12 " " -			78.00										
13 " " -			144.00										
14 " " -			22.00										
14 " " - Taxi (NYC)		29.00											
14 " " - (SFP)		16.00		19									
16 Harper's													
8 Discs + F1 Bbous								44.13					
19 Back-up Hard Disc													
22 Compaq									486.00				2217.00
22 " - Peripherals													478.92
22 Floppies								66.00					
22 Compaq - Adapter Etc										60.00			77.14
24 Basta - Taxi (Sr.Paul)	16.00												
24 Drinks + US/Meals	26.00												
24 Basta (500/1) Meals	6.00												
SUB-TOTALS	596.00	616.04	340.20	19	67.14	71.70	195.00	110.13	651.00	60.00	—		2833.06

EXPENSES
MAY 1989 (PAGE 2)

NOTES	1 RESEARCH	2 TRAVEL	3 BUSINESS MEALS + ENTERTAINMT	4 DUES + PUBS	5 BOOKS	6 OFFICE + POSTAGE	7 CLASSES/CONT ED	8 SUPPLIES	9 SMALL EQUIPMENT	10 COMMISSIONS TO INDEP. CONTRS	11 BUSINESS GIFTS	12	13 MISC.
SUB-TOTALS FROM PAGE 1 :	596.00	616.04	340.20	1.50	67.44	71.70	195.00	110.73	651.00	60.00	1		2833.06
25 BATA : LOCAL TRANSPORT	4.00												
25 " : M+L	24.00												
26 " : M+L	30.00												
27 " : M+L	29.00												
28 " : M+L	31.00												
28 " : LOCAL TRANSPORT	49.50												
29 " : M+L	18.00												
29 " : LOCAL TRANSPORT	32.00												
30 " : M+L	16.00												
31 " : M+L	31.00												
TOTAL EXPENSES : 5802.19	855.50	616.04	340.20	1.50	67.44	71.70	195.00	110.73	651.00	60.00	1		2833.06
CUMULATIVE EXPENSES :	1402.70	946.10	467.50	146.92	412.7	149.27	310.00	286.12	651.00	320.00	47.11		3417.83
CUMULATIVE TOTAL = 8595.52													

Figure 1.e. Sample Expense Record for a Writer (2nd page)

over five years). Of the two options, in order to hold down tax liability the writer will probably expense the computer if 1989 is going to be a highly profitable year.

Sample Expense Record for a Graphic Designer

The expense record in Figure 1.f provides the best backup documentation in case of an audit. It shows use of a double-entry form of bookkeeping, which means that figures are entered twice: first, as the amount of the check written, and again as the expenditure by cost category.

Double-entry bookkeeping is required for partnerships and corporations as a check against embezzlement. What the double-entry system offers the sole proprietor is a sophistication that will undoubtedly impress any IRS auditor as well as a down-to-the-penny reconciliation of accounts. This system is recommended only for those comfortable with bookkeeping practices who have well-established businesses where fiscal control is the primary method of increasing profits.

As a rule, checks are written for all items. Each month, the ledger is started by entering the upcoming sequence of checks. (In May, checks 378 to 380 were not used and hence were crossed out at the bottom.) A column identifies whether or not the designer obtained a receipt for the item purchased. At audit time, checks can be pulled from their sequential order and substantiated by receipts, which are grouped in separate envelopes.

With the reconciliation in the lower left-hand column, there is complete conformity between the expense ledger and the designer's books. All income is accounted for (under Deposits) and can be reconciled with the designer's income sheets. Both expense and income records can be reconciled with bank statements.

Sample Expense Record for a Video Artist

The art world breathed a collective sigh of relief when the Internal Revenue Service exempted most artists from capitalization rules. Filmmakers and video artists proved unlucky in being left to deal with the law and its regulations. Briefly, capitalization requires expenses to be attributed to a product and deducted only when that product is sold.

While most artists were excluded by the 1988 Technical and Miscellaneous Revenue Act (TAMRA) from capitalization provisions included in the Tax Reform Act of 1986, artists involved in "printing, photographic plates, motion picture films, video tapes, or similar items" were explicitly required to capitalize their expenses.

Not only direct costs, but indirect costs incurred in running a business had to be allocated to specific projects. Allocating was easy enough to do for direct costs—the costs for materials and labor that go into making a finished product. Film and film processing, wages or payments to independent contractors, set design and manufacture, props, and studio rental were closely identified with a given project. Indirect costs posed a different problem. How do you allocate the cost of a professional membership, attending a theater production or professional development seminar, or rent on a studio office to the three or four film projects you've worked on all year?

After capitalization, only a few expenses can still be deducted in the year incurred: advertising, marketing, and distribution expenses; bidding expenses; depreciation on capital assets acquired in previous years and already on a depreciation schedule (Form 4562); and articles purchased for resale. The rest must be allocated among projects and deducted as each project is sold.

Filmmakers and video artists have the option of using the safe harbor provision issued by IRS Bulletin 88-62. This allows artists to deduct 50 percent of direct and indirect costs in the year the costs are incurred, and the other 50 percent over the next two years.

EXPENSES
MAY 1989

	Initials	Date
Prepared By		
Approved By		

DATE	NOTES	1 CHECK #	2 CHECK AMT	3 SEPARATE RECEIPT (✓)	4 TYPE/STATS/ PRINTING	5 ADV	6 DUES/PUBS/ BOOKS	7 BUSI MEALS + ENT	8 OFFICE + POSTAGE	9 SUPPLIES	10 TOOLS + SM. EQUIPMT	11 PMTS TO INDEP. CONTRACTORS	12 BANK CHARGES	13 MISC.
3		364	22.00	✓					22.00					
6	WILSON, FABER (½)	365	1647.22	✓	1647.22									
6	J.C. WILSON	366	28.00	✓				28.00						
8	NIBS	367	16.20							16.20				
8	SEC'AL	368	45.00									45.00		
1	NEWSLETTER	369	75.00			75.00								
4	NAGDA	370	100.00				100.00							
6	WILSON, FABER (BAL + OVERRUN)	371	1946.50	✓	1946.50									
7		372	8.46	✓						8.46				
12		373	14.27	✓						14.27				
5	G. SIMMONS / CH PALACE	374	30.00	✓				30.00						
29	BERTHOLD, RULING	375	17.42	✓			17.42							
30	— VOID —	~~376~~												
31	WYATT / FRANCESCO'S	377	22.00	✓				22.00						
		~~378~~											6.85	
		~~379~~												
		~~380~~												
	TOTAL EXPS:		3972.07		3593.72	75.00	117.42	80.00	22.00	38.93	-0-	45.00	6.85	-0-
			+ 6.85 BANK											
			3978.92											
	CUMULATIVE:		16479.53		14191.70	330.00	415.95	467.50	110.00	698.68	129.50	100.00	36.20	-0-
	MAY 1987													
	PREVIOUS BALANCE =	727.41												
	+ DEPOSITS =	4620.00												
	NEW BALANCE =	5347.41												
	— EXPENDITURES =	3978.92												
	END BALANCE	1368.49	OK.											
	IN CHECKBOOK:	1368.49												

Figure 1.f. Sample Expense Record for a Graphic Designer

What do you do as a filmmaker or video artist? Begin by analyzing the kind of work you do. Are you involved in making your own films, or do you shoot for someone else and charge by the day? If you make your own films, you probably should elect the safe harbor provision, because there is a likelihood the film you're making will never sell, or will sell for less than it cost to make, leaving you with expenses you may never be able to deduct. If, on the other hand, you are essentially a "hired gun" and work for someone else who is making their own films or videos, then implicitly you meet the original requirements of capitalization because what you're doing is starting and finishing a series of small projects throughout the year. Since each of the projects is "sold" (read: You are paid your daily rate) as soon as it's completed, your expenses incurred in running your business are deductible within that calendar year. This reading of the capitalization rules is not as strained as it might appear. If push came to shove, a film or video artist could produce books that conform to capitalization rules.

The filmmaker or video artist who sells expertise to someone engaged in the production of a film or video work begins with a master ledger, similar to any of the other expense ledgers described in this section. From that master ledger flow mini-ledgers for each of the shoots undertaken by the artist in the current year. Costs clearly incurred for a specific shoot are copied from the master ledger to the mini-ledger for that shoot. Costs that cannot be clearly identified, or overhead costs are moved to a "mixed" mini-ledger. This process of copying costs from the master ledger to mini-ledgers is continued until all costs are copied from one to one of the others.

At this point, what the filmmaker or video artist has is a master ledger, a mini-ledger for each individual project, and a "mixed" ledger for overhead costs. If the artist worked on fourteen projects in 1989, in theory that artist would have sixteen ledgers: one master, fourteen minis, and one mixed. See the flow chart of ledgers in figure 1.g. The sum of the expenses in the fourteen minis and one mixed would equal the expense total on the master, since the minis and mixed ledgers contain nothing more or less than appears in the master ledger. If the same artist worked on thirty-two projects in 1989, that artist would potentially have thirty-four sets of books for 1989.

Are we talking about an administrative nightmare here? Yes and no. The people responsible for writing the regulations spelling out how capitalization will operate are adamant that the product (in this case films and videos) makes the individual subject to capitalization requirements. Hence, the "hired guns" used in this example must capitalize expenses.

But if and when push comes to shove, which is another way of saying when the filmmaker or video artist is audited, a reasonable auditor should accept the logic presented above. The unreasonable auditor may require a breakout of information from a master ledger to minis, but that will probably never occur. The allocation of indirect expenses from the "mixed" ledger to each of the mini-ledgers could be done on the basis of income proportion represented by each project.

Let's say filmmaker Baker earned $50,000 in 1989 from her video work in four separate projects from which she was paid as an independent contractor. Project A paid $15,000; B paid $10,000; C paid $20,000; D paid $5,000. Direct expenses were $2,000 for A; $1,000 for B; $5,000 for C; and nothing for D. Indirect expenses for the year totaled $18,000, itemized as follows:

—studio rent = $3,600

—telephone and business long distance = $1,200

—equipment = $3,000

—dues, publications, memberships, films = $1,500

—payments to independent contractors = $2,000

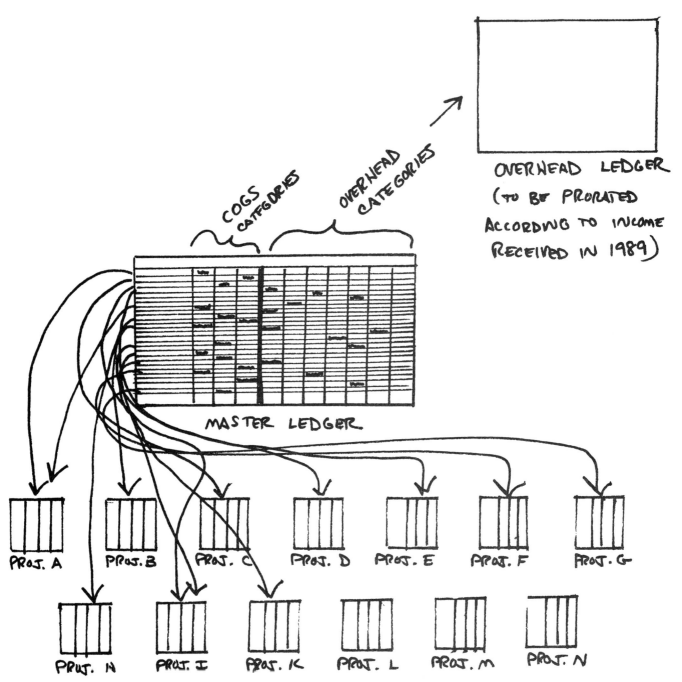

COGS CATEGORIES

OVERHEAD CATEGORIES

OVERHEAD LEDGER
(TO BE PRORATED
ACCORDING TO INCOME
RECEIVED IN 1989)

MASTER LEDGER

PROJ. A   PROJ. B   PROJ. C   PROJ. D   PROJ. E   PROJ. F   PROJ. G

PROJ. H   PROJ. I   PROJ. K   PROJ. L   PROJ. M   PROJ. N

Figure 1.g. Sample Expense Record for a Video Artist (using Standard Capitalization per IRC Sec. 263A).

Flow chart for Ledgers: From Master to Minis and to Mixed

—business interest = $400

—travel and entertainment = $1,200

—bank charges = $100

—office expense = $1,900

—small equipment = $1,500

—insurance on equipment = $600

—auto expense = $1,000

(To be sure, nothing in real life is this simple. Expense figures are rarely round numbers. The example is for illustration purposes only.)

Indirect expenses would be allocated to each project in the same proportion that project brought income to Baker: 30 percent to A; 20 percent to B; 40 percent to C; and 10 percent to D. Since Baker was paid for all projects in 1989, all costs would be deductible in 1989.

What about the other kind of filmmaker or video artist? What if you're shooting your own films, and perhaps hiring "guns" to work for you? You're stuck with the safe harbor provision. Set up and keep books as described for the other artists in this section. At tax time, make the kinds of changes described in Part II of this book. Remember that the safe harbor election is irrevocable. You cannot choose to use safe harbor rules in 1989, 1990, and 1991, and then switch to regular capitalization rules because you're working for some other filmmaker on a project basis in 1992.

Other Expense Records

The possible combinations of expense records for practicing artists is limitless. What is true, however, is that most self-employed professionals have the following expense categories:

—Dues, Publications, and Books

—Travel

—Business Meals and Entertainment

—Office Supplies and Postage

—Supplies

—Tools and Small Equipment

—Conferences, Continuing Education, Training

—Payments to Independent Contractors (commissions)

—Miscellaneous, for the occasional expenditure that doesn't fit comfortably under these categories.

To customize your expense records, use any one of the examples displayed on the preceding pages, or, if none is appropriate to your needs, remember to enter in the first several columns the materials used in your product, and then complete your expense record with the headings listed above.

A sculptor, for example, might have the following expense categories: bronze/casting materials; finishing materials; foundry costs; plus the categories listed above. A potter or ceramicist could have clay; glazing materials; utilities; plus the categories listed above. A video artist could have tapes; equipment rentals; video supplies; repairs; plus the categories listed above. A composer or musician could have sheet music; instruments/supplies; repairs; plus the categories listed above. What is most important is that your books reflect your business.

Sample Income Record for a Photographer

The income record in Figure 2.a shows one method of keeping track of income besides listing it by order of receipt.

The Notes column identifies the event generating the income by name of participant. Weddings, portraits, reprints of the artist's work in local or national publications, limited-edition releases by the artist (fine arts), and "other" cover the possible sources of income the photographer may wish to track.

At the outset of a business, which this income record represents, division of income by segment may seem unnecessary. But the column headings lay the basis for a later evaluation of the business and serve, more immediately, to wean the artist away from reliance on the bottom line to a more sophisticated and useful method of analyzing income.

Suppose, for example, that during the first year of business 35 percent of income over time comes from shooting weddings. Then the photographer needs to take a hard look if, during a three-month period, only 15 percent of his income comes from weddings. There is more to worry about if there are few engagements scheduled. Perhaps there is trouble with the business, or the photographer may be making a conscious effort to break away to new areas of emphasis. In either case, the numbers give early warning that something different is happening. Whether that difference is intentional or accidental, the photographer can make changes to correct the deficiency or to continue the acceleration toward a new focus.

Sample Income Record for a Graphic Designer

The income record in Figure 2.b shows how to keep track of income by industry segment.

The Notes column is used to identify the product that generates the revenue. Corporate work, consisting primarily of annual reports and marketing-presentation materials, is the largest single source of income for this graphic designer. Other income comes from local or national publications, individuals (perhaps long-standing clients for whom this designer still does occasional work), nonprofit organizations, and "other."

Other Income Records

How you keep track of income depends on the age of your business. As you start out, making income is more important than identifying where it comes from. As your business matures, containing costs assumes a higher priority. In a mature business, the sole proprietor's objective is to maintain existing accounts, to weed out the weaker ones and replace them with new accounts, and to safeguard income base.

The two examples on the following pages are the primary vehicles for assessing your income. The first stresses the type of event that generates income; the second the market sector from which income is derived. Whether you are a dancer or a designer, one of the two systems should be adaptable to your needs.

Dancers and poets are more like the photographer, in that they should track income by type of event. Income categories to use would be ticket sales, performances, individuals, and "other."

The second set of income categories, analyzing income by source, could be used comfortably by writers or systems analysts. Sculptors, potters, and ceramicists would change the categories to consignment, fairs and exhibitions, wholesale, and "other."

INCOME
MAY 1989

DATE	NOTES	WEDDINGS	PORTRAITS	LOCAL/NAT'L PUBLICATIONS	FINE ART	OTHER	
2	SMITH + WESSON	175.00					
6	ALBY'S NEW DOGS		45.00				
6	MONICA SANCHEZ		60.00				
6	SOPHIE'S GRADUATION		245.00				
9	HOPE + GARDNER	250.00					
9	ROYSON + EVANS	160.00					
16	MILLER + FREDRICKS	200.00					
16	FONT + GABRIEL	180.00					
16	JONES + SINCLAIR	200.00					
18	ALBY PRINTS		66.40				
21	MIKE'S NEW SON		50.00				
22	TWINS' BABY				75.00		
23	ALYSON + DREISER	175.00					
23	NICHOLS + MAYER	190.00					
23	BARTHOLOMEW + DIXON	200.00					
24	GOLDBERG + MEIER	200.00					
26	LTD ED / TWINS BABY → MN MKTG ASSN					500.00	
28	SOPHIE PRINTS		110.90				
	TOTAL INCOME = 3082.30	1930.00	577.30		75.00	500.00	-0-

Figure 2.a. Sample Income Record for a Photographer (Income by event)

INCOME
MAY 1989

DATE	NOTES	CORPS. (INTERNAL)	PUBLICATIONS	INDIVIDUALS	NON-PROFIT ORGS.	MISC.	
6	3M ANNUAL REPORT	7500⁰⁰					1
11	½ ON MW MONTHLY		1200⁰⁰				2
14	BILL SCANLAN / CARDS			140⁰⁰			3
17	UA FLYER				200⁰⁰		4
24	BAL ON MW MONTHLY		1200⁰⁰				5
26	LINDA HETGES / CARDS + LETTHEAD			90⁰⁰			6
31	TC MAG		500⁰⁰				7
31	C. SCHMIDT CONCERT			450⁰⁰			8
							9
							10
	TOTAL INCOME =	7500⁰⁰	2900⁰⁰	680⁰⁰	200⁰⁰		11
	11280⁰⁰						12

Figure 2.b. Sample Income Record for a Graphic Designer
(Income by market sector)

4

Books as Business Tools

Keeping books regularly gives you statistics that allow you to assess business performance. Does this sound too far-fetched for a fine artist? Consider a sculptor whose medium is bronze. Does it make sense for this artist to use information from his books on the cost of producing a particular piece to assist him in pricing his product? Does it make sense for the portrait painter to understand what hourly rate is implied by her fee schedule? Are you curious about how much you make per hour at your art?

For many artists the party line is that money does not concern the true artist. The reality is closer to the plight of the working poor—scrimping to make ends meet and to afford some basic amenities. Money matters to the working poor and, in the end, it matters to most artists who expect to make a living from their art. "Making a living" are the key words. Can you support yourself by your art or do you need a full-time job to support this ancillary activity from which you draw your lifeblood?

Artists offer something to the world that bankers cannot, and vice versa. But the IRS draws no such fine distinctions. It insists only that one set of rules be followed for businesses run for the purpose of making a profit, and another set for hobbies run for pleasure and diversion.

The IRS's increasingly strident insistence on the distinction between business and hobby challenges the artist's contention that art is a lifestyle issue, but only to the extent the artist wishes to use losses incurred in the production of art to offset other income. The artist as hobbyist is free to keep the government at bay by reporting hobby income and deducting expenses up to the limit of that income. The business artist, however, must meet more stringent qualifications to justify the loss from one activity to offset income from another.

Are other segments of society subject to such stringent control? Yes. Losses from a limited partnership, once wholly deductible, are now subject to annual limitations that will eventually phase out their usefulness. Even when losses from limited partnerships were wholly deductible, their activities fell under close government scrutiny.

And what about those stories of people paying no income tax due to tax shelters? In the main, they're not accurate anymore. Besides, there is more to tax shelters than meets the eye. While it is true that tax shelters can postpone tax liabilities for two or three years in a row, the fact remains that tax shelters simply shift tax liabilities to a later time.

In short, it has become increasingly difficult to avoid paying taxes. Artists are not singled out for government scrutiny. The bottom line is that anyone who wants certain privileges needs to follow the rules. Does this mean that deducting losses from art work is a privilege? Yes. Artists who are self-employed are a special class. They are autonomous, as are people who participate in limited partnerships or who derive their livelihood from a trust. They are not bound by the confines of a W-2-type income.

The government does not spend a great deal of time eyeing the person who works for a corporation and has two children, a home in the suburbs, and two savings accounts. Even if she owns shares in a mutual fund, the government knows just about everything it needs or wants to know about her. Add self-employment to the formula, however, and you've thrown in a huge unknown, prompting scrutiny and government inquiry.

So, some individuals invite review by the government. Who gets it? Usually those who forget to report and pay tax on income they receive. Next in line are those whose income is not under someone else's control—for example, self-employed people. Next are those who are awarded income from a third party—for example, fellowship recipients. Fourth are those who participate in limited partnerships. Do artists fall into one or more of these categories? Does it snow in Minnesota?

To summarize, making art must now be conducted as a business or as a hobby. There is no in between. As a business, it should be conducted as a profit-making endeavor, with good financial records. This does not mean all artists make a profit, although the IRS says that you must show a profit in three of any five years or, prima facie, your activity can be deemed a hobby. From this it follows that the more you know about how your business is run, the more effectively you will be able to defend yourself against charges of being a hobbyist.

Well and good for the IRS, but the underlying issue for you is whether or not you enjoy doing your art. What does enjoyment entail? Year after year of waiting tables in order to spend all their money on painting may work for young people. But it grows wearisome for those in their thirties and positively oppressive for those who want to have a family while still in their forties. In other words, your biological clock will catch up with you if the government doesn't. Enjoyment is limited by your financial requirements. At some point you will realize you want to be paid for what you're contributing. Fine. Many people contribute far less and reap far more. Ours is an affluent society, one in which you can share without abandoning your soul or artistic precepts. Understanding how to run your art as a business can give you some more of the amenities without degrading your artistry and artistic intent.

To return to the pricing example: Art is a discretionary item. People will buy art for reasons of prestige or social standing, for decoration, or perhaps because they like or relate to the piece. Because the purchase of art is discretionary, its value is subjective. At a minimum, however, you need to cover your costs. (Sometimes this is not possible, but then you face a host of other problems, not the least of which is the IRS assuming you are running a hobby instead of a business.)

If you cover only your costs, you have said your time is worth nothing. This is not true. How much is your time worth? A plumber earns $55 an hour in Saint Paul. A plumber keeps water inside the pipes. Buying a plumber's time is usually not discretionary. On the other hand, people usually enjoy a vase or a painting on the wall longer than they enjoy a pipe that no longer leaks. So how do you price your work? Your books are a start. They allow you to identify the costs of production and the costs of the environment in which the goods are produced (that is, overhead). Production plus time plus a percentage of the overhead costs equals the cost to you of the item produced.

You know the production costs from your books. A time log, taken over a period of two weeks, will tell you how many hours on average you spend to produce a piece of work. Use a spiral notebook, one page per day. Jot down in quarter-hour increments how you use the full twenty-four-hour period. Distinguish between production time and overhead, administrative, and other non-income-producing time. After two weeks, you should arrive at some accurate measure of how many hours you spend in productive income-producing work.

Your books tell you how much money you spend on overhead. You can calculate as follows: If you produce twenty works in a year, divide total overhead by twenty. If your work comes in fits and starts, divide total overhead by twelve to arrive at a monthly overhead figure. Then apply that figure against the length of time it took to complete a particular project.

What's left after you subtract production costs and overhead from your gross income is your net income. From it you can calculate what you earn on an hourly basis. This equation works best for projects that are already completed. But it can also be the basis on which you bid a project. As a professional you know what the raw materials will cost. You know how long it will take you to complete it, so you can factor in your overhead. If you need to hire assistants, you know how much you will pay them. You calculate time spent in design and execution, put an hourly factor on it, and come up with a preliminary total. Don't forget taxes, retirement plan contributions, and profit. Finally, add a 10 percent "slush factor" and voilà!—the bid.

Of course, it helps to temper that bid with reality. You can bid the project and come in with a winning bid on the basis of your presentation or the extras you add. And it helps to know whether you really want the job or not. In the latter case you can bid up the price until the commission to be gained exceeds your physical or artistic pain threshold. Even if your bid is accepted, you'll be paid enough to overcome your doubts about doing the project.

If you win the bid, your planning abilities are called into play—can you bring in the project on the budget you set, knowing that if you can't, the only slush factor is the money earmarked for you?

Part of the beauty of working for yourself is setting your own hours. The larger beauty, however, is testing yourself against your own standards. No one else calls the shots, and no one else sets limits on your performance. The business you create is one you mold to meet your objectives. To an extent you respond to the external market, but you are the ultimate controller of how fast your business grows and how far it goes. Does this help place the idea about artist as entrepreneur in a more acceptable context?

Once you understand and accept the need to be paid for your time, you've lost some of your innocence. You've also come to understand the need to keep books and to use them to explain your business. While it may be true that some people do not keep books out of fear of making mistakes, other people do not keep books because they have the luxury of running their art as a sideline, a hobby—money does not matter to them. They, in the end, are the mouthpiece of the philosophy that true artists care nothing for money. They, in the end, are the enemies of art by the people and, presumably, for the people. Real people, in the end, need money to live.

So your books can tell you about pricing; what else can they do? They can tell you:

1. Which client segment provides you with the most revenue, allowing you to determine marketing to this segment, sensitizing you to changes in this segment, or redirecting your business if this lucrative but not intellectually fulfilling segment can occupy less of your time.

2. How to cut costs, especially on overhead. Mature businesses will focus on cost-cutting in production areas, newer businesses on overhead costs.

3. How to protect market segments you want to retain and discourage those you don't.

4. How to keep unpaid bills at a minimum.

What do you need to do with your books to gain greater insight into your business? Not much more than what has already been discussed. For the dollar total in each column, calculate a percentage of total expenditures or total income; for each cumulative total, the same. Percentages are easier to manipulate than raw figures; differences (called "variances" in statistics) are easier to detect.

The most elementary form of business evaluation checks for variances of more than 5 percent in any monthly expense or income category from the average for that expense or income category, determined by at least eighteen months' experience.

During the first six months of a business, expenses and income will fluctuate wildly as you spend money on whatever seems to be needed and take in money from any source offering it. As your business matures, you begin to channel expenses, pinpointing areas where spending is essential, not discretionary, and controlling income so it is more predictable, both as to source and frequency. After the first year or year and a half, both expenses and income become somewhat predictable and hence measurable in terms of deviation from the norm. If the expense total for a particular column in a particular month, then, deviates from the norm more than 5 percent, you should review that month's expenditures to see if they were all necessary or if you are becoming somewhat slack in your fiscal management.

Similarly, if you can predict that 30 percent of your monthly income comes from a certain corporation, and in August that percentage dips to 18 percent, you may have cause for alarm. Perhaps someone with whom you schedule business is simply on vacation; but maybe they didn't like your last project. Your books can alert you to changes in your business atmosphere before you become consciously aware of them.

A third way your books can be used to evaluate your business involves determining trends and requires statistics over a two- or three-year period. Likely areas for trend analysis are:

1. Cost of production versus income

2. Income by month or quarter, comparing several years

3. Expenses versus income by month

4. Percentage of overhead expense, by month, over several years

The following pages show how your books can be used to evaluate your business activities.

Evaluation from an Expense Record

If you want to use your books to evaluate your business every month, you must first convert the raw data to percentages. Using the expense record for a painter reproduced in Figure 3, follow along as we build the evaluation model.

First, divide the expense total for each column by the total expenses for the month. That gives you the percentage of the month's expenses represented by each expense category.

$$\text{Example:} \quad \frac{\text{brushes + paints}}{\text{total May expenses}} = \frac{\$78.19}{\$792.94} = 9.9 \text{ percent}$$

Next, divide the cumulative expense total for each column by the total cumulative expenses. That gives you the percentage of cumulative expenses represented by each expense category.

$$\text{Example:} \quad \frac{\text{cum. canvas/paper}}{\text{total cumulative expenses}} = \frac{\$792.18}{\$2713.30} = 29.2 \text{ percent}$$

The cumulative expense percentage figures give you a broad indication of the amounts you historically spend on a particular expense category over the course of time. As such it becomes a standard against which to compare and evaluate the current month's expenditures. Using these percentage figures, compare the month's percentage for each expense column with the cumulative percentage for each expense column. Deviations of more than 5 percent are noted. For the painter in May, the following self-analysis might take place:

EXPENSES
MAY 1989

#	NOTES	BRUSHES + PAINTS	CANVAS / PAPER	OTHER SUPPLIES	FREIGHT	TOOLS + SMALL EQUIPMENT	DUES, PUBS + BOOKS	TRAVEL	BUSS MEALS + ENTERTAINMENT	OFFICE + POSTAGE	PMTS TO INDEP. CONTRACTORS	COMPS / CONT ED	MISC
1	JANSON												
6	MAGENTA, SIENNA, 2 FUSCHIA	16⁸⁰										
6	4 NAT. BRISTLE - VAR.	18⁶²										
7	TURP			3ᵗᵉ			49⁹⁵						
7	H. McGUIRE / SCREENS												
9	4 (?M. ART SYMPOSIUM								8⁰⁰		320⁰⁰	8⁰⁰	
1	FRAMING (JOAN)		86⁴²										
16	MAT												
22	→NYC EXHIBIT				142²⁰								
12	INSURANCE PRE-SALE	42⁴⁴				7⁷²	22⁰⁰						66⁰⁰
24	BASESTOCK / RE-ORDER												
25	ARTPAPER SUB												
29	X-ACT-O KNIVES												
	TOTAL EXPENSES: 792.⁴⁴	78¹⁹	86⁴²	3¹⁶	241⁸²	7⁷²	71⁹⁵		8⁰⁰	I	320⁰⁰	8⁰⁰	99⁶⁰
	% OF MAY EXPENSES	9.9	11.0	0.4	17.9	1.0	9.1	-0-	1.1	-0-	40.4	1.0	8.4
	CUMULATIVE EXPENSES 416.⁸⁴	416⁸⁴	792¹⁸	46³⁰	142²⁰	16⁴⁸	111⁴⁵	327¹⁰	109²¹	26¹¹	480⁰⁰	38⁰⁰	206⁵⁰
	CUMULATIVE TOTALS 271336												
	% OF CUMULATIVE EXP:	15.4	29.2	1.7	5.2	0.6	4.1	12.1	4.0	1.0	17.7	1.4	7.6

© WILSON JONES COMPANY U.S.A. — "COLUMN WRITE" — G7613C PADDED   WG7613C "WYRING" BOUND ·

Figure 3. Business Evaluation from an Expense Record

1. Brushes and paints are more than 5 percent lower than usual. Am I letting supplies run too low? Or am I using my supplies better?

2. Canvas/paper usually runs about 30 percent of a month's expenses. This month they represent only 11 percent. Am I working less? Am I using other media?

3. Other supplies are okay.

4. Freight is way up. I did ship those materials to the New York exhibit. Was the $142.20 justified in terms of real prospects, or am I on an ego trip? What follow-up must I do with the New York people to make this investment pay off as I expect?

5. Tools and small equipment are okay.

6. Dues and publications are okay, though on the border. I need to watch large purchases (such as the $49.95 Janson text. Nice, but hardly necessary.).

7–9. Travel looks good, as do business meals and entertainment. Office and postage are okay.

10. Payment to independent contractors is really up. Was the $320 in framing necessary? Refer to New York exhibit and make this trip pay off!

11. Conferences and continuing education are also okay.

12. The insurance for the New York show makes the total cost for that exhibit $528.80, not including supplies or my time. And I didn't even go to New York! This gives me a good idea of what a lot of shows will cost me over time.

A second way of analyzing data from an expense sheet is to draw a dividing line between categories of expense that contribute to saleable goods and overhead categories. In the example of the painter, freight could be considered in either category, but for the purpose of this discussion it will fall into the cost of goods sold category. Adding up the May percentages, the painter has 39.2 percent of the month's expenses in the cost of goods sold category.

The cumulative percentages for the same cost categories are 51.5 percent of year-to-date expenses. Again, there is a deviation of more than 5 percent. Is work slowing down? Has the glamour of the New York exhibit dried up the creative juices? Perhaps there's an error in the way the cost categories are set up. The framing is really a cost of goods sold expense. A change may be needed to keep framing costs on the left, or cost of goods sold, side of that dividing line.

If framing expense were moved to the cost of goods sold side, the May cost of goods sold percentages total would be 79.6 percent. The cumulative percentages may not be changed automatically. The $160 spent on independent contractors in the January-to-April period needs to be identified as an overhead or cost of goods figure. If it is more framing, then the historical cost of goods percentages total is more like 69.2 percent. While there is still more than a 5 percent deviation in the monthly versus the cumulative percentage totals, the error at least is on the side of work, not overhead. Beware, however, of the trap that counts labor done by others as your own.

As a footnote, calculating the cost of goods sold percentage makes it easy to calculate the percentage of expenditures on overhead. Simply subtract the cost of goods sold percentage from 100 percent. For May, overhead is 60.8 percent; for the year-to-date period, overhead is 48.5 percent.

Notice that the May percentage figures add up to 100.2 percent, due to rounding. This is close enough for purposes of this exercise.

The guidelines to follow in using an expense record to perform some business evaluation require that you use the figures you create intelligently. It's not enough to crank out percentages and expect the statistics to do the talking for you. In this case, payments to independent contractors were really a cost of goods sold expense instead of an overhead expense. You need to think through your books and think through the entries you make and the rationale you use for putting an expense in a particular category. Only with care and attention can your books become a reliable data base and measurement of your business growth.

Evaluation from an Income Record

Evaluation from an income record uses the same procedures as evaluation from an expense record. What you're looking for is different. In evaluating an expense record, you are looking for signs of decreased or increased output, and productive (cost of goods sold) expenditures versus unproductive (overhead) expenditures. In evaluating an income record, you are looking for signs of lack of attention to a particular market or market sector. In the case of the photographer (event-directed income record) or the graphic designer (market-sector-directed record), the comparison of current-month percentages versus cumulative percentages can tell you:

1. If you've subconsciously moved away from working in a given area

2. If you need to advertise for more business of a particular kind

3. If you have alienated a vendor or group of vendors by a change in work style or manner, or by the people you have hired to assist you

4. What area provides the best remuneration

5. What area provides the most comfortable working conditions

6. How many jobs you need to do each month to maintain a certain standard of living (to be determined by you)

7. What types of work pay off best for you

8. To what extent job satisfaction and professional growth are compatible with the requirements of earning a living

Businesses in their early development (up to three years old) usually evaluate expense records more than income records. As a business matures (three to five years) and reaches its potential (five to seven years), the focus switches to income record evaluation. From income records work schedules are set, which, in turn, are based on budgets, pricing analyses, and projections of income needed.

Trend Analysis

Over a period of time, your business records can provide you with data on how your business is evolving. Graphing is easy and provides a picture of your business. What you need to create these pictures of business activity are monthly expense and income reports. The rest is up to you, and the possibilities are limitless. The graphs reproduced on the following pages are just some of the possibilities.

Figure 4.a graphs monthly income by monthly expenses for 1988 and 1989. The connecting lines have nothing to do with the time of the year in which you spent or earned money, but do show the relation between income and expenses. In this kind of graph you want each succeeding year's line to fall to the left of the preceding year's. In other words, you want your expenses to shrink while your income remains approximately the same.

In this example, monthly income for the second year never drops below $1,000. It peaks at $3,500 for both years. For 1988, there are six entries at the $2,000 income level or above;

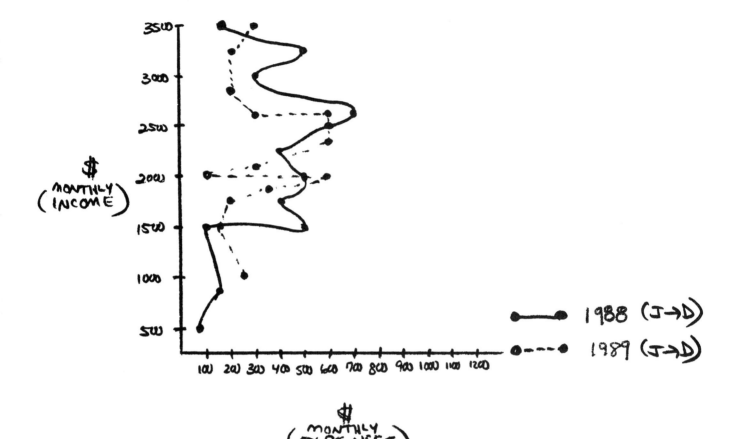

Figure 4.a. Business Evaluation—Graphing Income vs. Expenses, 1988–1989

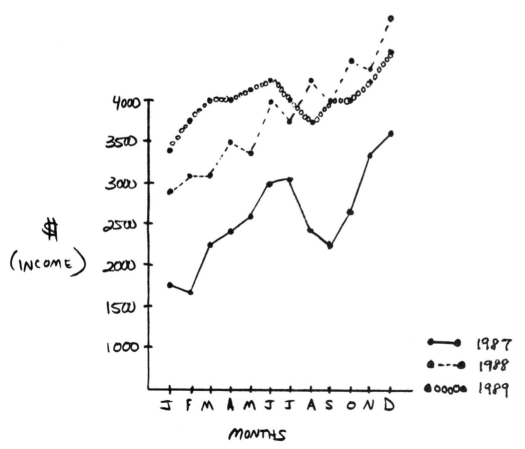

Figure 4.b. Business Evaluation—Graphing Monthly Income, 1987–1989

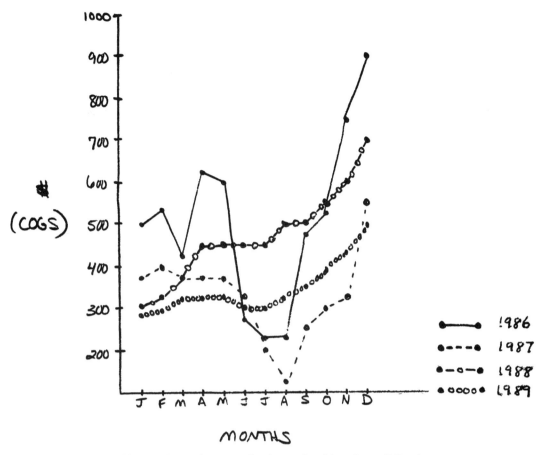

Figure 4.c. Business Evaluation—Graphing Cost-of-Goods-Sold, 1986–1989

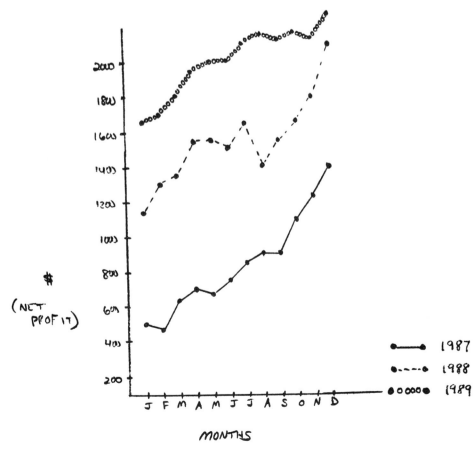

Figure 4.d. Business Evaluation—Graphing Net Profit, 1987–1989

in 1989, there are nine such entries. On the expense side, seven of the 1988 data points are at $300 per month or more. 1989 is the same.

What can you conclude from such a graph? Because the expense figures are approximately the same, even though the 1989 income points are higher than the 1988 income points, 1989 was a significantly better year. If your net profit for 1988 was $18,870 and your net profit for 1989 was $27,600, you already knew that 1989 was a better year. But did you know *why* it was a better year? The graph gives you new information.

Figure 4.b compares income, by month, over three years. The solid line represents 1987, perhaps the first year in business. Notice how January income for 1988 picks up almost where 1987 ended. A graph like this shows progress. There's a bit of a lull at year's end but the overall trend is upward. There's a drop in July and August of 1989—a vacation, perhaps? This artist earned it!

Figure 4.c shows still another way of using the data in your financial records. Here, the monthly cost of goods sold is graphed over four years of business history. This is the kind of graph a mature business would generate. Income and overhead are presumably predictable; the only other factor to watch is the cost of goods sold, on which future profits depend.

If your business purchases raw materials from a wholesaler you may not notice small price increases over a period of months or even years. What you do notice is that your business doesn't seem to be paying you very much, especially in light of how long you've been at it. Rather than get mad at your business, try this kind of graph to see if you can determine the source of the problem.

In this example, 1986 and 1987 show a marked drop in the summer months. In 1988, however, the sole proprietor found an alternative market for those months. Cost of goods also increases near the end of each year, no doubt because of the holiday season. But why are the increases more gradual in 1988 and 1989 than they were in 1986 and 1987? Herein lies part of the solution to the profit dilemma. As the owner and primary worker, you know how your business operates. But perhaps you didn't notice that the industry as a whole changed after 1987, possibly because the cost of the raw materials dropped due to increased competition. You might have noticed some small price decreases, but figured they were nothing to get excited about. Graphing can sometimes restore that excitement. In this case, if profits 1988–89 haven't increased over 1986–87, you should do some more analysis, since a drop in the overall cost of goods sold should spell higher net incomes.

A fourth example is shown in Figure 4.d, which graphs net profit, by month, over three years. In this business, most of the money is made near the end of the year. Each succeeding year picks up about where the last one dropped off, a sign of a healthy business. For 1988 the net profit levels are all above any monthly level in a previous year, another sure sign of business success.

If this business is new (and it may well be), the owner should concentrate in 1989 on cutting costs, especially overhead costs. Cutting the cost of goods used in your product is viable only if there has been an industry-wide price decrease or you have found an alternative provider. Using cheaper goods in an established product line is the second fastest way to ruin a business. Only embezzlement or fraud destroy it faster.

5

Reporting Requirements

When you are in business for yourself, there are several reporting requirements you must meet in order to comply with the law. Some are reports you must file on behalf of other people; others are reports you must file to keep yourself one step ahead of the tax collector.

Reports to File for Others

Whenever you pay an independent contractor more than $600 in a calendar year, you must file a Form 1099-MISC by January 31 of the following year. The original Form 1099-MISC is filed with the federal government; one copy is filed with the payee; one copy remains in your records as proof you complied with the law. This form must be filed by January 31 of the year following the year the services were performed. Failure to file the report, or filing it late, will result in a fine to the payer of fifty dollars per incident, and may lead, in case of audit, to the disallowance of the claimed deduction for services rendered.

Form 1099-MISC must be sent to the government with a cover sheet, Form 1096. Examples of these forms appear in Figures 5 and 6.

Whether an individual is an employee or an independent contractor hinges on the unpredictability of work available and the project nature of the work assigned. While states are more concerned about the status of a worker than is the federal government, it is best to follow certain guidelines in determining whether or not an individual is an independent contractor or an employee.

In general, if a person works for you on your premises more than half time for more than seventeen weeks per year, he is an employee. As such, he is entitled to have you pay half his Social Security payments and all his Workers' Compensation and unemployment insurance. If you also provide medical or retirement plan coverage, he must be included in your group plans. A person who works for you only a few hours per week on a regular basis is your employee. Since these amount to a considerable outlay annually, it's important to determine early on whether the person you hire will be an independent contractor or employee.

An independent contractor controls his hours of work and usually works on his own premises. All you do is control the quality of the work performed. Work is intermittent and project-oriented. Work may be seasonal.

Given the additional expense of having an employee, it's probably best to try the person out as an independent contractor on a temporary basis before offering regular employment. It is only fair to explain before you hire him, however, that an independent contractor is responsible for payments of quarterly taxes and any and all insurance premiums so that rude surprises do not await him at tax time or when he is injured on the job.

Being honest up front is the best policy and will make for a better employee if you find the demands of your business require the presence of a part-time or full-time employee who is on your business premises, under your control, for definable work times, for an indefinite period.

6969

☐ CORRECTED

| Form **1096**
Department of the Treasury
Internal Revenue Service | **Annual Summary and Transmittal of
U.S. Information Returns** | OMB No. 1545-0108

19**89** |

⌐ Type or machine print FILER'S name (or attach label)

Matthew Dillon

Street address **PLACE LABEL HERE**
200 Main Street

City, state, and ZIP code
Dodge City, KS   77667   ⌐

►

If you are not using a preprinted label, enter in Box 1 or 2 below the identification number you used as the filer on the information returns being transmitted. Do not fill in both Boxes 1 and 2.

Name of person to contact if IRS needs more information

Telephone number
(   )

For Official Use Only

☐☐☐☐☐☐☐ ☐☐

| 1 Employer identification number | 2 Social security number
345 67 8901 | 3 Total number of documents   2 | 4 Federal income tax withheld
$ | 5 Total amount reported with this Form 1096
$ 1,550. |

Check only one box below to indicate the type of forms being transmitted.   If this is your FINAL return, check here . . . . . ☐

W-2G 32	1098 81	1099-A 80	1099-B 79	1099-DIV 91	1099-G 86	1099-INT 92	1099-MISC 95	1099-OID 96	1099-PATR 97	1099-R 98	1099-S 75	5498 28
☐	☐	☐	☐	☐	☐	☐	☒	☐	☐	☐	☐	☐

Under penalties of perjury, I declare that I have examined this return and accompanying documents and, to the best of my knowledge and belief, they are true, correct, and complete.

Signature ► *Matthew Dillon*   Title ► SHERIFF   Date ► 1/18/90

Please return this entire page to the Internal Revenue Service. Photocopies are NOT acceptable.

Instructions

Purpose of Form.—Use this form to transmit Forms W-2G, 1098, 1099, and 5498 to the Internal Revenue Service.

Completing Form 1096.—If you received a preprinted label from IRS with Package 1099, place the label in the name and address area of this form inside the brackets. Make any necessary corrections to your name and address on the label. However, do not use the label if the taxpayer identification number (TIN) shown is incorrect. If you are not using a preprinted label, enter the filer's name, address, and TIN in the spaces provided on the form. **The name, address, and TIN you enter on this form must be the same as those you enter in the upper left area of Form 1099, 1098, 5498, or W-2G.** A filer includes a payer, a recipient of mortgage interest payments, a broker, a barter exchange, a person reporting real estate transactions, a trustee or issuer of an individual retirement arrangement (including an IRA or SEP), and a lender who acquires an interest in secured property or who has reason to know that the property has been abandoned. Individuals not in a trade or business should enter their social security number in Box 2; sole proprietors and all others should enter their employer identification number in Box 1. However, sole proprietors who are not required to have an employer identification number should enter their social security number in Box 2.

Group the forms by form number and submit each group with a separate Form 1096. For example, if you must file both Forms 1098 and Forms 1099-A, complete one Form 1096 to transmit your Forms 1098 and another Form 1096 to transmit your Forms 1099-A.

In Box 3, enter the number of forms you are transmitting with this Form 1096. Do not include blank or voided forms in your total. Enter the number of correctly completed forms, not the number of pages, being transmitted. For example, if you send one page of three-to-a-page Forms 5498 with a Form 1096 and you have correctly completed two Forms 5498 on that page, enter 2 in Box 3 of Form 1096. Check the appropriate box to indicate the type of form you are transmitting.

No entry is required in Box 5 if you are filing Form 1099-A or 1099-G. For all other forms, enter in Box 5 of Form 1096 the total of the amounts from the specific boxes of the forms listed below:

Form W-2G	Box 1
Form 1098	Box 1
Form 1099-B	Boxes 2, 3, and 6
Form 1099-DIV	Boxes 1a, 5, and 6
Form 1099-INT	Boxes 1 and 3
Form 1099-MISC	Boxes 1, 2, 3, 5, 6, 7, 8, and 10
Form 1099-OID	Boxes 1 and 2
Form 1099-PATR	Boxes 1, 2, 3, and 5
Form 1099-R	Boxes 1 and 8
Form 1099-S	Box 2
Form 5498	Boxes 1 and 2

If you will not be filing Forms 1099, 1098, 5498, or W-2G in the future, either on paper or on magnetic media, please check the "FINAL return" box.

If you are filing a Form 1096 for corrected information returns, enter an "X" in the CORRECTED box at the top of this form.

For more information about filing, see the separate Instructions for Forms 1099, 1098, 5498, 1096, and W-2G.

For Paperwork Reduction Act Notice, see separate Instructions for Forms 1099, 1098, 5498, 1096, and W-2G.   Form **1096** (1989)

Figure 5.

9595 ☐ VOID ☐ CORRECTED For Official Use Only

Type or machine print PAYER'S name, street address, city, state, and ZIP code	1 Rents	OMB No. 1545-0115	
Matthew Dillon 200 Main Street Dodge City, KS 77667	$	**1989**	**Miscellaneous Income**
	2 Royalties $	Statement for Recipients of	

PAYER'S Federal identification number 345 67 8901	RECIPIENT'S identification number 470 36 9258	3 Prizes and awards $	4 Federal income tax withheld $	**Copy A** **For Internal**
Type or machine print RECIPIENT'S name (first, middle, last) Wyatt J. Earp		5 Fishing boat proceeds $	6 Medical and health care payments $	**Revenue** **Service Center**
		7 Nonemployee compensation $ 1,200.	8 Substitute payments in lieu of dividends or interest $	For Paperwork Reduction Act Notice and
Street address P. O. Box 111				instructions for completing this
City, state, ZIP code Kansas City, MO 68888		9 Payer made direct sales of $5,000 or more of consumer products to a buyer (recipient) for resale . . . . ▶ ☐		form, see Instructions for Forms 1099,
Account number (optional)		10 Crop insurance proceeds $	////////	1098, 5498, 1096, and W-2G.

Form **1099-MISC**   Do NOT Cut or Separate Forms on This Page   Department of the Treasury - Internal Revenue Service

---

9595 ☐ VOID ☐ CORRECTED For Official Use Only

Type or machine print PAYER'S name, street address, city, state, and ZIP code	1 Rents	OMB No. 1545-0115	
Matthew Dillon 200 Main Street Dodge City, KS 77667	$	**1989**	**Miscellaneous Income**
	2 Royalties $	Statement for Recipients of	

PAYER'S Federal identification number 345 67 8901	RECIPIENT'S identification number 470 36 9259	3 Prizes and awards $	4 Federal income tax withheld $	**Copy A** **For Internal**
Type or machine print RECIPIENT'S name (first, middle, last) Cyrus Holliday, M.D.		5 Fishing boat proceeds $	6 Medical and health care payments $	**Revenue** **Service Center**
		7 Nonemployee compensation $ 350.	8 Substitute payments in lieu of dividends or interest $	For Paperwork Reduction Act Notice and
Street address 100 Main Street				instructions for completing this
City, state, and ZIP code Dodge City, KS 77667		9 Payer made direct sales of $5,000 or more of consumer products to a buyer (recipient) for resale . . . . ▶ ☐		form, see Instructions for Forms 1099,
Account number (optional)		10 Crop insurance proceeds $	////////	1098, 5498, 1096, and W-2G.

Form **1099-MISC**   Do NOT Cut or Separate Forms on This Page   Department of the Treasury - Internal Revenue Service

---

9595 ☒ VOID ☐ CORRECTED For Official Use Only

Type or machine print PAYER'S name, street address, city, state, and ZIP code	1 Rents	OMB No. 1545-0115	
	$	**1989**	**Miscellaneous Income**
	2 Royalties $	Statement for Recipients of	

PAYER'S Federal identification number	RECIPIENT'S identification number	3 Prizes and awards $	4 Federal income tax withheld $	**Copy A** **For Internal**
Type or machine print RECIPIENT'S name (first, middle, last)		5 Fishing boat proceeds $	6 Medical and health care payments $	**Revenue** **Service Center**
		7 Nonemployee compensation $	8 Substitute payments in lieu of dividends or interest $	For Paperwork Reduction Act Notice and
Street address				instructions for completing this
City, state, and ZIP code		9 Payer made direct sales of $5,000 or more of consumer products to a buyer (recipient) for resale . . . . ▶ ☐		form, see Instructions for Forms 1099,
Account number (optional)		10 Crop insurance proceeds $	////////	1098, 5498, 1096, and W-2G.

VOID (handwritten annotation with arrow)

Form **1099-MISC**   Department of the Treasury - Internal Revenue Service

Figure 6.

Once you have an employee, your reporting requirements, as well as your financial requirements, increase. The first step is to open a separate payroll account at the bank. Make sure the checks come with two detachable check stubs to record withholding information—one stub to go to the employee with the check, the other to remain in your payroll book. The second step is to apply for a Federal Employer Identification Number. File Form SS-4 with your IRS district office. A number will be issued in approximately four weeks and will trigger the sending of reporting forms to you. You also need to apply for a state and/or city tax identification number if you live in a state or city that levies a separate tax. You will then be filing quarterly reports on how much tax you withheld from your workers. More about those reports later.

In order to write out a payroll, you need to know some things about your workers. What you need to know is on Form W-4 and includes Social Security number and number of withholding allowances. Make sure you have a signed Form W-4 for each employee. Now you're ready to write your first payroll.

The withholding information you enter on the payroll stubs are the federal, state, and Social Security taxes withheld from each paycheck you write. Hence, if you pay your worker monthly, you must withhold money to pay his share of these taxes each time you write him a paycheck.

The money you pay each worker equals the gross amount earned less federal and state/local withholding and Social Security tax. The amounts of federal and state tax are determined by marital status and number of withholding allowances and can be looked up in a catalog sent to you after applying for your federal and state identification numbers. The Social Security tax is 7.51 percent of gross earnings in 1989 and 7.65 percent in 1990.

These amounts, plus the employer's portion of Social Security tax (same percentage), must be deposited at a Federal Reserve bank in your area. (Most banks that handle business accounts are federal depositories.) Use your federal deposit coupon (Form 8109) when you receive it to make a deposit each time you write out a payroll. Deposit payroll taxes as you go. That way you won't be tempted to use the withheld funds for operating expenses, which can leave you in a financial bind and trigger punitive penalties if you are caught borrowing workers' money.

Because writing out a payroll is time-consuming, set up a monthly payroll system so you're faced with the task only once a month.

Thirty days after the end of each quarter (March, June, September, December) you are required to file Form 941 (Employer's Quarterly Federal Tax Return) with the IRS. This report reconciles the amounts withheld and deposited with the amounts that should have been withheld and deposited, and allows you to make up any small discrepancies. (Any state or city with its own tax has its own reporting form. Local due dates generally conform to federal due dates.)

Annually, you are required to file Form W-2 for each employee by January 31 of the following year. Form W-2 is a five- or six-part form with forms for three employees on each sheet. The top (colored) copy is sent to the Social Security Administration in your district with Form W-3 as a cover sheet. The last copy is yours to keep; the middle three or four copies go to the employee to file with her individual income tax return.

The other annual federal reporting requirements include Form 940 (FUTA—the federal unemployment tax form), also due by January 31. Most states have their own unemployment tax form and Workers' Compensation insurance as well. Once you have your federal and state identification numbers, these report forms will come to you automatically.

If possible, complete Form 941, Forms W-2/W-3, Form 940, and all the state forms during the first week of January while business is still slow due to the holiday lull. That way a large part of the bookwork will be out of the way and you can focus on your own tax return.

Reports to File for Yourself

If you are self-employed, you are earning income from which no tax has been withheld. Because there is no withholding at the source and no employer is making periodic payments of your money on your behalf, you must make those payments yourself. You make periodic estimated tax payments using Form 1040-ES. Chances are good that, if you need to make federal quarterly payments, you also need to make state payments. Check with your state tax office for the appropriate forms to file for estimated state taxes.

Self-employed people pay estimated taxes quarterly, on the fifteenth day of April, June, September, and January. (State deadlines usually conform to federal deadlines.) If the fifteenth falls on a Sunday or holiday, the deadline is moved to the following business day. Failure to make payments on time results in interest penalties. A postmark is considered proof of filing on time.

There are two ways to make tax payments: through withholding and through quarterly estimated payments. Any combination of the two can cover your liability. If you are wholly self-employed and have no regular employment on which withholding is taken, then, of course, your entire tax payment must come from quarterly filings of estimated payments.

The estimated tax payment is just that—an estimate of how much tax you need to pay for a given year. But what sounds easy is difficult to calculate. At a minimum you need to know the rules on deductibility and to keep scrupulously accurate books. If on March 2, 1990, you calculate your total tax liability for 1989 to be $10,000 and you've paid only $8,000 in quarterly tax payments, you may be facing an underpayment penalty on that $2,000 shortfall, which could run as much as $200 or more.

In the example above, if you had paid $9,000 in quarterly tax payments, you would still owe the IRS another $1,000 but at least you would be able to file Form 2210 with your tax return to exempt you from the penalty for underpaying your 1989 tax bill. Form 2210 provides exemption from the penalty for underpaying your taxes under either of two conditions: 1. Payment of 90 percent of the current year's tax liability (this is the exemption you would use in the situation described above); or 2. Payment of an amount equal to the previous year's tax liability.

If you had paid only $8,000 of the $10,000 owing in 1989, you would try to use the second exemption to avoid the underpayment penalty. Your total federal tax liability for 1988 appears on line 53 of Form 1040. If that figure is $8,000 or less, there will be no penalty for underpaying your 1989 tax, although you will still need to cough up the additional $2,000.

Let's assume you escaped unscathed in 1989. How do you plan your quarterly payments for 1990, the first of which is due April 15, 1990? There are two ways to calculate your payments. The first involves more work and a strong grasp of tax law and is risky; the other is simple and sure, but may result in an overpayment to the IRS during the year.

With the first method you calculate your tax liability at four points during the year: March 31, May 31, August 31, and December 31. Calculate your tax liability for each period, prorating your deduction and personal exemptions. The figure you come up with for each date will be the amount you need to pay for that quarter. At the end of the year, if you owe the IRS more than $500, use the worksheet accompanying Form 2210 (annualized income worksheet) to see if you can escape the penalty or, at least, to see where your calculations failed you.

A more certain method for calculating your estimated tax payments is to base your payments on the current tax year's liability. If you know in March 1990 that your 1989 tax liability is $10,000, divide that figure by four and use that $2,500 figure as your quarterly payment. When you prepare your 1990 tax return, file Form 2210 to claim exemption from the penalty by having paid an amount equal to the previous year's tax liability.

What happens in 1990 if your business drops off and you don't make nearly as much as you did in 1989? Do you still need to send the $2,500 each quarter? No. If by December 1990 you know your net profit is well below the previous year's, or you've added a part-time job and had taxes withheld, you may decrease that last payment. Alternatively, you can skip the January 15 payment altogether provided you file your 1990 return and pay any outstanding liability in full by January 31, 1991.

Practically, it's unusual for income to drop. Income generally increases from year to year. What this means for your quarterly estimated taxes is that you are paying the minimum required by law. By April 15 of the following year, you need to pay up the remaining balance due and make the first payment on the following year's tax liability. And so it goes, year after year.

What happens in a given year if you overpay your quarterly taxes and the IRS ends up owing you $200 or $300? Generally you roll this amount over toward the first quarter estimated payment (which then is $200 or $300 lower than the other three) to avoid checks crossing in the mail or a slip-up in recordkeeping.

It's difficult to get on the quarterly payment bandwagon because the first year of self-employment usually sets you back financially. You need to pay up on the previous year's taxes and then also make a dent in the upcoming year's tax liability. It's tough, but those who pay quarterly not only avoid throwing money away on penalties (it's cheaper to borrow against a credit card) but also avoid having to come up with large sums of cash on demand as they discipline themselves to anticipate these payments. Paying quarterly estimated taxes is about as much fun as going to the dentist, and about as necessary, too.

PART II

Your 1989 Tax Return

6

What's New about the 1989 Tax Forms

Retrospective on the 1986 Tax Reform Act

Tax forms filed for 1989 represent the third year the Tax Reform Act (TRA) of 1986 has been in effect. Three years ago that act promised to be the most revolutionary piece of tax legislation in this nation's history. In its first two years, it had already lived up to that promise.

Under TRA, hundreds of thousands of lower-income taxpayers were removed from the tax rolls. Middle-income taxpayers found themselves paying more taxes, unless they had large families. Upper-income taxpayers found the largest increases in tax liability, largely because of limitations placed on deductions they had used to full advantage under previous tax codes. More taxpayers (especially single people) found out the Internal Revenue Service considered them richer (and hence subject to higher taxes) than they thought they were.

• Capitalization Update

Congress kept its word not to tamper with this revolutionary piece of legislation, making only minor adjustments to TRA. One such adjustment concerns artists directly. Under TRA, artists were subject to capitalization requirements; that is, they were not able to deduct expenses in the year the expenses were incurred but had, instead, to wait until their art was sold to deduct the expenses connected with producing an art piece.

Responding to a groundswell of protest from national and local art organizations, Congress exempted most artists from capitalization requirements. Artists not covered by this exemption include artists in two categories: those who produce works where the utilitarian value exceeds the aesthetic value (potters and jewelers, for example) and those involved in the video and film industry. A description of how these artists should handle tax preparation is included in the Schedule C discussion to come.

• Update on TRA Phase-In Provisions

TRA was phased in over five years. The 1989 tax forms show the third-year limitations established by TRA. Deductions that prior to TRA were unlimited (such as consumer interest paid and losses from limited partnerships or rental property, to name the major areas of change) are limited to 20 percent on the 1989 forms. In the case of investment property (that is, limited partnerships and rental property), the other 80 percent is carried over to future years, to be applied against future profits or deducted when the investment is sold.

Consumer interest deductions not allowed in 1989 can never be recovered. They represent wasted money. When TRA limited interest deductions, individuals responded by changing spending habits and restricting credit card debt to an extent no one had predicted. Credit card debt has decreased per capita, while consumer buying has remained strong, a situation that undoubtedly will force economists back to the drawing table. The phenomenon of decreased use of consumer credit is a powerful reminder of the effect tax law has on the way individuals run their daily lives.

The personal exemption for 1989 has been fully phased in and is worth $2,000 per exemption claimed on the front of Form 1040. The standard deduction (used by taxpayers not itemizing their personal deductions) is $3,100 for a single person, $5,200 for a married couple filing a joint return, and $4,550 for a head of household (unmarried person with dependent child in the house). For future tax years, these figures will be adjusted for inflation, ending the "bracket creep" that eroded salary increases under prior tax laws.

● Electronic Filing

For the first time, taxpayers expecting a refund in any state in the country can file their 1989 tax returns using electronic filing. Electronic filing allows tax practitioners to transmit tax returns to one of three national processing centers by telephone modem.

From the IRS's perspective, electronic filing cuts the volume of paper the IRS is forced to store, eliminates the IRS's responsibility to keypunch tax information, and assures a mathematically correct return. For the taxpayer, refunds should be processed approximately three weeks sooner. For the practitioner, new equipment and additional staff to monitor the electronic filing process mean new costs. Part of the new costs can be absorbed internally as a part of better client services, but part of the cost is certainly passed along to the consumer. Filing returns electronically is sure to speed refunds for all taxpayers.

● Update on Auditing

In 1985 the IRS undertook a massive computerization of its recordkeeping and issued new requirements for third-party payments (among them, banks that pay you interest, agencies or individuals who hire you as an independent contractor). Artists saw an increase in the number of 1099-MISC forms issued to them and also began to see penalties assessed against them for not issuing 1099-MISC forms to independent contractors they employed.

Better records of who is being paid what allowed the IRS to expand its auditing capabilities. The IRS is fond of boasting that the percentage of returns audited has dropped annually, but it's referring only to the number of office or field audits (where you go to their office, or the IRS comes to yours, respectively), and not to the total number of returns changed.

Computer-generated reports and 1099 forms have resulted in "mail" audits, through which the IRS informs you by mail it has reports of income you did not report on your tax return. Included in the notice is the amount the IRS expects you to pay for the oversight. Absent substantiation from you that the report to the IRS is incorrect or that, somewhere in your return, you did report the income, this becomes a liability you must pay.

The increase in reports from third-party payers has allowed the IRS to monitor the typical taxpayer with unusual accuracy. The "typical" taxpayer has a W-2 job, several bank accounts, a mortgage, maybe a mutual fund, and possibly a child or two. This person poses no surprises to the IRS: the IRS has already received almost every tax document this person needs to file a tax return before that person summarizes the information through filing the return itself. Knowing through reports filed by computer what the "typical" taxpayer has earned and what the "typical" taxpayer owes means the IRS has been able to focus its audit attention on people in business for themselves—and this includes artists. The function of an audit is to ascertain that you have reported all your taxable income and have taken only legitimate deductions.

The percentage of returns audited still makes the threat of audit the greatest, most effective compliance tool in the IRS arsenal. After all, the IRS can't audit all small-businesspeople. But if you are audited, the auditor will confront you on the legitimacy of your deductions. Even if you come out of the audit "clean," the auditor has the option of checking a box on the internal audit form to recommend a subsequent-year audit.

Auditors are also more up to date on tax-law code and regulations than in the past. Increased training has led to more successful compliance efforts (which means more money for the IRS). More than ever before, an artist or small-businessperson needs to spend some time becoming familiar with tax law to achieve some level of sophistication in completing a tax return or working effectively with a tax accountant.

Computerization since 1986 has made tax filing a rigorous exercise. Take your legitimate deductions, but:

—Don't press your luck in the hope of "outsmarting" the IRS

—Don't estimate expenses

—Keep adequate documentation, including a mileage log for business miles driven, a contemporaneous log for cash expenditures, and receipts or cancelled checks for any other expenses

—Keep track of your income as you receive it, taking care to separate the W-2 income from independent-contractor income (there's withholding on the former, not on the latter)

Good recordkeeping habits will keep you out of tax trouble.

● Update on Enforcement

Some laws, on the books for years, are not enforced by auditors. From tax district to tax district across the country, enforcement attitudes differ. To protect yourself, know what the tax code says and how it's likely to be interpreted and applied to your case by an auditor. Your auditor has some discretion in how vigorously he or she pursues a certain item on a tax return.

In general, expenses in the following categories arouse the most attention and are most susceptible to an auditor's scrutiny and challenge:

—Travel

—Entertainment

—Major equipment purchases (especially those bought late in the year)

Don't try to deduct travel expenses unless you're enrolled in a structured program whose curriculum is directly and integrally related to your business purpose. Don't try to deduct entertainment where personal pleasure is a material factor. Make sure your equipment is in service (up and running, and you're using it) to claim it in a specific tax year.

● Changes for 1989

1. *Consumer Interest Deduction.* Limited to 20 percent of amount paid.

2. *Mortgage interest* on a primary residence. Fully deductible for the first $1 million in acquisition cost and $100,000 in home equity loans. For loans secured between October 22, 1986 and December 31, 1986, certain special rules apply.

   Mortgage interest on a second home. Fully deductible as long as the second home has running water and kitchen facilities.

3. *Losses on rental property.* Limited to $25,000 per return filed by individuals (single or married filing jointly). For pre-1986 property, an additional 20 percent of the loss above $25,000 can be deducted in 1989; for property purchased after 1986, losses in excess of $25,000 are suspended. To qualify for the $25,000 loss limitation, losses must be allocated among all properties owned.

4. *Losses on passive investments.* Limited to 20 percent on investments purchased prior to 1986; suspended on investments purchased after 1986.

5. *Limitation on employee business expenses.* If you work for a corporation that reimburses you for business expenses, or if you incur business expenses in your regular

line of work, those expenses now are considered miscellaneous deductions. They should be entered on Form 2106, where the net deduction is calculated. The net deduction then is transferred to Schedule A where it is deductible only to the extent it exceeds 2 percent of your adjusted gross income. A change for 1989: if your employer requires you to document expenses, the reimbursement will not appear on your Form W-2, and you do not need to file Form 2106. You still need to use Form 2106 if: a. your employer gives you a per diem, or allows you to keep any excess reimbursement; or b. you claim business expenses in excess of your employer's reimbursement.

Actors who have at least two W-2 jobs and whose adjusted gross income is less than $16,000 in 1989 can list their expenses from Form 2106 directly on line 30 of Form 1040. Actors whose adjusted gross income is more than $16,000 and all other taxpayers must include their Form 2106 expenses in the Miscellaneous Deductions section of Schedule A, subject to the 2-percent threshold.

Remember, do not use Form 2106 unless you are a paid employee who receives a W-2 form. Business expenses for self-employed artists belong on Schedule C.

6. *Changes affecting children.* First, a Social Security number is required for any child born before January 1, 1988. Second, for children subject to the "kiddie tax," parents may now opt to include the child's income on their own tax return by filing Form 8814 and attaching it to their return. This results in an increase in the parents' adjusted gross income (which limits some deductions) but eliminates the need for a separate tax filing for the child.

Claiming the child care credit on Form 2441 when parents work or are enrolled full-time in school now requires the Social Security number (or Federal Employer Identification Number) of each daycare or child-care provider. Even if you participate in a pretax childcare program through your employer, you must have this information to complete Form 2441.

● **Reminders for Self-Employed Artists**

1. *Strict enforcement of recording requirements for deducting automobile costs.* You must keep a log book of business, commuting, and personal mileage. Mileage information is entered on Form 4562, which allows you to deduct automobile expenses on Schedule C. Be aware of the IRS definition of commuting mileage: the first trip from your home and the last trip back to your home, each day. Artists who have studios or work spaces ("offices") in their homes and who can deduct the costs associated with them are being considered as "commuting" on the first trip away from the home studio and the last trip back to it.

2. *Profitability.* An artist must now show a profit in three of any five consecutive tax years to escape IRS scrutiny. Anything less may result in an audit and an IRS ruling that the activity is a hobby and hence subject to rules limiting the deductibility of losses. Rulings can be made retroactively.

3. *Grants and fellowships.* These awards are taxable income. List the amount you received on the "other income" line on the front of Form 1040, where it is not subject to Social Security tax. Do not include it in your Schedule C income because it is not earned income.

4. *Activity code.* Be sure to enter on Schedule C a code from the list on the back of the schedule. Failure to do so causes the IRS computers to select your tax return for review.

5. *Selling business equipment, including automobiles.* Sale of business equipment or automobiles is reported on Form 4797. Be sure to calculate depreciation included in the standard mileage rate used for automobile deductions, and to figure profit or loss only on the business portion of the automobile.

Let's look at the schedules and forms you'll need to complete your 1989 tax return. They'll show how the changes come through to affect individual taxpayers.

7

Forms

Form 1040

Every tax return filed by a self-employed individual revolves around Form 1040, replicated on the following pages.

For 1989 Form 1040 has the same format:

—Filing Status

—Exemptions

—Income

—Adjustments to Income
This is where you take your deductions for retirement-plan contributions, alimony if you pay it, and other miscellaneous deductions from gross income.

—Tax Computation

—Credits

—Other Taxes
Most frequently applicable to self-employed people. Includes self-employment tax (also known as FICA or Social Security and calculated on Schedule SE), and recapture of the investment tax credit (calculated on Form 4255 when a business asset is sold on which investment tax credit was taken in prior years).

Important to artists who are also waiters is the Social Security tax levied on tips, when a waiter does not declare 8.5 percent of his or her gross receipts as tip income. The amount "imputed" for tips by the employer appears on Form W-2 and must be separately listed as income; on Form 4137 the Social Security tax is calculated and that tax is entered here.

Of general interest in this section is the alternative minimum tax (to which more people will be subject in the past, due to the rollback of many tax preference items) and the penalty on early withdrawals from retirement savings plans (applicable in 1989 to IRAs, annuities, Keoghs, and 401(k) or 403(b) plan withdrawals).

—Payments

—Refund or Amount You Owe

Form 1040 may look similar to past years' versions, but there are noteworthy differences. Here they are.

1. *Spouse's name.* There is now room for listing two names on the tax return, helpful for married couples who have different last names.

2. *Social Security numbers.* Any dependent born before January 1, 1988 must have a Social Security number listed on the 1989 Form 1040. Use Form SS-5 to request a Social Security number; allow at least six weeks' processing time.

Form **1040** Department of the Treasury—Internal Revenue Service
U.S. Individual Income Tax Return **1989** (4)

For the year Jan.–Dec. 31, 1989, or other tax year beginning _____, 1989, ending _____ 19__ | OMB No. 1545-0074

Label
Use IRS label. Otherwise, please print or type.

L A B E L / H E R E	
Your first name and initial	Last name	Your social security number
If a joint return, spouse's first name and initial	Last name	Spouse's social security number
Home address (number and street). (If a P.O. box, see page 7 of Instructions.)	Apt. no.	
City, town or post office, state and ZIP code. (If a foreign address, see page 7.)		

For Privacy Act and Paperwork Reduction Act Notice, see Instructions.

Presidential Election Campaign ▶
Do you want $1 to go to this fund? . . . . Yes ☐ No ☐

If joint return, does your spouse want $1 to go to this fund? . Yes ☐ No ☐

Note: Checking "Yes" will not change your tax or reduce your refund.

Filing Status
Check only one box.

1 ☐ Single
2 ☐ Married filing joint return (even if only one had income)
3 ☐ Married filing separate return. Enter spouse's social security no. above and full name here. _____
4 ☐ Head of household (with qualifying person). (See page 7 of Instructions.) If the qualifying person is your child but not your dependent, enter child's name here. _____
5 ☐ Qualifying widow(er) with dependent child (year spouse died ▶ 19___). (See page _ of Instructions.)

Exemptions
(See Instructions on page 8.)

6a ☐ **Yourself** If someone (such as your parent) can claim you as a dependent on his or her tax return, do not check box 6a. But be sure to check the box on line 33b on page 2 . .

b ☐ **Spouse** . . . .

c Dependents:

(1) Name (first, initial, and last name)	(2) Check if under age 2	(3) If age 2 or older, dependent's social security number	(4) Relationship	(5) No. of months lived in your home in 1989

If more than 6 dependents, see Instructions on page 8.

d If your child didn't live with you but is claimed as your dependent under a pre-1985 agreement, check here ▶ ☐
e Total number of exemptions claimed . . . .

No. of boxes checked on 6a and 6b _____
No. of your children on 6c who:
• lived with you _____
• didn't live with you due to divorce or separation (see page 9) _____
No. of other dependents on 6c _____
Add numbers entered on lines above ▶ ☐

Income
Please attach Copy B of your Forms W-2, W-2G, and W-2P here.

If you do not have a W-2, see page 6 of Instructions.

Please attach check or money order here.

7	Wages, salaries, tips, etc. (attach Form(s) W-2)	**7**
8a	Taxable interest income (also attach Schedule B if over $400)	**8a**
b	Tax-exempt interest income (see page 10). DON'T include on line 8a 8b	
9	Dividend income (also attach Schedule B if over $400)	**9**
10	Taxable refunds of state and local income taxes, if any, from worksheet on page 11 of Instructions . .	**10**
11	Alimony received	**11**
12	Business income or (loss) (attach Schedule C)	**12**
13	Capital gain or (loss) (attach Schedule D)	**13**
14	Capital gain distributions not reported on line 13 (see page 11)	**14**
15	Other gains or (losses) (attach Form 4797)	**15**
16a	Total IRA distributions . . 16a____ 16b Taxable amount (see page 11)	**16b**
17a	Total pensions and annuities 17a____ 17b Taxable amount (see page 12)	**17b**
18	Rents, royalties, partnerships, estates, trusts, etc. (attach Schedule E)	**18**
19	Farm income or (loss) (attach Schedule F)	**19**
20	Unemployment compensation (insurance) (see page 13)	**20**
21a	Social security benefits. 21a____ 21b Taxable amount (see page 13)	**21b**
22	Other income (list type and amount—see page 13) _____	**22**
23	Add the amounts shown in the far right column for lines 7 through 22. This is your **total income** ▶	**23**

Adjustments to Income
(See Instructions on page 14.)

24	Your IRA deduction, from applicable worksheet on page 14 or 15	24
25	Spouse's IRA deduction, from applicable worksheet on page 14 or 15	25
26	Self-employed health insurance deduction, from worksheet on page 15	26
27	Keogh retirement plan and self-employed SEP deduction . .	27
28	Penalty on early withdrawal of savings	28
29	Alimony paid. **a** Recipient's last name _____	
	and **b** social security number . . _____	29
30	Add lines 24 through 29. These are your **total adjustments** . . . . . . ▶	**30**

Adjusted Gross Income
31 Subtract line 30 from line 23. This is your **adjusted gross income**. If this line is less than $19,340 and a child lived with you, see "Earned Income Credit" (line 58) on page 20 of the Instructions. If you want IRS to figure your tax, see page 16 of the Instructions . . ▶ | **31**

Tax Compu-tation	32 Amount from line 31 (adjusted gross income)	32
	33a Check if: ☐ **You** were 65 or older ☐ Blind; ☐ **Spouse** was 65 or older ☐ Blind. Add the number of boxes checked and enter the total here . . . . ▶ 33a	
	b If someone (such as your parent) can claim you as a dependent, check here . . ▶ 33b ☐	
	c If you are married filing a separate return and your spouse itemizes deductions, or you are a dual-status alien, see page 16 and check here . . . . ▶ 33c ☐	
	34 Enter the { ● Your **standard deduction** (from page 17 of the Instructions), **OR** larger { ● Your **itemized deductions** (from Schedule A, line 26). of: {　　If you itemize, attach Schedule A and check here . . ▶ ☐ }	34
	35 Subtract line 34 from line 32. Enter the result here	35
	36 Multiply $2,000 by the total number of exemptions claimed on line 6e	36
	37 **Taxable income.** Subtract line 36 from line 35. Enter the result (if less than zero, enter zero) . .	37
	Caution: If under age 14 and you have more than $1,000 of investment income, check here ▶ ☐ and see page 17 to see if you have to use Form 8615 to figure your tax.	
	38 Enter tax. Check if from: **a** ☐ Tax Table, **b** ☐ Tax Rate Schedules, or **c** ☐ Form 8615. (If any is from Form(s) 8814, enter that amount here ▶ **d** _____)	38
	39 Additional taxes (see page 18). Check if from: **a** ☐ Form 4970　**b** ☐ Form 4972	39
	40 Add lines 38 and 39. Enter the total . . . . ▶	40

Credits (See Instructions on page 18.)	41 Credit for child and dependent care expenses (attach Form 2441)	41	
	42 Credit for the elderly or the disabled (attach Schedule R) . .	42	
	43 Foreign tax credit (attach Form 1116)	43	
	44 General business credit. Check if from: **a** ☐ Form 3800 or　**b** ☐ Form (specify) _____	44	
	45 Credit for prior year minimum tax (attach Form 8801) . .	45	
	46 Add lines 41 through 45. Enter the total		46
	47 Subtract line 46 from line 40. Enter the result (if less than zero, enter zero) . . . . . ▶		47

Other Taxes (Including Advance EIC. Payments)	48 Self-employment tax (attach Schedule SE)	48
	49 Alternative minimum tax (attach Form 6251)	49
	50 Recapture taxes (see page 18). Check if from: **a** ☐ Form 4255　**b** ☐ Form 8611 . . .	50
	51 Social security tax on tip income not reported to employer (attach Form 4137)	51
	52 Tax on an IRA or a qualified retirement plan (attach Form 5329)	52
	53 Add lines 47 through 52. Enter the total . . . . ▶	53

Medicare Premium	54 Supplemental Medicare premium (attach Form 8808)	54
	55 Add lines 53 and 54. This is your **total tax** and any supplemental Medicare premium . . . . ▶	55

Payments Attach Forms W-2, W-2G, and W-2P to front.	56 Federal income tax withheld (if any is from Form(s) 1099, check ▶ ☐)	56	
	57 1989 estimated tax payments and amount applied from 1988 return	57	
	58 Earned income credit (see page 20)	58	
	59 Amount paid with Form 4868 (extension request)	59	
	60 Excess social security tax and RRTA tax withheld (see page 20)	60	
	61 Credit for Federal tax on fuels (attach Form 4136) . . .	61	
	62 Regulated investment company credit (attach Form 2439) . .	62	
	63 Add lines 56 through 62. These are your **total payments** . . . . ▶		63

Refund or Amount You Owe	64 If line 63 is larger than line 55, enter amount **OVERPAID** . . . . ▶	64
	65 Amount of line 64 to be **REFUNDED TO YOU** . . . . ▶	65
	66 Amount of line 64 to be **APPLIED TO YOUR 1990 ESTIMATED TAX** ▶	66	
	67 If line 55 is larger than line 63, enter **AMOUNT YOU OWE.** Attach check or money order for full amount payable to "Internal Revenue Service." Write your social security number, daytime phone number, and "1989 Form 1040" on it	67
	68 Penalty for underpayment of estimated tax (see page 21) . . .	68	

Sign Here (Keep a copy of this return for your records.)	Under penalties of perjury, I declare that I have examined this return and accompanying schedules and statements, and to the best of my knowledge and belief, they are true, correct, and complete. Declaration of preparer (other than taxpayer) is based on all information of which preparer has any knowledge. ▶ Your signature ／ Date ／ Your occupation ▶ Spouse's signature (if joint return, BOTH must sign) ／ Date ／ Spouse's occupation

Paid Preparer's Use Only	Preparer's signature ▶ ／ Date ／ Check if self-employed ☐ ／ Preparer's social security no. Firm's name (or yours if self-employed) and address ▶ ／ E.I. No _____ ／ ZIP code _____

3. *Exemptions.* If you have a full-time college student in the house (or you provide more than half the student's support), you can claim that student only if he or she is less than 24 years old on December 31, 1989. If the student is older than 24 years of age on December 31, 1989, you can claim the student as a dependent only if you provide more than half the student's support *and* the student has less than $2,000 gross income.

4. *Income section.* There are no changes here from the 1988 forms. Remember to list tax-exempt interest on line 8b, IRA distributions on line 16a, and pension distributions on line 17a (even if you roll over the distribution to another retirement account). Only the part you keep is listed on line 16b or 17b. That part is also subject to early withdrawal penalty. Complete Form 5329 to compute the penalty. Use line 22, the Other Income line, to list grants or fellowships you received during 1989. Also, if you are filing Form 8814 to claim your minor child's income on your own return, use line 22 to report that income.

5. *Adjustments to Income section.* Employee business expenses are no longer deductible on the front of Form 1040. The deduction, still calculated on Form 2106, is now taken on the Miscellaneous section of Schedule A. An exception is made for actors with more than two W-2 employers and with an adjusted gross income of less than $16,000, who list their Form 2106 business expense deduction on line 30 of the 1989 Form 1040. Enter "Form 2106—Qual. perform. artist" on the dotted line after the phrase *total adjustments.*

6. *Tax Computation.* This section is the same as it was in 1988, except that the standard deduction is larger: $3,100 for a single person, $5,200 for a married couple filing a joint return, and $4,550 for a head of household (unmarried person with dependent child in the house). The personal exemption is also higher than it was in 1988. For 1989, claim $2,000 for each exemption listed in the exemption section on the front of Form 1040. If you file Form 8814 to claim your minor child's income, enter the additional tax on line 38 of this section.

7. *Credits.* This section is unchanged from the 1988 forms. Remember that more information is needed to qualify for the child care credit than in past years.

8. *Other taxes.* Two lines are appended to this section for the Supplemental Medicare premium. Use Form 8808 to calculate the surtax if you are a senior eligible for Social Security benefits, pending Congressional action amending this law.

9. *Payments.* Unchanged from the 1988 forms.

10. *Refund or Amount You Owe.* Unchanged from the 1988 forms.

● Completing your 1989 Form 1040

PRELIMINARIES
Use the label sent to you by the IRS. It speeds processing of your return and ensures accuracy. If your address is different from the address on the label, cross it out and neatly enter the new address. If your name has changed, cross out the incorrect information and enter the correction. If you and your spouse have different names, enter one name on the top line and the other name on the second line. Enter your Social Security number at the end of the name line. Do the same for your spouse.

FILING STATUS
Enter your filing status. If you are married but you and your spouse are filing separate returns, you must enter your spouse's name and Social Security number. Failure to do so will slow the processing of your return and may result in a penalty.

If you are separated from your spouse, you may file as single under the following circumstances: you have a state-issued separation decree or separate maintenance decree or; you have a minor child and did not live with your spouse for any day during the last six months of the calendar year. If you don't qualify under either of these circumstances and you are still legally married on December 31, 1989, you must file jointly or separately.

EXEMPTIONS

You are entitled to claim yourself as an exemption unless you can be claimed as a dependent on someone else's tax return. Claim an exemption for each dependent child who lived in your household and for whom you provided more than one-half the support. You do not have to provide more than one-half the support if you are the custodial parent of a child awarded to you under a divorce decree issued after 1985.

If you are a pre-1985 custodial parent, your divorce decree should stipulate which parent is eligible to claim the exemption. If the decree does not, the parent providing more than one-half the support can claim the child. If neither parent provides more than one-half the support (and Aid to Dependent Children and Social Security benefits count as support), neither is eligible to claim the child as an exemption.

If you are the noncustodial parent under a post-1985 divorce decree, the only way you can claim a child as a dependent is to obtain from your former spouse a waiver and attach it to your tax return. Use Form 8135 for this purpose.

INCOME

Enter on **line 7** the income reported to you on Form W-2. Only W-2 income belongs on this line. If you are self-employed you do not receive a W-2 report on your self-employment income. The only place to report self-employment income (which includes income paid to you and reported on a Form 1099-MISC) is Schedule C.

On **lines 8 and 9** report interest and dividend income. Interest income is reported to you on Form 1099-INT; dividend income, on Form 1099-DIV. Tax-exempt interest income will also be reported to you on a separate Form 1099-INT and must be entered on **line 8b.** Information sent to you on a 1099 form has already been sent directly to the government. Keep track of your investments so you can report this income accurately on your tax return. Failure to do so frequently results in an audit.

On **line 10** list the amount of your state tax refund only if you itemized personal deductions on your 1988 Schedule A of your 1986 return. State tax refunds usually are reported to you on a 1099 form. If you received a 1099 form indicating you were issued a state tax refund, but you didn't itemize personal deductions, you must list the refund on line 10 and then back it out (as a negative figure) on line 22, the "Other income" line. If you did not itemize personal deductions on Schedule A, your state tax was never deducted in calculating your federal tax liability and so you do not report any refund (which represents an excess deduction) as income.

Enter any alimony you receive on **line 11.** Child-support payments never count as income to the recipient or as a deduction to the payer. If you receive a "familial maintenance payment," your divorce decree should stipulate how much of it is earmarked for child support; if it does not, the entire payment is considered alimony. If your ex-spouse is behind in payments, any payments made are considered child-support payments first, then alimony payments.

Line 12 is used by self-employed individuals to report their self-employment profit from Schedule C. If you are self-employed, follow the separate instructions provided in this chapter for that schedule.

Capital gains and losses are calculated on Schedule D and reported on **line 13.** The 1989 Schedule D has been expanded to two pages (four sides) to allow for a complete listing of transactions. Do not summarize your stock trades. Remember that sale of mutual fund shares constitutes a taxable transaction and must be reported on Schedule D. Sales of shares in tax-exempt mutual funds will trigger a Form 1099-B.

Make sure you report all trades on schedule D. You will receive a Form 1099-B report for each taxable transaction. Like all 1099s, the one you receive has already been sent to the government. Be sure you calculate profit or loss on each transaction for which you receive a Form 1099-B. IRS publication 564 "Mutual Fund Distributions" explains options for figuring the basis of mutual fund shares sold.

Line 14 allows you to report capital gains distributions separately from other dividend income. If you live in a state where capital gains are taxed at a lower rate than other income, report the regular dividends on line 9 of Form 1040 and the capital gains portion on line 14. If your state treats all dividend income the same, report the "gross dividend" figure from the Form 1099-DIV on line 9 and skip line 14.

Use **line 15** to report gains or losses from the sale or disposition of business property. Calculate the gain or loss on Form 4797 and then transfer the information from that form to this line. Remember to use Form 4797 to calculate the gain or loss on an automobile used in business. You need to take into account the amount of business usage (whether you used the actual expense method or the standard mileage deduction) to calculate the gain or loss.

Enter on **lines 16a and 16b** any IRA distributions you received during 1989. A distribution means you withdrew money from the retirement account. If you received an IRA distribution and were not at least 59½ years old when you received it, you are subject to a 10 percent penalty on the amount withdrawn. This penalty is calculated on Form 5329 and is imposed on top of the tax due on the amount withdrawn.

To calculate the taxable amount of any IRA distribution, enter the amount received on line 16a. The difference between the figure on line 16a and the taxable amount on line 16b is the amount you rolled over to another qualified retirement plan within sixty days of receiving the distribution. The sixty days is counted from the day you constructively receive the funds (the day you receive the money or have it available to you), not the day your IRA trustee issues you the check. Keep good records in case of IRS challenge. The amount you list on line 16b is the amount subject to 10 percent penalty on Form 5329.

Use **lines 17a and 17b** to report distributions from any pension or annuity fund (including Keogh plans). Enter the gross amount distributed on line 17a. The difference between lines 17a and 17b is the amount of your after-tax contributions to the pension or annuity plus any amount rolled over to another qualified retirement account within sixty days of constructive receipt of the funds.

For withdrawals from pension or annuity funds, the amount subject to early withdrawal penalty on Form 5329 is the amount on line 17b, unless you were at least 59½ years old when you withdrew the money. Also, certain Employee Stock Option Plans (ESOPs) are not subject to this withdrawal penalty, but all voluntary contributions are unless you meet the age requirement.

Income from rental property, partnerships and S-corporations, and royalties on oil and gas properties is reported on **line 18.** Royalties on works you create are considered self-employment income and can be reported only on Schedule C. See the separate instructions later in this chapter on Schedule E.

Profit (or loss) from running a farm is calculated on Schedule F and reported on **line 19.**

Unemployment compensation is fully taxable. Report any benefits on **line 20.** Few states withhold federal or state taxes from unemployment compensation, which may result in your owing a penalty for underpaying your estimated taxes. If you receive unemployment insurance payments, make estimated tax payments or increase your withholding by decreasing the number of allowances claimed when you go back to work. This may work to provide enough additional payments to cover the liability from the unemployment insurance compensation. If you are unemployed a long time, you should file estimated tax forms.

Social Security benefits must be reported on **line 21a.** As in the past, only part of these benefits may be taxable, but in any case no more than 50 percent of the total benefits received are subject to taxation. Use the worksheet in the tax instruction booklet to determine how much, if any, of your Social Security benefits are taxable. List that amount on **line 21b.**

Other income can be listed on **line 22.** Examples of entries on this line are: jury duty pay; fellowships, grants, prizes, and awards; honoraria for academicians; your minor child's income (if you choose to file Form 8814). Do not use this line for any self-employment income.

ADJUSTMENTS TO INCOME
Individual Retirement Account contributions may still be deductible on **lines 24 and 25.** An individual can contribute up to $2,000 per year to an IRA; a married couple $4,000, provided both spouses work and each earns at least $2,000. For a married couple where one spouse works and the other does not, the maximum contribution is $2,250 (split any way they choose, up to $2,000 for one of them). If, however, one spouse is self-employed and shows a loss, the maximum contribution for that couple is $2,000. An IRA contribution cannot exceed earned income. For IRA eligibility only, alimony is considered earned income.

The deductibility of a 1989 IRA contribution is subject to income limitations described as follows:

If a single person is covered by a pension plan (indicated by a check mark in the "pension plan" box of the W-2 form) and if that individual has more than $35,000 adjusted gross income (prior to the IRA deduction), that person can claim no deduction for the IRA contribution.

If his or her adjusted gross income is between $25,000 and $35,000, the deductibility of the IRA contribution decreases $200 for every $1,000 his or her income exceeds $25,000, so that the deduction is gradually phased out. Where an IRA contribution is only partially deductible, Form 8615 needs to be completed and filed with the tax return. In addition to Form 8615, the taxpayer should in a separate ledger track the nondeductible contributions from year to year so that taxes aren't paid on those nondeductible amounts when the taxpayer begins to withdraw IRA funds. *Note:* the IRS has ruled it will consider distributions as coming proportionately from all IRA accounts. This means that taxpayers cannot earmark withdrawals as coming from an account consisting exclusively of nondeductible contributions. If this single person has income over $35,000, no part of the IRA contribution is deductible, though the earnings are tax-deferred until the funds are withdrawn.

To summarize: For a single person covered by a pension plan and having income under $25,000, an IRA of $2,000 is fully deductible. At $30,000, a $2,000 IRA contribution results in a $1,000 tax deduction. At $35,000 and beyond, no part of the IRA contribution is tax deductible. If that single person is not covered by a pension plan at work and does not have a pension plan as a self-employed person, that person is eligible to fully deduct an IRA contribution of up to $2,000 per year.

For a married couple filing jointly, the deductibility phase-out begins at $40,000, with no IRA contribution eligible for deduction if adjusted gross income (before the IRA deduction) exceeds $50,000, as long as one spouse is covered by a pension plan where he or she works. "Covered" by a pension plan is defined as being eligible for coverage, regardless of whether or not an individual is fully or partially or not at all vested in 1989.

Adjusted gross income, for purposes of figuring the IRA deduction, is the sum of all income less the sum of all adjustments to income, except for the IRA deduction. A self-employed individual who has a Keogh or Simplified Employee Pension (SEP) retirement plan can still have an IRA if he or she meets the income limitations listed above.

Where one spouse is covered by a pension plan and the other is not, some strategizing about long-term objectives is required as to whether the deductible contribution should be claimed on line 24 or line 25. Particularly where one spouse has served as homemaker for a period of time, that spouse could claim the $2,000 limit in order to build up his or her account, while the working spouse could use other methods to build up his or her retirement account.

Participation in a pretax retirement plan—a 401(k) or 403(b) plan or annuity—results in your being classified as a "covered" employee. Sometimes you can contribute enough to one of these pretax plans to reduce your income enough to have a fully deductible IRA as well.

If your income puts you squarely into the 28 percent bracket, you may want to consider a nondeductible IRA contribution as a good investment. Remember that IRA contributions remain practically untouchable until you are 59½ years old due to the early-withdrawal penalty. This means you should not use an IRA as a type of savings account. The funds are meant for retirement. Period.

If you're self-employed, report 25 percent of your health insurance premiums you pay on **line 26,** up to the net profit you show on line 12 of Form 1040. (Report the remaining 75 percent of your health care premiums on Schedule A.) If you are married and your spouse pays for your health care coverage through his or her employer, you are not eligible to claim this adjustment to income.

Self-employed individuals who regularly produce a sizeable net profit from their trade or business should establish a Keogh retirement plan or SEP plan to shelter some of their income from taxation. This should be done once an individual outgrows the $2,000 annual limit on IRA contributions. Contributions to a Keogh or SEP plan are listed on **line 27.**

If a person who has a regular W-2 job is also self-employed, a Keogh or SEP plan can be used to make retirement plan contributions and also reduce taxable income without regard to whether that person is a "covered" employee, since contributions are based exclusively on net profit from self-employment activities.

By the same token, if a self-employed person has a part-time W-2 job and is "covered" by a pension plan at that job, the maximum deductible IRA contribution depends on adjusted gross income, as described above. Contributions to a SEP or Keogh plan remain independent of everything except net profit from self-employment activities.

Most Keogh plans are one of two types: profit sharing or defined contribution. Under the former, an individual can contribute up to 15 percent of after-contribution net profit (or 13.043 percent of net profit) to a retirement account. Under the latter, an individual must contribute the same percentage of net profit to the plan each year. With a defined-contribution Keogh plan, the self-employed person selects a percentage when the plan is established. Annually, that minimum percentage of net profit must be contributed to the Keogh account. You can contribute more but never less than the minimum percentage established.

The overall limit on Keogh contributions is 20 percent of net profit annually, through a combination of profit sharing and defined-contribution plans, up to $30,000 per year. The overall limit on SEP contributions is 13.043 percent of net profit, up to $30,000 per year.

The benefits of a Keogh plan over a SEP plan depend on how old you are and where you are in your business life. For those whose businesses are well established and who are in their late thirties or older, the advantages of a Keogh are obvious. For top-bracket earners, the defined-contribution plan should be selected for maximum contributions. For middle-or lower-bracket earners, the profit-sharing version should be selected until you're comfortably able to contribute more than 13.043 percent of your net profit, which is when you need to switch to a Keogh plan.

A Keogh plan requires annual reporting; a SEP plan does not. Keogh participants must file an annual report with the IRS (Form 5500 series) by July 31 of the year following the tax year whether or not they made a contribution that year. A fifty-dollar-per-day penalty is assessed for late filing.

Line 28 allows you to deduct the penalty you incur when you withdraw savings prematurely from a savings program (usually a Certificate of Deposit). You should have no premature-withdrawal penalty on any savings plan you inherit. If a bank levies such a penalty on an inherited piece of property, meet with bank officials in order to resolve the issue before filing a formal complaint with the federal bank regulatory agency.

Alimony you pay to your ex-spouse can be deducted on **line 29**. Make sure this is alimony only. Child support is not deductible. List your ex-spouse's name on **line 29a** and Social Security number on **line 29b** to guarantee the deductibility of these payments.

Use **line 30** only if you are a performing artist qualified to report business expenses from Form 2106 directly on the front of Form 1040. On the dotted line following "total adjustments" enter the words "Qual. perform. artist, Form 2106" and be sure to attach Form 2106 identifying your business expenses to your tax return.

ADJUSTED GROSS INCOME
Income (**line 23**) less adjustments to income (**line 30**) equals your adjusted gross income (**line 31**).

TAX COMPUTATION
Use **line 33a** to identify your (or your spouse's) eligibility for additional deductions if you are older than 65 years of age or blind. The additional deduction comes in the form of an increased standard deduction, and is not available to taxpayers who itemize their personal deductions.

Check the box on **line 33b** if you are claimed as a dependent on another taxpayer's return. Remember that you are not eligible to claim a personal exemption for yourself if someone else is claiming one for you.

Check the box on **line 33c** if you and your spouse are filing separate tax returns and your spouse has elected to itemize personal deductions. That election forces you to itemize personal deductions as well, even if the standard deduction would be more beneficial to you.

On **line 34** enter the larger of the standard deduction allowed or your personal itemized deductions from Schedule A (discussed below).

Claim on **line 36** a $2,000 deduction for each exemption listed on the front of Form 1040. The result is your taxable income on **line 37.** Use this figure to determine your 1989 federal income tax by referring to the tax tables printed in the tax instruction booklet. Taxpayers with high incomes may need to use other tax tables or computation methods. See the instructions if you cannot readily assess the amount of your tax liability from the tax tables.

Check one box on **line 38** to identify the method used to determine your 1989 tax liability. Also, if you use Form 8814 to report income belonging to a minor child, be sure to enter "Form 8814" on the dotted line and add the child's liability to your own on line 38.

Additional taxes (**line 39**) most often result from using five-year averaging on a pension distribution (Form 4972). Additional tax liabilities can also accrue due to trust income (Form 4970).

Your total federal income tax liability appears on **line 40.**

CREDITS

Credits allow you to reduce your tax liability. The most frequently used credit is the child care credit. Complete Form 2441 to determine how much you can deduct. Income is no bar to receiving this credit, but both spouses must work. Status as a full-time student is construed as full-time employment worth $2,400 per year for the purpose of determining credit amount.

Note the change this year to Form 2441: Identification numbers are required for every daycare or child-care provider whose payments you are applying toward the credit. Either a Social Security number or Federal Employer Identification Number must be provided on Form 2441. If you fail to supply a number, you must document your attempts to secure the number or risk disallowance of the credit. If a provider refuses to give you an identification number, that fact must be documented on Form 2441.

The child care credit is deducted on **line 41.**

Qualifying for the credit for the elderly and/or disabled is difficult. If you think you might qualify, complete Schedule R. Enter any allowable credit on **line 42.**

Other credits include the foreign tax credit (Form 1116) and the general business credit (Forms 3800, 3468, 5884, 6478, 6765, or 8586). Enter these credits on **line 43** for the former and **line 44** for the latter.

You'll use **line 45** if you had to prepay taxes on sale of business property using a long-term contract. The amount prepaid comes back to you in the form of a credit to the extent the actual liability comes due annually. See Form 8801 if you sold property for more than $150,000 in 1989.

These credits cannot lower your tax liability to below zero. Also, they cannot result in a refund in and of themselves.

OTHER TAXES

If you are self-employed, you have already used Schedule C to figure your net profit or loss. In either case, you transferred the figure on **line 30** of Schedule C to **line 2** of Schedule SE. You also transferred any profit or loss from a partnership to **line 2** of Schedule SE.

If the profit from your self-employment activities (sole proprietorships and partnerships) exceeds $400, you must pay Social Security tax on that profit. The 1989 FICA rate is 13.02 percent on the first $48,000 of earned income (W-2 income or profit from self-employment or partnerships). Use Schedule SE to calculate your Social Security tax liability and then enter that tax on **line 48.**

The alternative minimum tax (AMT) was introduced in 1984 to prevent high-income individuals from avoiding tax liabilities due to a multitude of tax-sheltering activities. Certain tax deductions were labeled tax preference items, subject to inclusion when the alternative minimum tax was figured. By and large, if you are an individual earning less than $25,000 per year or a married couple earning less than $40,000 per year, you needn't concern yourself with the AMT and Form 6251. If, however, you earn more than that or participate in certain limited partnerships, you must file Form 6251 to determine whether or not you will owe more tax than you have previously calculated. Enter any AMT amount on **line 49.**

Line 50 is tax from recapture of investment tax credit. The investment tax credit, repealed for 1986 and later, applied to purchases of some business assets from 1981 through 1985. Investment tax credits from assets sold prior to the end of their useful lives (equal to the depreciable life of the asset, if it was depreciated; or the potential depreciable life, if it was expensed) are subject to recapture. Use Form 4255 to calculate this recapture amount.

Waiters who do not declare 8.5 percent of their daily gross receipts as tips may have their employers "impute," or attribute to them, a certain tip income on the basis of averages used in that business. Wages paid the waiter are reported in box 10 of Form W-2, with the "attributable" tip income reported in box 6. Whenever a figure appears in box 6 of Form W-2, that amount must be included in W-2 income on **line 7** of Form 1040, and it must also be used on Form 4137 to calculate the Social Security tax on those tips. That tax is entered on **line 51.**

If you are a waiter, you are better off reporting 8.5 percent of your receipts as tip income. The alternative forces you to keep additional records to prove your case, should the "imputed" amount reported by your employer exceed the tips you actually received.

Any withdrawals from a qualified retirement plan are subject to a 10 percent early-withdrawal penalty. Calculate the penalty on Form 5329 and enter that additional tax on **line 52.**

Line 53 shows your total 1989 federal tax liability.

Line 54 is new this year. Highly controversial, this tax is levied on people eligible for Medicare and is an attempt by Congress to fund catastrophic health plan coverage for Medicare-eligible people. Use Form 8808 to calculate the surtax if you are eligible for Medicare.

PAYMENTS

Enter federal tax withholding shown on your W-2 on **line 56.** Do not include any FICA taxes in this amount.

Line 57 shows the estimated tax payments you made on April 15, June 15, and September 15, 1989, plus the January 15, 1990 payment if you have made at least one of the earlier payments. Also included in this line is any money rolled over from overpayment of your 1988 taxes.

You may be eligible for an earned income credit if your 1989 adjusted gross income is less than $19,340 and you have a dependent child in your household. Use tables in the tax instruction book to determine your earned income credit. Enter the credit on **line 58.**

If you applied for an extension to file your 1989 tax return by filing Form 4868 on or before April 15, 1990, you had to calculate your 1989 tax liability prior to filing the form and pay any excess liability with Form 4868 for the extension to be granted. List whatever amount you sent with Form 4868 on **line 59.**

If you had two or more employers, they may have withheld excess Social Security or railroad retirement fund taxes. If your W-2 income is less than $48,000, don't worry; if it's more, check your FICA withholding to see if you are entitled to a refund by entering the excess withholding on **line 60.** (Note that if you have only one employer who overwithholds Social Security, you must apply for a refund to that employer.)

Lines 61 and 62 refer to special credits for commercial fuel use (Form 4136) and to regulated investment companies (Form 2439). You may be eligible for the former if you purchased a diesel-fueled automobile in 1989.

Line 63 shows the total payments you have made toward your 1989 tax liability. If your payments exceed the total tax liability shown on **line 55** you have a refund (**line 64**). That refund can be sent to you (**line 65**) or rolled over to your 1990 estimated tax payments (**line 66**) or split any way you choose.

If, on the other hand, your liability exceeds your payments, you owe the federal government some money which you must send along with your return, or in any event no later than April 15, 1990. If that amount exceeds $500, you may also be subject to a penalty for underpaying your taxes.

If the amount on **line 68** is greater than $500, complete Form 2210 to see if you are exempt from the penalty for underpaying your taxes or, if you are not, to calculate the size of that penalty. If you do not meet the standards for exemption from the penalty, you must include the penalty in the amount you send to cover your 1989 tax liability.

Generally, only two conditions qualify you to be excused from the penalty for underpaying your taxes. The first is that you paid in a timely manner—through withholding and/or estimated taxes—an amount equivalent to 90 percent of your 1989 tax liability. Unless you keep extremely reliable books on your business and investments and know more than a smattering of tax law, this figure is difficult to predict reliably.

The second condition is easier to meet. It requires that you pay—again, via withholding and/or estimated tax payments—an amount equivalent to your previous year's tax liability.

Here's how it works: If you paid in 1989—through withholding or estimated tax payments—an amount equal to one-fourth of your 1988 tax liability each quarter, then you owe no penalty for underpaying your 1989 taxes, even if your underpayment amounts to tens of thousands of dollars. You still have a major tax liability but there is no penalty on top of it. This second exemption to the penalty is the most convenient method of keeping your tax payments reasonable while simultaneously insuring you will not fall into the penalty situation for underpaying your taxes.

Why is it important not to underpay your taxes? For 1989 the penalty for failure to make timely payments is 11 percent annually, from April 15, 1989 (the date of the first quarterly payment) until the total liability is paid. Compound this with a state late-filing penalty and you can see why it's easier to borrow against a credit card than from the government.

This concludes our discussion of Form 1040. Of course, a Form 1040 is only as good as the forms and schedules that accompany it, and it is to these supporting documents that we now turn our attention.

Forms 1040A and 1040EZ

These are not included in this book. If you are self-employed you cannot use them.

Form 2106

Form 2106 is used to report business expenses you incur as a result of being someone else's employee. The 1989 Form 2106 is streamlined due to changes in reporting requirements. Beginning in 1989, if you substantiate expenses to your employer and are reimbursed only the amount you substantiate, the reimbursement will not appear on your W-2 form.

Use Form 2106 only if your employer provides you with a per diem (no substantiation required from you; you can keep whatever you don't spend) or if you want to claim expenses your employer does not reimburse (such as mileage reimbursement or seminars related to your job). Remember that if you choose not to submit a claim for reimbursement to your employer and if your employer would reimburse you for expenses if you submitted a claim, you cannot claim a deduction for these expenses on your tax return.

If you have regular paid employment in addition to self-employment income, you need to keep separate expense records for each kind of employment. Regular employment expenses are recorded on Form 2106; self-employment expenses are recorded on Schedule C. If your jobs overlap (for example, an arts administrator for a state government and a practicing artist), determine for which activity an expense was primarily incurred and list the expense in the books for that activity.

Form 2106 is replicated on the following page.

Use Part II to calculate your deduction for business use of your automobile. Then go back to Part I to identify other business expenses.

Enter in **Part II, Section A, line 14** the date your automobile was placed into service. "Service" is defined as the date you purchased the vehicle, whether or not you used it for business. Enter on **line 15** the total number of miles you drove the car in 1989. Take this from your mileage log by subtracting the year-end odometer reading from the start of the year odometer reading.

If you have two automobiles you use for business, enter the data for one car in column (a) and the data for the other in column (b). You should have separate mileage logs and separate expenses records for each car.

Your business miles on **line 16** are the sum of each day's log of miles driven for business purposes. Remember that you have business mileage as a regular employee only if you are traveling from one job site to another. Commuting is defined as your first trip out in the morning and your last trip home at night and is not business mileage. An exception is made if your first trip is outside the normal radius of your home area, a distance arbitrarily determined to be thirty-five miles.

Line 17 is simple division to determine percentage of business use. **Lines 18, 19, and 20** are intended to keep you honest. The sum of lines 16, 19, and 20 equals the total mileage on line 15. Everyone now, by definition, has commuting mileage. If you work at a W-2 job 5 days per week, 50 weeks per year, your entry on line 19 is 5 times 50 times the average round-trip commuting distance on line 18.

Questions on **lines 21, 22, and 23a and 23b** qualify your automobile as a business vehicle. You must answer these questions. If you did not keep daily odometer readings, do not attempt to write off business mileage unless you can reliably reconstruct mileage records from your appointment book.

Once you've completed Part II Section A, complete either Section B or Section C. If this is the first year you've used your automobile for business, then you have a choice to use Section B or Section C. If you've ever used the actual expense method of claiming business expenses for automobile use, you must use Section C. If you own the car whose expenses you are claiming, also use Section D. A leased vehicle is eligible only for the actual expense method of deducting operating expenses; no entry is permitted for leased vehicles in Section D since you do not own a leased vehicle.

The standard mileage rate for 1989 is 25.5 cents per business mile for the first 15,000 business miles, and 11 cents per mile for anything more.

If this is the first year you're using your car for business, use these criteria to decide which method is better for you in the long run. If you anticipate using your car more than 50 percent for business (without commuting mileage) for at least the next three years, and you have a moderately expensive to expensive vehicle that you will trade in within five years, use the expense method. If you bought a used vehicle that you will drive for the foreseeable (long) future and you are unsure of your actual business usage, use the standard mileage rate.

Whether or not your employer reimburses you for automobile expenses has no bearing on your choice of deduction method.

For the standard deduction method, complete **Part II, Section B, line 24** by entering the number of business miles, up to 15,000 miles. (The excess miles go on **line 25**.) Up to 15,000 business miles per year is calculated at 25.5 cents per mile (**line 26**); anything in excess at 11 cents per mile (**line 27**). (Note that once you have more than 60,000 business miles on a car, all miles are calculated at 11 cents per mile.) The total standard mileage deduction is entered on **line 28** and transferred to Part 1, line 1 of Form 2106.

The standard mileage rate is intended to cover the costs of running your vehicle and thus includes gas and oil, repairs and maintenance, and insurance. A depreciation factor is included in the standard mileage rate. To the standard mileage rate deduction can be added (on line 2 of Part I) business parking costs.

Form **2106**

Department of the Treasury
Internal Revenue Service

Employee Business Expenses

▶ See separate Instructions.

▶ Attach to Form 1040.

OMB No. 1545-0139

1989

Attachment Sequence No. **54**

Your name	Social security number	Occupation in which expenses were incurred

Part I Employee Business Expenses

STEP 1 Enter Your Expenses

		Column A Other Than Meals and Entertainment		Column B Meals and Entertainment	
1 Vehicle expense from Part II, line 28 or line 35	1				
2 Parking fees, tolls, and local transportation, including train, bus, etc. . .	2				
3 Travel expense while away from home, including lodging, airplane, car rental, etc. **Do not** include meals and entertainment	3				
4 Business expenses not included on lines 1 through 3. **Do not** include meals and entertainment	4				
5 Meals and entertainment expenses. (See Instructions.)	5				
6 Add lines 1 through 5 and enter the **total expenses** here	6				

Note: *If you were not reimbursed for any expenses in Step 1, skip lines 7–9 and enter the amount from line 6 on line 10.*

STEP 2 Enter Amounts Your Employer Gave You For Expenses Listed In STEP 1.
(See the Instructions for lines 7 and 8.)

7 Enter amounts your employer gave you that were **not** reported to you on Form W-2 (see Instructions)	7				
8 Enter amounts your employer gave you that were reported to you in **Box 16** of Form W-2 (see Instructions)	8				
9 Add the amounts on lines 7 and 8. Enter the total here	9				

STEP 3 Figure Expenses To Deduct on Schedule A (Form 1040)

10 Subtract line 9 from line 6	10				
Note: *If both columns of line 10 are zero, stop here. If Column A is less than zero, report the amount as income. See the Instructions for how to report.*					
11 Enter 20% (.20) of line 10, Column B	11				
12 Subtract line 11 from line 10	12				
13 Add the amounts on line 12 of both columns and enter the total here. **Also** enter the total on Schedule **A (Form 1040), line 20.** (Qualified performing artists and handicapped employees, see Instructions for special rules on where to enter the total.) . . . . ▶	13				

For Paperwork Reduction Act Notice, see Instructions.

Form **2106** (1989)

Part II Vehicle Expenses (Use either your actual expenses (Section C) or the standard mileage rate (Section B).)
(Rural mail carriers, see page 1 of the Instructions.)

Section A.—General Information

			(a) Vehicle 1	(b) Vehicle 2
14	Enter the date vehicle was placed in service	14	/ /	/ /
15	Total mileage vehicle was used during 1989	15	miles	miles
16	Miles included on line 15 that vehicle was used for business	16	miles	miles
17	Percent of business use (divide line 16 by line 15)	17	%	%
18	Average daily round trip commuting distance	18	miles	miles
19	Miles included on line 15 that vehicle was used for commuting	19	miles	miles
20	Other personal mileage (add lines 16 and 19 and subtract the total from line 15).	20	miles	miles

21 Do you (or your spouse) have another vehicle available for personal purposes? ☐ Yes ☐ No

22 If your employer provided you with a vehicle, is personal use during off duty hours permitted? ☐ Yes ☐ No ☐ Not applicable

23a Do you have evidence to support your deduction? ☐ Yes ☐ No. **23b** If "Yes," is the evidence written? ☐ Yes ☐ No

Section B.—Standard Mileage Rate (Do not use this section unless you own the vehicle.)

24	Enter the smaller of line 16, or 15,000 miles (Rural mail carriers, see Instructions.).	24	miles
25	Subtract line 24 from line 16	25	miles
26	Multiply line 24 by 24¢ (.24) (see Instructions if vehicle is fully depreciated)	26	
27	Multiply line 25 by 11¢ (.11)	27	
28	Add lines 26 and 27. Enter total here and on Part I, line 1	28	

Section C.—Actual Expenses

			(a) Vehicle 1	(b) Vehicle 2
29	Gasoline, oil, repairs, vehicle insurance, etc	29		
30	Vehicle rentals.	30		
31	Value of employer-provided vehicle (applies only if included on Form W-2 at 100% fair rental value, see Instructions)	31		
32	Add lines 29 through 31.	32		
33	Multiply line 32 by the percentage on line 17	33		
34	Depreciation from lines 36 and 37, column (f) (see Instructions)	34		
35	Add lines 33 and 34. Enter total here and on Part I, line 1	35		

Section D.—Depreciation of Vehicles
(You can only claim depreciation for a vehicle you own. There is a limit on the amount of depreciation and Section 179 deduction you can claim. See the instructions for the limit. **If line 17 above is 50 percent or less, you cannot claim the Section 179 deduction and you must figure depreciation using the straight line method over 5 years.**)

	Cost or other basis (a)	Basis for depreciation (Business use only—see Instructions) (b)	Method of figuring depreciation (c)	Depreciation deduction (d)	Section 179 deduction (e)	Total column (d) + column (e) (enter in Section C, line 34) (f)
36 Vehicle 1						
37 Vehicle 2						

Interest on a car loan for an automobile used in business is deductible only as consumer interest on Schedule A (limited, in 1989, to 20 percent of the amount actually paid). Also enter on Schedule A the fee you pay for an automobile license, provided you live in a state that assesses fees on the basis of automobile value. If you do, the amount exceeding the base rate for an auto license is deductible as a personal itemized deduction on Schedule A.

The actual expense method, by contrast, allows you to deduct a percentage of the actual costs of running the vehicle. The percentage is the figure on **line 17.**

List actual costs on **line 29** of Part II, Section C. If you need to hire a rental vehicle, those costs can be entered on **line 30.** If you have a company car, your employer may have included the value of that car in your W-2 wages, in which case you need to use **line 31** to back out part of that perquisite.

Total expenses to operate the vehicle appear on **line 32.** Multiply line 32 by the actual percentage business use from line 17 to determine the business portion of your actual expenses (**line 33**). If you own the vehicle, add the depreciation figured in Section D for the total allowable automobile deduction on line 35.

To use Section D, enter the cost of the vehicle in column (a). Column (b) is column (a) multiplied by the business percentage use from line 17. The method of figuring depreciation in column (c) is "S/L" or "ACRS" or "MACRS," along with the lifetime you have assigned the vehicle—five years for vehicles placed in service in 1987 or later. (See the discussion of Form 4562 for an explanation of these depreciation methods.) Refer to the appendix for more specific information on depreciation, since it is one of the more complicated aspects of tax preparation.

The depreciation deduction (column (d)) is current-year depreciation. If this is the first year a vehicle is in service, you may elect to write off part of the cost directly. This is the "Section 179 expense" referred to in column (e). The maximum deduction for an automobile placed in service in 1989 is $2,560. This assumes 100 percent use of the automobile (which is impossible, unless you're driving a taxicab or other commercial vehicle, since you will have commuting mileage). If you use your car less than 100 percent for business, you must reduce the maximum Sec. 179 deduction proportionately.

The sum of depreciation deduction and Section 179 deduction can never be more than $2,560 for a car's first year of business use. Other limits apply for subsequent years' use. See the instructions for Form 4562 for those other limitations.

Your total vehicle expense, whether it's from the standard mileage method (**line 28**) or the actual expense method (**line 35**) is transferred to the front of Form 2106. **Part I, line 1** is your business vehicle expense figure for 1989.

To this vehicle cost can be added on **line 2** parking fees, tolls, and local transportation costs. **Line 3** covers your travel costs away from your tax home overnight. On **line 4** enter your other business expenses. Note that meals and entertainment on overnight travel must be calculated separately on **line 5, column B,** since they are only 80 percent deductible.

Line 6 is your total business expense (column A) and total expense for meals and entertainment (column B). If you received reimbursements from your employer, report them on **line 7** if your employer did not include these anywhere on your W-2 form. If your employer reported your reimbursement for documented expenses in box 16 of Form W-2, enter that figure on **line 8. Line 9** is the sum of lines 7 and 8.

If **line 10** turns out to be a negative figure, you were reimbursed more than you legitimately spent. This will happen when an employer's mileage reimbursement exceeds the amount the IRS allows. Report this additional income on line 22 on the front of Form 1040 (the "other income" line).

If your expenses exceed your employer's reimbursements, you have a deduction on **line 13.** Enter this figure on line 20 of Schedule A as a miscellaneous personal deduction.

If you are a performing artist with adjusted gross income totaling less than $16,000 and you had at least two W-2 employers who paid you at least $200 each, then you can enter the line 13 deduction directly on the front of Form 1040. Use line 30 in the Adjustments to Income section and write "Qual. perform. artist/Form 2106" on the dotted line next to the entry.

Remember that Form 2106 is used only for expenses you incur in your role as someone else's employee.

Form 4562

Use Form 4562 to claim depreciation expense on real property you use in your business. The form is replicated on the next pages.

Depreciation is one of the trickier parts of tax law, due primarily to the changes made over the past ten years. The Tax Reform Act of 1986 introduced the Modified Accelerated Cost Recovery System (MACRS). MACRS uses the double declining balance method of calculating depreciation deductions. While the method itself is described in the Glossary, use the Form 4562 instructions on the table in the Glossary to identify the exact percentage to use in any given year.

For equipment put into service prior to 1989, use the same depreciation method you used in prior years. A 1985 purchase, for example, would be depreciated under Accelerated Cost Recovery System (ACRS). Assuming it was five-year property (a computer or piece of video equipment), 1989 would be the last year of depreciation. A piece of equipment purchased in 1985 for personal use and converted to business use in 1989 would require the use of MACRS tables.

If you bought business equipment in 1989, you have the choice of depreciating it or expensing it. "Expensing" means you deduct the cost in the year of purchase, instead of deducting parts of the cost over each of several successive years ("depreciating"). Use Part I of Form 4562 to expense up to $10,000 in business assets purchased in 1989.

Notice the $200,000 lifetime limit on expensed property (**Part I, line 3**). Most artists will never reach this threshold.

If you're part of a partnership, the partnership can also expense business assets. That expensing, like a partnership's profit or loss, would be passed along to you as an individual and would count toward your $10,000 annual limit. Make sure your partnership return is prepared early enough to give you plenty of time to decide between expensing and depreciation. The same is true if you're part of an S-corporation.

Describe the property on **line 6** in tax terms and in colloquial terms. If you buy a kiln, for example, enter on line 6: "5-year recovery property/Kiln." Such a description satisfies the IRS and identifies for you the equipment you bought. This is especially helpful when you sell the equipment. For a VCR or camera, list the maker and model type as well.

Date placed in service, column (b), is the date of purchase. Column (c) is the purchase price. Column (d) is the amount of that cost you choose to expense, or write off, in the year of purchase.

Line 7 of Part I requires a separate accounting of listed property. "Listed property" includes an automobile, or film and video equipment, or cameras, or computers, or equipment not used 100 percent for business. Listed property is handled in Part III of Form 4562.

If you have listed property you think you may want to expense, you must complete Part III before finishing Part I. Anyone who wants to claim an automobile expense on Schedule C also must complete Part III.

Form **4562**	**Depreciation and Amortization**	OMB No. 1545-0172

Form **4562**

Department of the Treasury
Internal Revenue Service   (4)

Depreciation and Amortization

▶ See separate instructions.
▶ Attach this form to your return.

OMB No. 1545-0172

1989

Attachment Sequence No. **67**

Name(s) as shown on return

Identifying number

Business or activity to which this form relates

Part I Depreciation (*Use Part III for automobiles, certain other vehicles, computers, and property used for entertainment, recreation, or amusement.*)

Section A.—Election To Expense Depreciable Assets (Section 179)

1 Maximum dollar limitation	1	$10,000
2 Total cost of section 179 property placed in service during the tax year (see instructions)	2	
3 Threshold cost of section 179 property before reduction in limitation	3	$200,000
4 Reduction in limitation (Subtract line 3 from line 2, but do not enter less than -0-.)	4	
5 Dollar limitation for tax year (Subtract line 4 from line 1, but do not enter less than -0-.)	5	

(a) Description of property	(b) Date placed in service	(c) Cost	(d) Elected cost
6			

7 Listed property—Enter amount from line 28	7	
8 Tentative deduction (Enter the lesser of: (a) line 6 plus line 7; or (b) line 5.)	8	
9 Taxable income limitation (Enter the lesser of :(a) Taxable income; or (b) line 5) (see instructions)	9	
10 Carryover of disallowed deduction from 1988 (see instructions)	10	
11 Section 179 expense deduction (Enter the lesser of: (a) line 8 plus line 10; or (b) line 9.)	11	
12 Carryover of disallowed deduction to 1990 (Add lines 8 and 10, less line 11.) ▶ 12		

Section B.—MACRS Depreciation

(a) Classification of property	(b) Date placed in service	(c) Basis for depreciation (Business use only—see instructions)	(d) Recovery period	(e) Convention	(f) Method	(g) Depreciation deduction
13 General Depreciation System (GDS) (see instructions): *For assets placed in service ONLY during tax year beginning in 1989*						
a 3-year property						
b 5-year property						
c 7-year property						
d 10-year property						
e 15-year property						
f 20-year property						
g Residential rental property			27.5 yrs.	MM	S/L	
			27.5 yrs.	MM	S/L	
h Nonresidential real property			31.5 yrs.	MM	S/L	
			31.5 yrs.	MM	S/L	
14 Alternative Depreciation System (ADS) (see instructions): *For assets placed in service ONLY during tax year beginning in 1989*						
a Class life					S/L	
b 12-year			12 yrs.		S/L	
c 40-year			40 yrs.	MM	S/L	

15 Listed property—Enter amount from line 27	15	
16 GDS and ADS deductions for assets placed in service before 1989 (see instructions)	16	

Section C.—ACRS and/or Other Depreciation

17 Property subject to section 168(f)(1) election (see instructions)	17	
18 ACRS and/or other depreciation (see instructions)	18	

Section D.—Summary

19 Total (Add deductions on line 11 and lines 13 through 18.) Enter here and on the appropriate line of your return (Partnerships and S corporations—see instructions.)	19	
20 For assets shown above and placed in service during the current year, enter the portion of the basis attributable to section 263A costs (see instructions).	20	

For Paperwork Reduction Act Notice, see page 1 of the separate instructions.

Form **4562** (1989)

Part II | **Amortization**

(a) Description of property	(b) Date amortization begins	(c) Cost or other basis	(d) Code section	(e) Amortization period or percentage	(f) Amortization for this year
21 Amortization for property placed in service **only** during tax year beginning in 1989					

22 Amortization for property placed in service before 1989	**22**	
23 Total. Enter here and on "Other Deductions" or "Other Expenses" line of your return	**23**	

Part III | **Listed Property.—Automobiles, Certain Other Vehicles, Computers, and Property Used for Entertainment, Recreation, or Amusement**

If you are using the standard mileage rate or deducting vehicle lease expense, complete columns (a) through (d) of Section A, all of Section B, and Section C if applicable.

Section A.—Depreciation   (Caution: *See instructions for limitations for automobiles.*)

24a Do you have evidence to support the business use claimed? ☐ Yes ☐ No | 24b If "Yes," is the evidence written? ☐ Yes ☐ No

(a) Type of property (list vehicles first)	(b) Date placed in service	(c) Business use percentage (%)	(d) Cost or other basis (see instructions for leased property)	(e) Basis for depreciation — business use only	(f) Recovery period	(g) Method	(h) Depreciation deduction	(i) Elected section 179 cost
25 *Property used more than 50% in a trade or business:*								
26 *Property used 50% or less in a trade or business:*								
							S/L	
							S/L	
							S/L	

27 Total (Enter here and on line 15, page 1.)	**27**	
28 Total (Enter here and on line 7, page 1.)	**28**	

Section B.—Information Regarding Use of Vehicles—*If you deduct expenses for vehicles:*
- *Always complete this section for vehicles used by a sole proprietor, partner, or other "more than 5% owner," or related person.*
- *If you provided vehicles to your employees, first answer the questions in Section C to see if you meet an exception to completing this section for those vehicles.*

	(a) Vehicle 1	(b) Vehicle 2	(c) Vehicle 3	(d) Vehicle 4	(e) Vehicle 5	(f) Vehicle 6
29 Total business miles driven during the year (DO NOT include commuting miles) . .						
30 Total commuting miles driven during the year						
31 Total other personal (noncommuting) miles driven						
32 Total miles driven during the year (Add lines 29 through 31)						

	Yes	No	Yes	No	Yes	No	Yes	No	Yes	No	Yes	No
33 Was the vehicle available for personal use during off-duty hours?												
34 Was the vehicle used primarily by a more than 5% owner or related person? . . .												
35 Is another vehicle available for personal use?												

Section C.—Questions for Employers Who Provide Vehicles for Use by Their Employees
(Answer these questions to determine if you meet an exception to completing Section B. Note: Section B must always be completed for vehicles used by sole proprietors, partners, or other more than 5% owners or related persons.)

	Yes	No
36 Do you maintain a written policy statement that prohibits all personal use of vehicles, including commuting, by your employees?		
37 Do you maintain a written policy statement that prohibits personal use of vehicles, except commuting, by your employees? (See instructions for vehicles used by corporate officers, directors, or 1% or more owners.)		
38 Do you treat all use of vehicles by employees as personal use?		
39 Do you provide more than five vehicles to your employees and retain the information received from your employees concerning the use of the vehicles?.		
40 Do you meet the requirements concerning qualified automobile demonstration use (see instructions)?		

Note: *If your answer to 36, 37, 38, 39, or 40 is "Yes," you need not complete Section B for the covered vehicles.*

Line 9 is a reminder of the other limit imposed on the decision to expense equipment purchased in 1989: the income limitation. You can expense equipment up to $10,000 per year or your net profit for that year, whichever is less. If you are self-employed and also a member of a partnership, add your profit (or loss) from the two businesses to determine the income limit to enter on this line.

Use **Part I, Section B** to depreciate property or equipment purchased in 1989. Remember that a home studio is depreciated as nonresidential real property over 31.5 years. Leasehold improvements must also be depreciated over 31.5 years, regardless of the length of your lease. If you move before the 31.5 years has elapsed, write off the balance of the leasehold improvements in the year you move.

Much equipment used by artists is listed property and can be entered only in Part III. Other equipment is likely to have a five-year life; office equipment has a seven-year life. Check the instructions for Form 4562 or Publication 534, "Depreciation," for further information on the expected life of a specific piece of equipment.

Enter on **line 16** the depreciation total for property purchased in 1987 or 1988 that is still being depreciated in 1989. Use **line 17** to enter depreciation of equipment or property purchased in 1980 or earlier that is still being depreciated in 1989. Use **line 18** to enter depreciation for equipment or property purchased between 1981 and 1986 that is still being depreciated in 1989. Make sure you keep some kind of worksheet in case of IRS audit to substantiate the entry on these lines.

Line 20 refers to a set-aside amount if you are subject to capitalization requirements. Ceramicists and potters and jewelers who mass-produce a line of goods and have an inventory carried over from the previous year where utility outweighs artistry may find themselves with a bookkeeping nightmare in allocating 1989 costs to inventory and to goods sold. If you are subject to capitalization requirements and have an inventory, consult a tax accountant for assistance in making these allocations.

Part II is used for amortized expenses. Expenses must be amortized for several reasons. The most common amortized costs are start-up costs (code section 195) and research and development costs (code section 174). Amortizing costs means you spread them out over a minimum of sixty months. Amortized costs are entered on the "other expense" line of the business involved—usually Schedule C in the case of the self-employed artist.

Part III is important to artists, since much of the equipment used in an artist's business is "listed property" to the IRS. You must answer the questions on **line 24a** and **line 24b.**

If you use an automobile or piece of equipment less than 100 percent in your business, you must keep a contemporaneous log of business usage. For the automobile, this means keeping a mileage log of daily odometer readings and business use, including commuting mileage. For a computer or camera or video recorder, this means a daily log of usage by time or volume.

Use **line 25** for property used more than 50 percent in your business; use **line 26** for property used less than 50 percent in your business. Notice that for listed property or equipment used less than 50 percent for business, you must depreciate the item using straight-line depreciation, usually over a longer period of time (five-year property becomes depreciable over seven years; seven-year property over twelve, and so on). Furthermore, no expensing is allowed on property used less than 50 percent in business.

If you include an automobile as listed property in Part III, and most artists will make that entry, be sure to complete **lines 29 through 35** for each vehicle you use in your business.

The sum of **line 29** (business miles) plus **line 30** (commuting miles) plus **line 31** (personal miles) equals **line 32** (total number of miles driven for the year). Make sure you have a mileage log to substantiate the entries on these lines.

Let's look at the specifics of completing Part III. In Section A, enter the types of listed property you have, beginning with your automobile. The date placed in service (column (b)) is the date you purchased the vehicle. Business percentage use in column (c) is calculated using your daily mileage log: divide the number of business miles you drove in 1989 by the total number of miles you drove in 1989. Also enter these figures in Part III, Section B, along with the number of commuting miles. Total miles less business and commuting miles equals personal miles driven.

If you use your car more than 50 percent for business, enter your automobile information on **line 25**; if less than 50 percent, use **line 26**.

Once you've determined the percentage business use for your vehicle (column (c)), you can complete Part III, Section A. Column (d) is the cost of the asset at time of purchase. Calculate the figure in column (e) by multiplying column (c) by column (d). The depreciable life of the vehicle is five years (column f); the depreciation method you use in column (g) is MACRS, if you purchased the vehicle in 1987, 1988, or 1989. Use ACRS for vehicles purchased between 1981 and 1986, and straight line (S/L, taking an equal amount in each year the vehicle is depreciated), for vehicles purchased prior to 1981.

The maximum deduction for an automobile placed in service (that is, purchased) in 1989 is $2,560, provided the vehicle costs more than $12,800 and is used 100 percent for business. The $2,560 decreases proportionately with actual cost and actual business use. The total deduction, however, can be split any way you like between columns (h) and (i) subject to the regular limitations on expensing.

If you have other listed equipment you use in your business, list this equipment following your automobile. If you elect to expense any part of your listed property, transfer the figure from column (i) to Part I, line 7. Regular depreciation for listed property is entered on Part I, line 15.

Once you've calculated your expense and depreciation totals in Part III, you can complete Part I (expensing) and move on to Part II (depreciation). Enter assets purchased in 1989 that you want to depreciate on line 13 of section B. **Line 13** provides a breakdown by life expectancy for business property placed into use during 1989. Refer to Publication 534, "Depreciation," to identify the life expectancy assigned to business property by the IRS.

In column (c), enter the cost of the property. This is your beginning basis in the property. The recovery period (column (d)) is the number of years you intend to depreciate the asset. Generally this will be the same number of years as the life expectancy of the asset. You can usually elect a longer life expectancy; you can never shorten the IRS-prescribed lifetimes.

Column (e), convention, refers to the half-year, quarter-year, or midmonth convention used for all classes of property. All property is subject to at least the half-year convention. This means that if you purchase a set of office furnishings on February 10, you can take a maximum of one-half year's depreciation in 1989. Worse, if you purchase most of your equipment in the last three months of the year, you must use the quarter-year convention. All residential property is subject to the midmonth convention.

Tables accompanying Form 4562 list the half-year convention. If you are subject to the quarter-year convention, use half of the half-year convention percentages. In column (e) enter "½" or "¼." Method, in column (f) is "MACRS." Enter the 1989 depreciation deduction in column (g).

A way around the whole "convention" issue is expensing property or equipment you purchase in 1989. But don't expense an asset simply because you don't want to fool with IRS tables. Some rules of thumb—If your income is low in 1989 and should be higher in 1990, you should probably depreciate the item. If you pay less than $1,000 for an item, you should probably expense it (if you can). If you haven't paid quarterly estimated taxes and expect to owe a lot of money by April 15, 1990, consider expensing simply to cut your current liability, even if it's not the best long-range strategy.

Other tax-planning considerations enter into the picture as well. It is important to remember that depreciation is a tax preference item. As such it can trigger payment of the alternative minimum tax, especially if you're an upper-bracket taxpayer. It also has ramifications when you sell the asset. Taking depreciation on a camera, for example, lowers your basis in the camera. You may sell the camera for less than you paid for it and yet, because of the depreciation taken on it over the years, end up with a taxable gain.

Similarly, for those who claim a home office in a home they own, the portion of the house attributable to business use during their entire period of ownership becomes business property. When the residence is sold, only part of any capital gain on the sale can be deferred— namely, the part attributable to the residential portion of the property. The part of the gain attributable to the business portion of the property falls due and payable in the year of sale.

The other important thing to remember about depreciation is that it is an "allowed" or "allowable" deduction. That is tax talk and it means you either take the deduction or you lose it. You cannot, for example, choose to claim an office in the home and deduct a portion of the mortgage interest, property tax, insurance, utilities, repairs, and maintenance, but forego the depreciation portion so as to avoid any capital gains payments when you sell the house. That depreciation deduction is allowable and will be counted against the property, whether or not you count it on a particular year's tax return.

Note that for any year in which you are not eligible to claim an office-in-the-home deduction, the depreciation is deferred onto the basis of the house. That means that, if you have no profit in 1989 and hence are ineligible to claim a home office or studio, the depreciation you normally would have taken in 1989 is added to the basis of the house. Against that is counted depreciation for all the years you actually took the depreciation deduction, plus the 1989 depreciation deduction that was allowable but that you could not take. If you've surmised the 1989 "deferral" balances out against the "allowable," you're right. That's the way the IRS wants it done.

This concludes the forms section. You may need other forms to complete your 1989 tax return, but a detailed treatment of the other forms is not possible within the confines of this volume.

On to the schedules!

8

Schedules

Schedule A

Schedule A is "Itemized Deductions" and is reprinted (along with Schedule B) on the following page. Especially for self-employed persons, read "itemized" as "personal itemized." The deductions listed on Schedule A pertain to your personal, not your business, life. They fall into the following categories:

— Medical and dental

— Taxes

— Interest paid

— Gifts to charity

— Casualty and theft losses

— Moving expenses

— Job expenses and miscellaneous deductions

Your business deductions as a self-employed person belong on Schedule C. Schedule A contains information on personal expenditures which may also be tax deductible. Whether or not you itemize your personal deductions has no bearing on whether or not you file the long form (Form 1040).

● Medical and Dental Expenses

Money you spend for prescribed medicines and drugs, along with premiums for health insurance, medical doctors and medical care, hospitals, and dentists are deductible on this section of Schedule A. This is money you spend for your own care and for that of your dependents, or persons you could consider dependents were it not for divorce. Thus, payments for your 12-year-old daughter who needs braces but who is in the custodial care of your ex-spouse are deductible to you (provided your payments are in addition to your child support payments). Payments for your 25-year-old son who is married but lives in your home as a self-sustaining adult are not deductible.

Costs of self-prescribed or health-regimen drugs are not deductible. Transportation costs are deductible at the rate of nine cents per mile if you use your own automobile, or the actual costs you pay someone else to get you to a hospital. Medical parking costs are deductible. Lodging is deductible if you need to remain overnight for the medical care of your dependent.

Remember to deduct 25 percent of the health insurance premiums you pay as a self-employed person on line 26 on the front of Form 1040.

Total medical costs (**line 2**) are deductible only to the extent they exceed 7.5 percent of your adjusted gross income.

● Taxes

Deductible taxes include state and local income taxes (withheld from your regular pay or paid via quarterly estimated taxes), property taxes on the home or recreational property you

SCHEDULES A&B
(Form 1040)
Department of the Treasury
Internal Revenue Service (4)

Schedule A—Itemized Deductions
(Schedule B is on back)

▶ Attach to Form 1040. ▶ See Instructions for Schedules A and B (Form 1040).

OMB No. 1545-0074

1989
Attachment
Sequence No. 07

Name(s) shown on Form 1040

Your social security number

Medical and Dental Expenses (Do not include expenses reimbursed or paid by others.) (See Instructions on page 23.)	**1a** Prescription medicines and drugs, insulin, doctors, dentists, nurses, hospitals, medical insurance premiums you paid, etc . .	**1a**		
	b Other. (List—include hearing aids, dentures, eyeglasses, transportation and lodging, etc.) ▶	**1b**		
	2 Add the amounts on lines 1a and 1b. Enter the total here .	**2**		
	3 Multiply the amount on Form 1040, line 32, by 7.5% (.075) . .	**3**		
	4 Subtract line 3 from line 2. If zero or less, enter -0-. **Total** medical and dental . . ▶	**4**		
Taxes You Paid (See Instructions on page 24.)	**5** State and local income taxes	**5**		
	6 Real estate taxes	**6**		
	7 Other taxes. (List—include personal property taxes.) ▶	**7**		
	8 Add the amounts on lines 5 through 7. Enter the total here. **Total** taxes . ▶	**8**		
Interest You Paid (See Instructions on page 24.)	**9a** Deductible home mortgage interest (from Form 1098) that you paid to financial institutions. Report deductible points on line 10.	**9a**		
	b Other deductible home mortgage interest. (If paid to an individual, show that person's name and address.) ▶	**9b**		
	10 Deductible points. (See Instructions for special rules.)	**10**		
	11 Deductible investment interest. (See page 25.)	**11**		
	12a Personal interest you paid. (See page 25.) .	**12a**		
	b Multiply the amount on line 12a by 20% (.20). Enter the result	**12b**		
	13 Add the amounts on lines 9a through 11, and 12b. Enter the total here. **Total** interest ▶	**13**		
Gifts to Charity (See Instructions on page 25.)	**14** Contributions by cash or check. (If you gave $3,000 or more to any one organization, show to whom you gave and how much you gave.) ▶	**14**		
	15 Other than cash or check. (You must attach Form 8283 if over $500.)	**15**		
	16 Carryover from prior year	**16**		
	17 Add the amounts on lines 14 through 16. Enter the total here. **Total** contributions . ▶	**17**		
Casualty and Theft Losses	**18** Casualty or theft loss(es) (attach Form 4684). (See page 26 of the Instructions.) . . . . ▶	**18**		
Moving Expenses	**19** Moving expenses (attach Form 3903 or 3903F). (See page 26 of the Instructions.) . . . . ▶	**19**		
Job Expenses and Most Other Miscellaneous Deductions (See page 26 for expenses to deduct here.)	**20** Unreimbursed employee expenses—job travel, union dues, job education, etc. (You MUST attach Form 2106 in some cases. See Instructions.) ▶	**20**		
	21 Other expenses (investment, tax preparation, safe deposit box, etc.). List type and amount ▶	**21**		
	22 Add the amounts on lines 20 and 21. Enter the total.	**22**		
	23 Multiply the amount on Form 1040, line 32, by 2% (.02). Enter the result here	**23**		
	24 Subtract line 23 from line 22. Enter the result. If zero or less, enter -0-. . . ▶	**24**		
Other Miscellaneous Deductions	**25** Other (from list on page 26 of Instructions). List type and amount ▶ .... ▶	**25**		
Total Itemized Deductions	**26** Add the amounts on lines 4, 8, 13, 17, 18, 19, 24, and 25. Enter the total here. Then enter on Form 1040, line 34, the LARGER of this total or your standard deduction from page 17 of the Instructions . . . . ▶	**26**		

For Paperwork Reduction Act Notice, see Form 1040 Instructions.

Schedule A (Form 1040) 1989

Name(s) shown on Form 1040 (Do not enter name and social security number if shown on other side.) | **Your social security number**

Schedule B—Interest and Dividend Income
Attachment Sequence No. **08**

Part I **Interest** **Income** (See Instructions on pages 10 and 27.)	If you received more than $400 in taxable interest income, you must complete Parts I and III. List ALL interest received in Part I. If you received, as a nominee, interest that actually belongs to another person, or you received or paid accrued interest on securities transferred between interest payment dates, see page 27.	

Interest Income

		Amount	
1	Interest income from seller-financed mortgages. (See Instructions and list name of payer.) ▶ **1**		
2	Other interest income. (List name of payer.) ▶		
	....		
	....		
	....		
	....		
	....		
	....		
	.... **2**		
	....		
	....		
	....		
	....		
	....		
3	Add the amounts on lines 1 and 2. Enter the total here and on Form 1040, line 8a. ▶ **3**		

Note: If you received a Form 1099-INT or Form 1099-OID from a brokerage firm, list the firm's name as the payer and enter the total interest shown on that form.

Part II **Dividend** **Income** (See Instructions on pages 10 and 27.)	If you received more than $400 in gross dividends and/or other distributions on stock, you must complete Parts II and III. If you received, as a nominee, dividends that actually belong to another person, see page 27.	

Dividend Income

		Amount	
4	Dividend income. (List name of payer—include on this line capital gain distributions, nontaxable distributions, etc.) ▶		
	....		
	....		
	....		
	....		
	....		
	.... **4**		
	....		
	....		
	....		
	....		
	....		
	....		
5	Add the amounts on line 4. Enter the total here **5**		
6	Capital gain distributions. Enter here and on Schedule D* . . . **6**		
7	Nontaxable distributions. (See the Instructions for Form 1040, line 9.) **7**		
8	Add the amounts on lines 6 and 7. Enter the total here **8**		
9	Subtract line 8 from line 5. Enter the result here and on Form 1040, line 9 . . . ▶ **9**		

Note: If you received a Form 1099-DIV from a brokerage firm, list the firm's name as the payer and enter the total dividends shown on that form.

*If you received capital gain distributions but do not need Schedule D to report any other gains or losses, see the Instructions for Form 1040, lines 13 and 14.

		Yes	No
Part III **Foreign** **Accounts** **and** **Foreign** **Trusts** (See Instructions on page 27.)	If you received more than $400 of interest or dividends, OR if you had a foreign account or were a grantor of, or a transferor to, a foreign trust, you must answer both questions in Part III.		
	10a At any time during 1989, did you have an interest in or a signature or other authority over a financial account in a foreign country (such as a bank account, securities account, or other financial account)? (See page 27 of the Instructions for exceptions and filing requirements for Form TD F 90-22.1.)		
	b If "Yes," enter the name of the foreign country ▶		
	11 Were you the grantor of, or transferor to, a foreign trust that existed during 1989, whether or not you have any beneficial interest in it? If "Yes," you may have to file Form 3520, 3520-A, or 926		

For Paperwork Reduction Act Notice, see Form 1040 Instructions.

own, and some personal property taxes. The most common personal property tax is your automobile license plate. The part of the fee you pay that is attributable to the value of the car is a personal property tax and deductible on **line 7.**

Remember that if you claim on Schedule C an office in the home deduction for the house you own and live in, the portion of property taxes you claim on Schedule A is the balance of the property tax paid less the amount you deduct on Schedule C.

● Interest

Mortgage interest incurred on your first or second home and paid to a bank is reported to you on Form 1098. Enter this interest on **line 9a.** Interest paid to an individual on a first or second home is entered on **line 9b** along with that individual's name and address. If you have other deductible interest on a first or second home, perhaps from using a personal line of credit to make a major home improvement, enter that on **line 9b** and be prepared to substantiate the deduction if the IRS asks you about it.

If you purchased a home in 1989 and paid points to reduce your mortgage interest rate and you paid cash for those points at closing, you can deduct those points on **line 10.** Points paid out of pocket to refinance your home are deductible over the life of the new mortgage. Deduct a proportion each year until the mortgage is paid off or the house is sold (in which case the balance of the points paid becomes deductible). When the cost of points is added to your original mortgage or refinanced mortgage, the points are not deductible but instead are added to the basis of your house.

A line of credit taken on your first or second home will result in a Form 1098 being issued to you at the end of the calendar year. This interest is deducted on **line 9a.** A line of credit taken on investments, by contrast, is not as easy to handle. You must track expenditures to prove deductibility because interest on a line of credit is reported to you as consumer interest.

To deduct interest incurred by borrowing against investments you own requires you to prove the money was used for taxable investments. The criterion the IRS uses is the first check written from an account to which you've transferred line-of-credit funds. If you go to the grocery store, you've eliminated the deductibility of the interest on the amount transferred, even if your second check is for the $10,000 you transferred from your line of credit to buy stocks. If you had written a check to buy the stocks immediately after transferring the money, the interest you subsequently paid would be eligible for deduction as investment interest on **line 11,** up to the income from that investment.

To protect the deductibility of interest incurred on line-of-credit funds, follow the tracking guidelines described in Publication 545, "Interest Expense." In general, the IRS recommends you keep a separate checking account for line-of-credit transfers and keep track of the investment expenses for which you use the line-of-credit funds. Commingling borrowed and earned funds (that is, line-of-credit funds and earned income) can be a recordkeeping nightmare.

Deductible "points" (**line 10**) include points for which you paid cash at closing when you purchased a first or second home. Points for refinancing are deductible only over the life of the refinanced loan (⅟₃₀ per year for a thirty-year mortgage).

An example of deductible investment interest (**line 11**) is interest on a margin account at a brokerage firm for which you have investment income (interest, dividends, capital gains) that exceeds this interest deduction.

Personal interest is all consumer interest—charge cards, auto loans, lines of credit. Enter the entire amount paid on **line 12a.** In 1989 only 20 percent of what you actually paid can be deducted. Enter the deductible portion of your consumer interest expense on **line 12b.**

- **Contributions**

There is no change from prior years in what or how much you can deduct. Remember that if you donate goods worth more than $500 you must attach Form 8283 to substantiate the deduction. If you donate goods worth more than $5,000 you must provide that form plus a written and signed appraisal from an independent appraiser.

- **Casualty and Theft Losses**

Use Form 4684 to try to deduct casualty or theft losses of personal property or business property. If the casualty or theft loss occurred to personal property, report it on Schedule A, **line 18**; if the casualty or theft involved business property, follow the instructions on Form 4684.

- **Moving Expenses**

Use Form 3903 to report your expenses, which then become part of your personal itemized deductions on **line 19** of Schedule A.

- **Job Expenses and Most Other Miscellaneous Deductions**

This hodgepodge of deductions is subject to a floor of 2 percent of adjusted gross income. That means that only the amount exceeding 2 percent of your adjusted gross income (line 31 on the front of Form 1040) is deductible on Schedule A. The remainder becomes what the IRS terms your normal cost of doing business.

Classified as a miscellaneous business expense are:

—Unreimbursed employee business expenses

—Tax preparation fees (even for self-employed persons, preparation of an individual tax return is considered a personal, not a business expense)

—Union and professional dues

—Books, journals, subscriptions, conferences, continuing education costs, secretarial services, long distance telephone—all those expenses you incur as someone's employee, as itemized on Form 2106. For teachers and other professionals, travel expenses are deductible only if they are directly related to your professional development and involve a seminar, symposium, or other structured program. Travel to gain firsthand knowledge of artifacts or ambience is not deductible.

Some miscellaneous expenses are not subject to the 2 percent floor, such as legal expense incurred to produce taxable income, but this line is rarely used.

To determine whether or not you should file Schedule A with your 1989 tax return, compare the figure on **line 26** with the standard deduction for your filing status ($3,100 for a single person; $5,200 for a married couple filing a joint return; $4,550 for a head of household). Use the method that provides a larger deduction for you.

Schedule B

Schedule B must be completed if a taxpayer receives more than $400 in interest or dividend income. (Schedule B was replicated opposite Schedule A.)

Part I requests names of payers and amounts of interest paid by each. Seller-financed mortgages are listed separately on **line 1.**

If you have a joint account with someone who is not your spouse and your Social Security number is listed on the account, you receive a Form 1099-INT for interest earned on the entire account. You must report this entire amount on your 1989 tax return. How do you back out the amount of interest income the other person received? Begin by reporting the payer's name and full amount on **line 2.** Then, once all payers and amounts are listed, total the interest received and call it "Sub-Total." Next, identify by name and Social Security number the person who shared the interest or any portion of it with you. Enter in parentheses the amount that person received in the "Amount" column and subtract that from the Sub-Total. The result is the Total you received on **line 3.** This figure is also entered on line 8a of Form 1040.

Use Part II of Schedule B to report dividend income. Payers and amounts paid should be identified per account. For example, if you have five accounts at Merrill Lynch, do not lump the dividend figures together from the five accounts. List each account separately to help you track information from year to year. If you close an account during 1989, enter "closed 1989" after the payer's name. The IRS doesn't require this, but you'll find it helpful when you prepare your 1990 taxes since you won't need to wonder why you have one less account than you had the year before.

As in the case of interest income, should you be identified as a recipient of dividends on a multiple-owner account, follow the procedure outlined above to back out the payments received by others.

When reporting dividend income, be sure always to use the "gross" figure, unless you live in a state where capital gains still receive favorable treatment. If you do, then enter the gross dividends figure from Form 1099-DIV in the amount column. On **line 6** of Schedule B, enter the "capital gains distribution" figure. From there, the capital gains portion of dividend income goes to Schedule D or directly on line 14 on the front of Form 1040. You must use Schedule D if you received a Form 1099-B for stock or mutual fund transactions; otherwise, transfer line 6 of schedule B directly to the front of Form 1040.

If your Form 1099-DIV indicates part of the gross dividends are nontaxable, enter the nontaxable portion on **line 7.** Remember to reduce the basis in any investment for which you claim nontaxable dividends.

Transfer the figure for total dividends received (**line 9**) to line 9 of Form 1040.

Before leaving Schedule B, be sure to complete Part III. Presumably the answers to each question are "No." Should you have foreign accounts with deposits in excess of $10,000 in U.S. funds, you must complete Form TD F90-22.1 and attach it to your return. Failure to do so may jeopardize any U.S. tax preferences you claim.

Schedule C

The heart of the return for any self-employed person, Schedule C determines annually the profit or loss from the business run by a sole proprietor. The schedule is replicated on pages 76 and 77.

Schedule C is broken into an informational section, Part I, which identifies income received; Part II, which summarizes business expenses; and Part III, which attributes costs and expenses to goods produced and keeps track of inventory.

● Informational Section
You are the proprietor of your business. As the proprietor, your name belongs in the "Name" section followed by your Social Security number in the box following the name section. Questions A through J describe the kind of business you operate.

Your principal business (**Question A**) is a type of business activity listed on the back of Schedule C. Each business has a business code (**Question B**) also on the back of Schedule C. You may find these descriptions difficult to use. They're based on standard industrial classifications that are intended to describe the totality of American economic life.

In general, as an artist you provide some type of service—business or personal—or you are in the entertainment field. If you're a potter or jeweler, you should identify yourself as a manufacturer, unless you create only one-of-a-kind pieces and are not subject to capitalization requirements, in which case identify yourself as category 8888: Fine arts/ceramic artist [or goldsmith, or whatever].

You have a name for the business, whether that is your own name or an assumed name under which you operate your business. "DBA" stands for "doing business as." If you have an external studio or office, that address would appear along with business name in **Question C.**

You will have an Employer Identification Number (**Question D**) only if you have employees or a Keogh retirement plan. You apply for an EIN by filing Form SS-4 with the regional IRS office to which you're assigned (see Form SS-4 instructions).

If you have an inventory, answer **Question E** by checking (2) Lower of cost or market. Any other choice requires tracking procedures far too complicated for a self-employed individual. If you have an inventory, you must also answer **Question G,** about whether or not you changed your inventory evaluating or counting procedures between the start and the end of the year. If you do not have an inventory (and as an artist creating one-of-a-kind works, you probably do not), check **Question E, box 4**—does not apply.

Question F asks you to identify your accounting procedure. If you record income when you receive a check for services rendered and record expenses when you pay a bill, then you are on a *cash* basis. If you record income when you bill it and record expenses when you receive a bill for services you ordered, then you are on an *accrual* basis. You may also be on another basis known as *hybrid* if you record income when you bill it and record expenses as you pay them.

Question H asks if you are claiming an office or studio in your home. You are eligible to do so only if you have a net profit for 1989. Claiming a home studio or office cannot generate a loss for you in 1989 on your self-employment activities or increase your loss, even if your home is the only place you work.

Question I asks about your level of participation in the business described on Schedule C. If you did not materially participate (which means investing money that is at risk in the business), you may not be able to deduct any loss the business engenders.

Question J probes the character of your business. If your business is part of a tax-shelter scheme, you must check this box and attach Form 8271. Perhaps one-tenth of 1 percent of artists will be involved in this circumstance. If you didn't consult a bevy of tax lawyers to establish your business, ignore Question J.

Following this preliminary information, Part I identifies income by source. **Gross receipts or sales (line 1)** is the total amount you sold or received in your sole proprietorship in 1989.

If, as part of your income, you were reimbursed by a customer for supplies you used to produce the item you sold, that reimbursement is part of the check you received and is included in this line. The cost of the supplies will be deducted in Part II of the form, or in Part III under "Cost of Goods Sold." It's important that your gross receipts or sales figure equals the sum of the checks and cash you received for your work.

If you were part of an informal collective (a trio or group who performed at a certain function with one check sent to you to split among the members), report the entire amount received. Back out payments to your colleagues on the "commissions" line of Schedule C.

If you refund part of a fee, deduct that figure on **line 2. Line 4** asks for the cost of goods sold. Calculate this amount using Part III of Schedule C, which is printed on the back of the schedule. You must use this part if you have an inventory. If you do not have an inventory, using the cost of goods sold section is optional.

SCHEDULE C (Form 1040)

Department of the Treasury
Internal Revenue Service (4)

Profit or Loss From Business
(Sole Proprietorship)

Partnerships, Joint Ventures, Etc., Must File Form 1065.

▶ Attach to Form 1040 or Form 1041.   ▶ See Instructions for Schedule C (Form 1040).

OMB No 1545-0074

1989

Attachment Sequence No. 09

Name of proprietor | Social security number (SSN)

A Principal business or profession, including product or service (see Instructions)

B Principal business code (from page 2) ▶

C Business name and address ▶ ....

D Employer ID number (Not SSN)

E Method(s) used to value closing inventory: (1) ☐ Cost (2) ☐ Lower of cost or market (3) ☐ Other (attach explanation) (4) ☐ Does not apply (if checked, skip line G)

F Accounting method: (1) ☐ Cash (2) ☐ Accrual (3) ☐ Other (specify) ▶ ....

	Yes	No
G Was there any change in determining quantities, costs, or valuations between opening and closing inventory? (If "Yes," attach explanation.)		
H Are you deducting expenses for business use of your home? (If "Yes," see Instructions for limitations.)		
I Did you "materially participate" in the operation of this business during 1989? (If "No," see Instructions for limitations on losses.)		

J If this schedule includes a loss, credit, deduction, income, or other tax benefit relating to a tax shelter required to be registered, check here. ▶ ☐
If you checked this box, you MUST attach **Form 8271.**

Part I Income

1 Gross receipts or sales	1	
2 Returns and allowances	2	
3 Subtract line 2 from line 1. Enter the result here	3	
4 Cost of goods sold and/or operations (from line 39 on page 2)	4	
5 Subtract line 4 from line 3 and enter the **gross profit** here	5	
6 Other income, including Federal and state gasoline or fuel tax credit or refund (see Instructions)	6	
7 Add lines 5 and 6. This is your **gross income** ▶	7	

Part II Expenses

8 Advertising	8		**22** Repairs	22	
9 Bad debts from sales or services (see Instructions)	9		**23** Supplies (not included in Part III)	23	
10 Car and truck expenses	10		**24** Taxes	24	
11 Commissions	11		**25** Travel, meals, and entertainment:		
12 Depletion	12		**a** Travel	25a	
13 Depreciation and section 179 deduction from **Form 4562** (not included in Part III)	13		**b** Meals and entertainment		
14 Employee benefit programs (other than on line 20)	14		**c** Enter 20% of line 25b subject to limitations (see Instructions)		
15 Freight (not included in Part III)	15		**d** Subtract line 25c from line 25b	25d	
16 Insurance (other than health)	16		**26** Utilities (see Instructions)	26	
17 Interest:			**27** Wages (less jobs credit)	27	
a Mortgage (paid to banks, etc.)	17a		**28** Other expenses (list type and amount):		
b Other	17b		....		
18 Legal and professional services	18		....		
19 Office expense	19		....		
20 Pension and profit-sharing plans	20		....		
21 Rent or lease:			....		
a Machinery and equipment	21a		....		
b Other business property	21b			28	

29 Add amounts in columns for lines 8 through 28. These are your **total expenses** ▶ | 29 | |

30 Net profit or (loss). Subtract line 29 from line 7. If a profit, enter here and on Form 1040, line 12, and on Schedule SE, line 2. If a loss, you MUST go on to line 31. (Fiduciaries, see Instructions.) | 30 | |

31 If you have a loss, you MUST check the box that describes your investment in this activity (see Instructions).
If you checked 31a, enter the loss on Form 1040, line 12, and Schedule SE, line 2.
If you checked 31b, you MUST attach **Form 6198.**

31a ☐ All investment is at risk.
31b ☐ Some investment is not at risk.

For Paperwork Reduction Act Notice, see Form 1040 Instructions.

Schedule C (Form 1040) 1989

Part III Cost of Goods Sold and/or Operations (See Instructions.)

32	Inventory at beginning of year. (If different from last year's closing inventory, attach explanation.)	32
33	Purchases less cost of items withdrawn for personal use	33
34	Cost of labor. (Do not include salary paid to yourself.)	34
35	Materials and supplies	35
36	Other costs	36
37	Add lines 32 through 36	37
38	Inventory at end of year	38
39	**Cost of goods sold and/or operations.** Subtract line 38 from line 37. Enter the result here and on page 1, line 4	39

Part IV Principal Business or Professional Activity Codes *(Caution: Codes have been revised. Check your code carefully.)*

Locate the major business category that best describes your activity (for example, Retail Trade, Services, etc.). Within the major category, select the activity code that most closely identifies the business or profession that is the principal source of your sales or receipts. **Enter this 4-digit code on page 1, line B.** **(Note:** *If your principal source of income is from farming activities, you should file **Schedule F (Form 1040), Farm Income and Expenses.)**

Construction

Code

0018 Operative builders (for own account)

General contractors
0034 Residential building
0059 Nonresidential building
0075 Highway and street construction
3889 Other heavy construction (pipe laying, bridge construction, etc.)

Building trade contractors, including repairs
0232 Plumbing, heating, air conditioning
0257 Painting and paper hanging
0273 Electrical work
0299 Masonry, dry wall, stone, tile
0414 Carpentering and flooring
0430 Roofing, siding, and sheet metal
0455 Concrete work
0885 Other building trade contractors (excavation, glazing, etc.)

Manufacturing, Including Printing and Publishing

0638 Food products and beverages
0653 Textile mill products
0679 Apparel and other textile products
0695 Leather, footware, handbags, etc.
0810 Furniture and fixtures
0836 Lumber and other wood products
0851 Printing and publishing
0877 Paper and allied products
1032 Stone, clay, and glass products
1057 Primary metal industries
1073 Fabricated metal products
1099 Machinery and machine shops
1115 Electric and electronic equipment
1883 Other manufacturing industries

Mining and Mineral Extraction

1511 Metal mining
1537 Coal mining
1552 Oil and gas
1719 Quarrying and nonmetallic mining

Agricultural Services, Forestry, Fishing

1933 Crop services
1958 Veterinary services, including pets
1974 Livestock breeding
1990 Other animal services
2113 Farm labor and management services
2212 Horticulture and landscaping
2238 Forestry, except logging
0836 Logging
2246 Commercial fishing
2469 Hunting and trapping

Wholesale Trade—Selling Goods to Other Businesses, Etc.

Durable goods, including machinery, equipment, wood, metals, etc.
2618 Selling for your own account
2634 Agent or broker for other firms— more than 50% of gross sales on commission

Nondurable goods, including food, fiber, chemicals, etc.
2659 Selling for your own account

2675 Agent or broker for other firms— more than 50% of gross sales on commission

Retail Trade—Selling Goods to Individuals and Households

3012 Selling door-to-door, by telephone or party plan, or from mobile unit
3038 Catalog or mail order
3053 Vending machine selling

Selling From Showroom, Store, or Other Fixed Location

Food, beverages, and drugs
3079 Eating places (meals or snacks)
3086 Catering services
3095 Drinking places (alcoholic beverages)
3210 Grocery stores (general line)
0612 Bakeries selling at retail
3236 Other food stores (meat, produce, candy, etc.)
3251 Liquor stores
3277 Drug stores

Automotive and service stations
3319 New car dealers (franchised)
3335 Used car dealers
3517 Other automotive dealers (motorcycles, recreational vehicles, etc.)
3533 Tires, accessories, and parts
3558 Gasoline service stations

General merchandise, apparel, and furniture
3715 Variety stores
3731 Other general merchandise stores
3756 Shoe stores
3772 Men's and boys' clothing stores
3913 Women's ready-to-wear stores
3921 Women's accessory and specialty stores and furriers
3939 Family clothing stores
3954 Other apparel and accessory stores
3970 Furniture stores
3996 TV, audio, and electronics
3988 Computer and software stores
4119 Household appliance stores
4317 Other home furnishing stores (china, floor coverings, etc.)
4333 Music and record stores

Building, hardware, and garden supply
4416 Building materials dealers
4432 Paint, glass, and wallpaper stores
4457 Hardware stores
4473 Nurseries and garden supply stores

Other retail stores
4614 Used merchandise and antique stores (except motor vehicle parts)
4630 Gift, novelty, and souvenir shops
4655 Florists
4671 Jewelry stores
4697 Sporting goods and bicycle shops
4812 Boat dealers
4838 Hobby, toy, and game shops
4853 Camera and photo supply stores
4879 Optical goods stores
4895 Luggage and leather goods stores
5017 Book stores, excluding newsstands
5033 Stationery stores
5058 Fabric and needlework stores
5074 Mobile home dealers
5090 Fuel dealers (except gasoline)
5884 Other retail stores

Finance, Insurance, Real Estate, and Related Services

5520 Real estate agents or brokers
5579 Real estate property managers
5710 Subdividers and developers, except cemeteries
5538 Operators and lessors of buildings, including residential
5553 Operators and lessors of other real property
5702 Insurance agents or brokers
5744 Other insurance services
6064 Security brokers and dealers
6080 Commodity contracts brokers and dealers, and security and commodity exchanges
6130 Investment advisors and services
6148 Credit institutions and mortgage bankers
6155 Title abstract offices
5777 Other finance and real estate

Transportation, Communications, Public Utilities, and Related Services

6114 Taxicabs
6312 Bus and limousine transportation
6361 Other highway passenger transportation
6338 Trucking (except trash collection)
6395 Courier or package delivery services
6510 Trash collection without own dump
6536 Public warehousing
6551 Water transportation
6619 Air transportation
6635 Travel agents and tour operators
6650 Other transportation services
6676 Communication services
6692 Utilities, including dumps, snowplowing, road cleaning, etc.

Services (Personal, Professional, and Business Services)

Hotels and other lodging places
7096 Hotels, motels, and tourist homes
7211 Rooming and boarding houses
7237 Camps and camping parks

Laundry and cleaning services
7419 Coin-operated laundries and dry cleaning
7435 Other laundry, dry cleaning, and garment services
7450 Carpet and upholstery cleaning
7476 Janitorial and related services (building, house, and window cleaning)

Business and/or personal services
7617 Legal services (or lawyer)
7633 Income tax preparation
7658 Accounting and bookkeeping
7518 Engineering services
7682 Architectural services
7708 Surveying services
7245 Management services
7260 Public relations
7286 Consulting services
7716 Advertising, except direct mail
7732 Employment agencies and personnel supply
7799 Consumer credit reporting and collection services

7856 Mailing, reproduction, commercial art and photography, and stenographic services
7872 Computer programming, processing, data preparation, and related services
7922 Computer repair, maintenance, and leasing
7773 Equipment rental and leasing (except computer or automotive)
7914 Investigative and protective services
7880 Other business services

Personal services
8110 Beauty shops (or beautician)
8318 Barber shop (or barber)
8334 Photographic portrait studios
8532 Funeral services and crematories
8714 Child day care
8730 Teaching or tutoring
8755 Counseling (except health practitioners)
8771 Ministers and chaplains
6882 Other personal services

Automotive services
8813 Automotive rental or leasing, without driver
8839 Parking, except valet
8953 Automotive repairs, general and specialized
8896 Other automotive services (wash, towing, etc.)

Miscellaneous repair, except computers
9019 TV and audio equipment repair
9035 Other electrical equipment repair
9050 Reupholstery and furniture repair
2881 Other equipment repair

Medical and health services
9217 Offices and clinics of medical doctors (MDs)
9233 Offices and clinics of dentists
9258 Osteopathic physicians and surgeons
9241 Podiatrists
9274 Chiropractors
9290 Optometrists
9415 Registered and practical nurses
9431 Other health practitioners
9456 Medical and dental laboratories
9472 Nursing and personal care facilities
9886 Other health services

Amusement and recreational services
8557 Physical fitness facilities
9597 Motion picture and video production
9688 Motion picture and tape distribution and allied services
9613 Videotape rental
9639 Motion picture theaters
9670 Bowling centers
9696 Professional sports and racing, including promoters and managers
9811 Theatrical performers, musicians, agents, producers, and related services
9837 Other amusement and recreational services

8888 Unable to classify

Part III, Cost of Goods Sold, is on the back of Schedule C. It must be used if you have an inventory for your business. By IRS regulation, if the cost of your inventory exceeds 10 percent of your gross revenues, you must report the value of that inventory at the end of your tax year. Inventory includes works in progress and raw materials. You must also use the accrual method of accounting. Most artists will turn out work as they receive orders for finished goods, thereby eliminating the need for a standing inventory of finished products and thus eliminating the need to use Part III of Schedule C.

But Part III can also be used to keep track of expenses that go directly into making the product you sell. Inventory at beginning of year (**Part III, line 32**) is the same figure you used as inventory at end of year on last year's schedule (Part III, line 7 of the 1988 Schedule C). If you don't have a standing inventory, both figures are zero.

Enter payments to independent contractors who worked in your business on **line 34** as the cost of labor; enter the cost of supplies that went directly into the finished product on **line 35.** Use **line 36** (other costs) for items such as freight if you're a sculptor, or advertising for a specific product line.

The total cost of the goods or services produced is the sum of inventory at beginning of year and 1989 purchases, less inventory at end of year. The cost of goods sold (COGS) figure appears on **line 39** of Part III of the 1989 Schedule C. From there it's transferred to **line 4** on the front of the schedule. Remember that if you have an inventory, you must use the same method to value it you used in the past.

Line 6 of Part I, "other income," includes recapture of excess depreciation (when business use of an automobile or other "listed" property slips to less than 50 percent and you have been depreciating the car using MACRS) or if you lease a luxury car and have income imputed to you.

Do not use **line 6** to report interest received on a business account. Interest received belongs on Schedule B since, as a sole proprietor, the identification number on the bank account is your Social Security number. The IRS runs a computer check between interest reported on Schedule B (or directly on line 8a on the front of Form 1040 if you're not required to file Schedule B) and thus will not pick up interest income you report elsewhere.

Your 1989 gross income from self-employment appears on **line 7.**

Part II identifies the business expenses you claim to reduce that 1989 gross income. Brief explanations and examples of the types of deductions included in each line follow.

Line 8 is the cost of advertising, including business cards, paid advertisements in publications, newspapers, or journals; videotapes or portfolios (if required to present your professional credentials).

Line 9 is the bad-debt figure for the year. To enter anything on this line, you must use the accrual method of accounting and have made a serious effort to collect the money owed you. A serious effort consists of three written contacts in an increasingly threatening tone. For larger amounts, legal action may be necessary to be considered sufficiently serious.

Use **line 10** to report car and truck expenses. A detailed discussion of options in deducting automobile expenses is provided in the Appendix, "A Quick Guide to Deductibility." Whether you use the standard deduction (25.5 cents per mile for 1989) or a percentage of the actual operating expenses, remember to add business parking costs to the figure you enter on this line.

On **line 11** enter the total commissions you paid to independent contractors in 1989. If you paid any independent contractor more than $600 during the year, you must send him or her a Form 1099-MISC. Be sure to keep the payer's copy of Form 1099-MISC with your copy of the 1989 tax return in case you're audited and asked to prove you filed the necessary reports.

Line 12, depletion, is rarely used by artists. An exception might be neon artists or ceramicists, where there is inevitable waste of some of the gases used in the manufacturing process. Considering the amounts involved, however, it's easier simply to write off supplies as they're purchased.

Line 13 identifies your depreciation expense for the year. The entry on this line comes directly from line 19 of the 1989 Form 4562.

If you have employees and have established an employee benefit program for them, enter the cost of these insurance or daycare benefits on **line 14.**

Freight costs are entered on **line 15.** Do not include standard postage costs or an occasional overnight delivery service on this line; they belong on line 19 as "office expense."

Line 16 (insurance) includes professional liability insurance, insurance on equipment, and insurance on your office or studio. Do not include health insurance premiums here (instead enter 25 percent of the premium cost on line 26 of Form 1040, and the remainder on line 1a of Schedule A), or disability insurance costs.

Deductible business interest is entered on **line 17a** and **line 17b.** Mortgage interest paid to financial institutions (line 17a) includes that portion of the mortgage interest on your home attributable to your office in the home. Mortgage interest paid via a contract for deed (also known as a land contract) should be entered on line 17b, along with other deductible business interest. Included in the latter category is the portion of interest on an automobile loan corresponding to business use of the vehicle or interest on credit cards used exclusively for business.

Enter the cost of legal and professional services on **line 18.** This category includes lawyers' and accountants' fees, as long as they pertain to operating your business. Tax preparation fees for sole proprietors are not deductible here and can be deducted only as part of miscellaneous deductions on line 21 of Schedule A.

If you are a photographer, do not enter film and developing expenses on this line, even if you use a professional laboratory for processing. That expense belongs under cost of goods sold, under supplies, or on line 28 itemized as "film and developing."

Office expense, on **line 19,** includes office supplies and postage. Also enter the cost of copying or printing here, as long as it is a minimal figure. If you've just had a book or a limited edition printed, you probably also have an inventory. The cost, in that case, should be entered in Part III of Schedule C.

Line 20, pension and profit-sharing plans, contains your contributions, as an employer, to such plans for your employees. Payments you make on your own behalf to an IRA/SEP account or to a Keogh Plan belong on line 24 and line 27, respectively, of Form 1040.

Rent on business property is subdivided on the 1989 Schedule C between amounts paid to rent or lease machinery and equipment (**line 21a**), and other business property (**line 21b**). Rent or lease payments on a copier, computer, fax machine, postage meter, or printing press are examples of deductions that would appear on line 21a.

Include rent on a studio you do not own or, if you claim office in the home, rent on an apartment where you have your studio on line 21b. If you rent your home, the deductible portion of the rental cost is the same as the percentage of home used as office multiplied by the total amount of rent paid.

Use **line 22** for repairs to business equipment.

Line 23 is the cost of supplies you use to produce the work you sell or service you provide. If you use the cost of goods sold section in Part III of Schedule C, this line includes all of the other supplies that, while not in the finished product itself, are necessary to make the product. Some artists refer to these supplies as "studio supplies" and may include light bulbs, lumber, X-acto blades, string, and the like. They're the kinds of items included in overhead—not related to the art you produce but necessary to its creation. If you do not use the cost of goods sold section in Part III, this line includes the supplies that go into making the product you produce, plus those so-called studio supplies.

Line 24 is the total amount of sales tax you paid to federal, state, or local authorities on products or services produced by your business or employer taxes. Examples include unemployment insurance, workers' compensation, and Social Security tax. Do not include here sales tax paid on individual items used in your business. The sales tax on a drawing pad, for example, is included in the total cost of the item, which is deducted as a supply on line 23 above.

Line 25 is divided among travel (**line 25a**) and meals and entertainment (**line 25b**). Refer to the Appendix, "A Quick Guide to Deductibility" for restrictions placed on what constitutes legitimate travel expenses. Make sure you have a daily log or appointment book to substantiate deductions on these lines. "Meals and entertainment" costs include the cost of business lunches or dinners plus the cost of meals on the road.

Since meals and entertainment costs are only partially deductible, **line 25c** backs out the disallowed percentage: 20 percent in 1989. Subtracting line 25c from line 25b gives you your meals and entertainment deduction on **line 25d,** equal to 80 percent of the amount actually spent on these items.

Business meals include meeting with a client or business associate over lunch or dinner for a specific business purpose. The IRS presumes you pay for the meal. If you "go dutch," there is no deductible business expense. If you meet with someone for convenience, there is no deductible business expense. If you grab a bite to eat on your way home from the theater at 11 P.M. because you haven't had time to eat all day, there is no deductible business expense.

The deductibility of entertainment expenses is also limited. Whether or not you can deduct the cost of a luxury skybox at a sports stadium will probably depend on the intestinal fortitude of your tax accountant or on records you keep showing business purposes discussed during time-outs. More to the point, business entertaining is now exceedingly difficult to justify and attracts IRS scrutiny if it appears luxurious. Moreover, for 1989, the amount you can deduct for luxury skyboxes is not the amount paid, but rather only the amount you would pay for a regular, nonluxury, ticket to the same event.

For more common circumstances, the price of tickets to an event that meets the clear business-purpose test is deductible only up to 80 percent of the face value of the tickets. As before, if you provide "freebies" to a business associate, you have no entertainment deduction.

Expenses for utilities are entered on **line 26.** Include in this figure the portion of heat, light, water, and trash collection charges attributable to your business portion of your home or, if you have a separate studio, the utilities charge at the studio.

Add to this your allowable telephone expense. In an urban area, this amounts to the base charge for a business telephone plus the charge for long-distance business calls. No portion of a personal telephone base charge is deductible, if that is the only telephone number in your home. This is true even if you live in a rural area (a change from the 1988 regulations).

If you have employees, enter the gross amount of the wages you pay them less any kinds of jobs credits on **line 27.**

Use **line 28** to list other expenses not covered by the categories listed above.

In the past, items such as bank charges on a business checking account or dues and publications used in your work had separate lines on Schedule C. These have been eliminated on the 1989 Schedule C. This signals another move toward tighter enforcement by the IRS, since the "other expenses" category has traditionally been a "hot button" for IRS computer matches of your deductions against profiles of reasonable expenses for businesses similar to yours. In entering expenses in this area, always be explicit. Never use the term "miscellaneous."

For expenses unique to your business, such as film and developing costs for photographers, on-site expenses other than meals for video artists shooting on location, props, costumes, or makeup for dancers or actors, or tools and small equipment for artisans, try to move these items to the "supplies" line. Keep the "other expenses" area dedicated to items that can't conceivably go elsewhere.

Enter bank service charges on **line 28.** This expense is frequently overlooked and can be a substantial amount. If you have a business account or a personal account used exclusively for business, your deduction is the sum of the monthly service charges plus the cost of check printing.

If you have a personal account with a per-check charge, you still have a deduction. To determine the amount you can deduct, count the number of checks you wrote for business (an easy task if you used some code in your check register to identify business deductions), multiply by the per-check charge you pay, and enter the result on line 8. If, in addition to the per-check charge, there's also a flat monthly fee, you can prorate the monthly fee and deduct that amount for each month you write business checks. Do not include overdraft or nonsufficient funds notices or any other kind of penalty in your deductible bank charges.

Also use **line 28** to enter the cost of dues, publications, and books. "Dues" includes payments to professional organizations, while "publications" includes the cost of newspapers or magazines you purchase in order to stay current in your field, as well as professional journals.

The cost of membership in professional organizations is usually deductible if the organization has a direct link to your professional activity. Membership in a writer's guild is clearly a necessary business expense for a writer.

Less clear is membership in a health club for a television announcer, still less clear is such a membership for a dancer or a pilot. Probably one of the most difficult membership expenses to justify is the one paid by a realtor for membership in a downtown business club or country club, though undoubtedly some business is conducted there.

If in doubt, keep a daily log of your activities (using the who-what-where-when-why system). By the end of the year you can determine whether or not the membership is primarily personal or primarily professional. If it turns out to be primarily professional, part of the dues may be deductible.

Publications are deductible as long as they are related to your profession. If, for example, you are a playwright, producer, or actor and subscribe to the local newspaper primarily to have ready access to theater reviews, the cost of that newspaper subscription is a deductible business expense. If, on the other hand, you are an athletic trainer who works on a contract basis at the local tennis club, your subscription to *Sports Illustrated* would probably not be deductible, while your subscription to *Sports Medicine* would be. The difference is that *Sports Illustrated* is a magazine for the sports generalist and has no direct relevance to the way you earn income. *Sports Medicine*, by contrast, has a direct link to your professional activities.

Laundry and cleaning costs had their own line on Schedule C in past years. Not so in 1989. Deduct the cost of cleaning costumes on **line 28.** Also use **line 28** for the expense of having your office professionally cleaned or, if you work out of your home, that portion of the cost of cleaning your home that equals the portion of your home used as an office.

If you are a filmmaker or video artist who has made the safe harbor election on deducting business expenses, enter the current year adjustment and prior year carryover on **line 28.** Also, if you are a filmmaker or video artist, be sure to label Schedule C clearly as to the method you're using to deduct expenses. Write across the top of Schedule C: "Original Capitalization per IRC 263A" if you are paid per project and do not work on your own films, or "Safe Harbor Election per IR Bulletin 88-62. Adopted [year you made the election]" if you made the safe harbor election in 1989 or earlier.

Your total business expense is entered on **line 29.** Gross income (**line 7**) less total deductions (**line 29**) equals your net profit for 1989 (**line 30**). Transfer this number to line 12 on the front of Form 1040 and to line 2 of Schedule SE (replicated on pages 84 and 85).

If you spent more in 1989 than you brought in, the figure on line 30 is a negative figure, enclosed in parentheses, and you have a net loss for the year. If you have a net loss, you must complete **line 31** by checking the box on **line 31a.** This indicates all the money you have put into the business is either spent or able to be spent on the debts the business has. Rarely will an artist not be "at risk" for the debts of the business (box on **line 31b**).

Even if you have a net loss, transfer the loss from line 30 of Schedule C to line 2 of Schedule SE. This makes for a complete tax return.

Schedule SE

Schedule SE is used to calculate your Social Security tax liability for the year. The back of Schedule SE is used only by ministers or Christian Science practitioners and does not pertain to this discussion.

Enter your profit (or loss) from line 30 of Schedule C on **line 2** of Schedule SE. If you are also involved in a partnership, you received a form K-1 reporting your partnership profit or loss. The amount of the profit or loss from a partnership is entered on Schedule E. Since these earnings are also subject to Social Security tax (FICA), they must be entered on Schedule SE along with your profit or loss from Schedule C.

If you work as a sole proprietor in two different occupations or if you actively participate in two or more partnerships, or any combination of these two, you need to add your profits and losses from all self-employment activities on line 2 of Schedule SE. The combined total on line 2 is your overall profit or loss from all self-employment activity (including partnerships in which you materially and actively participate) for 1989. Unless you're also engaged in farming, the number on **line 2** is the same as the number on **line 3.**

Line 4 is the maximum amount of earned income subject to Social Security tax. For 1989 the figure is $48,000. That means that if you have regular employment (a W-2 job) that pays you $48,000 or more, you have already paid the maximum amount in Social Security tax for 1989.

Most artists do not have outside jobs paying $48,000 or more, so they need to calculate how much of their self-employment profit (**line 2** of Schedule SE) is subject to self-employment tax. Enter on **line 5** the amount of Social Security wages from all W-2 forms issued to you for 1989. You'll find the Social Security wage figure in box 13 of each 1989 Form W-2.

When you subtract the amount of earned income already subject to Social Security tax (**line 5**) from the 1989 threshold ($48,000 on **line 4**), you have the remaining maximum amount still subject to Social Security tax on **line 6.** You pay self-employment tax on the lesser of the amounts on line 3 or on line 6. The lesser of those two amounts is entered on **line 7** and is multiplied by the 1989 Social Security tax rate for self-employed persons, which is 13.02 percent.

Your 1989 self-employment Social Security tax appears on **line 9** and is transferred from Schedule SE to **line 48** on the back of the 1989 Form 1040.

This completes the section on forms and schedules relating to self-employment activities. But since artists do not live by art alone, Schedules D and E are also described briefly.

Schedule D

Schedule D is used to report capital gains and losses that result from the sale of capital assets. Capital assets can include stocks, bonds, shares in a mutual fund, or real property (which includes property used in your business). Schedule D is replicated on pages 86–89.

For 1989, Schedule D has more room to report individual transactions. From a two-sided one-page schedule in prior years, it now is a two-sided two-page schedule. What's clear from the change is that the IRS doesn't want aggregate figures, that it now has the computing power to match individual transactions reported by brokers to individual transactions entered by taxpayers on Schedule D, and that any discrepancies will result in an IRS notice of additional tax liability.

Also affecting the 1989 Schedule D was a congressional battle resulting in lower tax rates for capital gains. How this affects the 1989 Schedule D will not be clear until after this book goes to market. In general, the schedule will probably remain unchanged except for an alternative method of calculating the tax on capital gains. Moreover, any 1989 change will be minimal, with the bulk of tax savings occurring in the 1990 and 1991 tax years.

Check the instructions that accompany your 1989 tax form packet for directives on how to deal with capital gains, should you need to file Schedule D.

Overall, this much is clear: For 1989, Schedule D is divided into six parts. Use Part I to report short-term capital gains from 1989; use Part II for long-term capital gains. Part III summarizes the cumulative gain or loss for 1989. Part IV provides detailed calculations for capital-loss carryovers (because you have exceeded the maximum allowable loss) from 1989 to the 1990 forms. Part V is used only if you sell property on a long-term contract and declare the note at less than face value (a rare occurrence). Use Part VI if the total figure from all Form 1099-Bs you receive differs from the transactions you reported in Parts I or II (totaled on **line 9c**).

Use **line 1** to report the total amount of potentially taxable stock and bond transactions. This is the sum of the figures reported to you on Form 1099-B. Whenever you receive a Form 1099-B, remember that a copy has already been sent to the IRS and that you must account for this transaction on Schedule D.

Use Part I of Schedule D for short-term capital gains and losses (if you owned the asset less than one full year), and use Part II for long-term gains and losses. Stock, bond, and mutual fund sales or redemptions for which you receive a Form 1099-B are reported on **line 2a** if held less than one year, or on **line 9a** if held more than one year.

Enter the sum of **line 2b** and **line 9b** on **line 9c**. This should equal the figure on line 1. If it does not, you need to provide a reconciliation explaining the difference in Part VI on the back of the schedule.

Other sales and distributions that constitute a long- or short-term gain or loss can be reported on **line 2c** or **line 9c.** You will not have a Form 1099-B for any of these transactions.

SCHEDULE SE	Social Security Self-Employment Tax	OMB No. 1545-0074
(Form 1040)	▶ See Instructions for Schedule SE (Form 1040).	**1989**
Department of the Treasury Internal Revenue Service (4)	▶ Attach to Form 1040.	Attachment Sequence No. **18**

Name of person with **self-employment** income (as shown on social security card)	Social security number of person with **self-employment** income ▶	⋮ ⋮

Who Must File Schedule SE

You must file Schedule SE if:

- Your net earnings from self-employment were $400 or more (or you had wages of $100 or more from an electing church or church-controlled organization); AND

- Your wages (subject to social security or railroad retirement tax) were less than $48,000.

Exception. If your only self-employment income was from earnings as a minister, member of a religious order, or Christian Science practitioner, AND you filed **Form 4361** and received IRS approval not to be taxed on those earnings, DO NOT file Schedule SE. Instead, write "Exempt–Form 4361" on Form 1040, line 48.

For more information about Schedule SE, see the Instructions.

Note: *Most people can use the short Schedule SE on this page. But, you may have to use the longer Schedule SE that is on the back.*

Who MUST Use the Long Schedule SE (Section B)

You must use Section B if ANY of the following applies:

- You choose the "optional method" to figure your self-employment tax (see Section B, Part II);

- You are a minister, member of a religious order, or Christian Science practitioner and you received IRS approval (from **Form 4361**) not to be taxed on your earnings from these sources, but you owe self-employment tax on other earnings;

- You were an employee of a church or church-controlled organization that chose by law not to pay employer social security taxes;

- You had tip income that is subject to social security tax, but you did not report those tips to your employer; OR

- You were a government employee with wages subject ONLY to the 1.45% Medicare part of the social security tax.

Section A—Short Schedule SE
(Read above to see if you must use the long Schedule SE on the back (Section B).)

1	Net farm profit or (loss) from Schedule F (Form 1040), line 36, and farm partnerships, Schedule K-1 (Form 1065), line 14a	**1**	
2	Net profit or (loss) from Schedule C (Form 1040), line 30, and Schedule K-1 (Form 1065), line 14a (other than farming). See the Instructions for other income to report	**2**	
3	Add lines 1 and 2. Enter the total. If the total is less than $400, **do not** file this schedule; you **do not** owe self-employment tax . . . . ▶	**3**	
4	The largest amount of combined wages and self-employment earnings subject to social security or railroad retirement tax (tier 1) for 1989 is	**4**	$48,000 | 00
5	Total social security wages and tips (from Form(s) W-2) and railroad retirement compensation (tier 1) . . .	**5**	
6	Subtract line 5 from line 4. Enter the result. If the result is zero or less, stop here; you **do not** owe self-employment tax . . . . ▶	**6**	
7	Enter the **smaller** of line 3 or line 6	**7**	
8	Rate of tax	**8**	×.1302
9	**Self-employment tax.** If line 7 is $48,000, enter $6,249.60. Otherwise, multiply the amount on line 7 by the decimal amount on line 8 and enter the result. Also enter this amount on Form 1040, line 48 . .	**9**	

For Paperwork Reduction Act Notice, see Form 1040 Instructions.   Schedule SE (Form 1040) 1989

Name of person with **self-employment** income (as shown on social security card)	Social security number of person with **self-employment** income ▶		

Section B—Long Schedule SE

    (Before completing, see if you can use the short Schedule SE on the other side (Section A).)

A   If you are a minister, member of a religious order, or Christian Science practitioner, AND you filed **Form 4361**, but you had $400 or more of **other** earnings subject to self-employment tax, continue with Part I and check here . . . . ▶ ☐

B   If your only earnings subject to self-employment tax were wages from an electing church or church-controlled organization that is exempt from employer social security taxes and you are not a minister or a member of a religious order, skip lines 1–3b. Enter zero on line 3c and go to line 5a.

Part I   Figure Social Security Self-Employment Tax

1	Net farm profit or (loss) from Schedule F (Form 1040), line 36, and farm partnerships, Schedule K-1 (Form 1065), line 14a	**1**		
2	Net profit or (loss) from Schedule C (Form 1040), line 30, and Schedule K-1 (Form 1065), line 14a (other than farming). See Instructions for other income to report. (Employees of an electing church or church-controlled organization **do not** enter your Form W-2 wages on this line. See the Instructions.) . .	**2**		
3a	Enter the amount from line 1 (**or,** if you elected the farm optional method, from line 11 below)	**3a**		
b	Enter the amount from line 2 (**or,** if you elected the nonfarm optional method, from line 13 below) . .	**3b**		
c	Add lines 3a and 3b. Enter the total. If the total is less than $400, **do not** file this schedule; you **do not** owe self-employment tax. (**Exception:** *If you were an employee of an electing church or church-controlled organization and the total of lines 3a and 3b is less than $400, enter zero and complete the rest of this schedule.*)	**3c**		
4	The largest amount of combined wages and self-employment earnings subject to social security or railroad retirement tax (tier 1) for 1989 is	**4**	$48,000	00

5a   Total social security wages and tips (from Form(s) W-2) and railroad retirement compensation (tier 1). **Note:** *Government employees whose wages were subject only to the 1.45% Medicare tax and employees of certain church or church-controlled organizations should **not** include those wages on this line. See Instructions* . . . . | **5a** | |

b	Unreported tips subject to social security tax (from Form 4137, line 9) or to railroad retirement tax (tier 1)	**5b**		
c	Add lines 5a and 5b. Enter the total	**5c**		
6a	Subtract line 5c from line 4. Enter the result. If the result is zero or less, enter zero and stop here; you **do not** owe self-employment tax . . . . ▶	**6a**		
b	Enter your Medicare qualified government wages. See the Instructions to see if you must use the worksheet in those instructions to figure your self-employment tax . **6b**			
c	Enter your Form W-2 wages of $100 or more from an electing church or church-controlled organization . **6c**			
d	Add lines 3c and 6c. Enter the total . . . . ▶	**6d**		
7	Enter the **smaller** of line 6a or line 6d	**7**		
8	Rate of tax	**8**	×.1302	
9	**Self-employment tax.** If line 7 is $48,000, enter $6,249.60. Otherwise, multiply the amount on line 7 by the decimal amount on line 8 and enter the result. Also enter this amount on Form 1040, line 48 . .	**9**		

Part II   Optional Method To Figure Net Earnings (See "Who Can File Schedule SE" in the Instructions.)

See Instructions for limitations. Generally, you may use this part **only** if:

A   Your **gross** farm income[1] was not more than $2,400; **or**

B   Your **gross** farm income[1] was more than $2,400 and your **net** farm profits[2] were **less** than $1,600; **or**

C   Your **net** nonfarm profits[3] were less than $1,600 and also **less** than two-thirds (⅔) of your **gross** nonfarm income.[4]

Note: *If line 2 above is two-thirds (⅔) or more of your gross nonfarm income[4], or if line 2 is $1,600 or more, you may **not** use the optional method.*

[1]From Schedule F (Form 1040), line 11, and Schedule K-1 (Form 1065), line 14b.   [3]From Schedule C (Form 1040), line 30, and Schedule K-1 (Form 1065), line 14a.
[2]From Schedule F (Form 1040), line 36, and Schedule K-1 (Form 1065), line 14a.   [4]From Schedule C (Form 1040), line 7, and Schedule K-1 (Form 1065), line 14c.

10	Maximum income for optional methods	**10**	$1,600	00
11	**Farm Optional Method**—If you meet test **A** or **B** above, enter the **smaller** of: two-thirds (⅔) of gross farm income from Schedule F (Form 1040), line 11, and farm partnerships, Schedule K-1 (Form 1065), line 14b; **or** $1,600. Also enter this amount on line 3a above	**11**		
12	Subtract line 11 from line 10. Enter the result	**12**		
13	**Nonfarm Optional Method**—If you meet test **C** above, enter the **smallest** of: two-thirds (⅔) of gross nonfarm income from Schedule C (Form 1040), line 7, and Schedule K-1 (Form 1065), line 14c; **or** $1,600; **or,** if you elected the farm optional method, the amount on line 12. Also enter this amount on line 3b above	**13**		

SCHEDULE D
(Form 1040)

Department of the Treasury
Internal Revenue Service   (4)

Capital Gains and Losses
(And Reconciliation of Forms 1099-B)

▶ Attach to Form 1040.   ▶ See Instructions for Schedule D (Form 1040).

▶ For more space to list transactions for lines 2a and 9a, get Schedule D-1 (Form 1040).

OMB No. 1545-0074

1989

Attachment
Sequence No. 12A

Name(s) shown on Form 1040

Your social security number

1   Report here the total sales of stocks, bonds, etc., reported for 1989 to you on Form(s) 1099-B or on an equivalent substitute statement(s). If this amount differs from the total of lines 2c and 9c, column (d), attach a statement explaining the difference. See the Instructions for line 1 for examples . . . . . . | 1 |

Part I   Short-Term Capital Gains and Losses—Assets Held One Year or Less

(a) Description of property (Example. 100 shares 7% preferred of "Z" Co.)	(b) Date acquired (Mo., day, yr.)	(c) Date sold (Mo., day, yr.)	(d) Sales price (see Instructions)	(e) Cost or other basis (see Instructions)	(f) LOSS If (e) is more than (d), subtract (d) from (e)	(g) GAIN If (d) is more than (e), subtract (e) from (d)
2a Stocks, Bonds, and Other Securities (Include all Form 1099-B transactions. See Instructions.)						
2b Amounts from Schedule D-1, line 2b (attach Schedule D-1) .						
2c Total (add column (d) of lines 2a and 2b). . ▶ 2c						
2d Other Transactions (Include Real Estate Transactions From Forms 1099-S.)						

3	Short-term gain from sale or exchange of your home from Form 2119, line 8a or 14 .	3		
4	Short-term gain from installment sales from Form 6252, line 22 or 30	4		
5	Net short-term gain or (loss) from partnerships, S corporations, and fiduciaries.	5		
6	Short-term capital loss carryover	6		
7	Add all of the transactions on lines 2a, 2b, and 2d and lines 3 through 6 in columns (f) and (g) . .	7	(	)
8	Net short-term gain or (loss), combine columns (f) and (g) of line 7	8		

Part II   Long-Term Capital Gains and Losses—Assets Held More Than One Year

	(b)	(c)	(d)	(e)	(f)	(g)
9a Stocks, Bonds, and Other Securities (Include all Form 1099-B transactions. See Instructions.)						
9b Amounts from Schedule D-1, line 9b (attach Schedule D-1) .						
9c Total (add column (d) of lines 9a and 9b). . ▶ 9c						
9d Other Transactions (Include Real Estate Transactions From Forms 1099-S.)						

10	Long-term gain from sale or exchange of your home from Form 2119, line 8a, 10, or 14 .	10		
11	Long-term gain from installment sales from Form 6252, line 22 or 30	11		
12	Net long-term gain or (loss) from partnerships, S corporations, and fiduciaries . .	12		
13	Capital gain distributions	13		
14	Enter gain from Form 4797, line 7 or 9	14		
15	Long-term capital loss carryover.	15		
16	Add all of the transactions on lines 9a, 9b, and 9d and lines 10 through 15 in columns (f) and (g) .	16	(	)
17	Net long-term gain or (loss), combine columns (f) and (g) of line 16	17		

For Paperwork Reduction Act Notice, see Form 1040 Instructions.   Schedule D (Form 1040) 1989

Name(s) shown on Form 1040 (Do not enter name and social security number if shown on other side.) | Your social security number

Part III   Summary of Parts I and II

18 Combine lines 8 and 17, and enter the net gain or (loss) here. If result is a gain, **stop here** and also enter the gain on Form 1040, line 13. If the result is a (loss), go on to line 19 . . . . | **18**

19 If line 18 is a (loss), enter here and as a (loss) on Form 1040, line 13, the **smaller** of:
a The (loss) on line 18; **or**
b ($3,000) or, if married filing a separate return, ($1,500) . . . . | **19** (   )

Note: When figuring whether 19a or 19b is **smaller,** treat both numbers as if they are positive.

Go on to Part IV if the loss on line 18 is more than $3,000 ($1,500, if married filing a separate return), OR if taxable income on Form 1040, line 37, is zero.

Part IV   Figure Your Capital Loss Carryovers From 1989 to 1990

Section A.—Figure Your Carryover Limit

20 Enter taxable income or loss from Form 1040, line 37. **(If Form 1040, line 37, is zero, see the Instructions for the amount to enter.)** . . . . | **20**

Note: For lines 21 through 36, treat all amounts as positive.

21 Enter the loss shown on line 19 . . . . | **21**
22 Enter the amount shown on Form 1040, line 36 . . . . | **22**
23 Combine lines 20, 21, and 22. If zero or less, enter zero . . . . . | **23**
24 Enter the **smaller** of line 21 or line 23 . . . . | **24**

Section B.—Figure Your Short-Term Capital Loss Carryover
(Complete this section only if there is a loss shown on line 8 and line 19. Otherwise, go on to Section C.)

25 Enter the loss shown on line 8 . . . . | **25**
26 Enter the gain, if any, shown on line 17 . . . . | **26**
27 Enter the amount shown on line 24 . . . . | **27**
28 Add lines 26 and 27 . . . . | **28**
29 Subtract line 28 from line 25. If zero or less, enter zero. This is your **short-term capital loss carryover from 1989 to 1990.** . . . . | **29**

Section C.—Figure Your Long-Term Capital Loss Carryover
(Complete this section only if there is a loss shown on line 17 and line 19.)

30 Enter the loss shown on line 17 . . . . | **30**
31 Enter the gain, if any, shown on line 8 . . . . | **31**
32 Enter the amount shown on line 24 . . . . | **32**
33 Enter the amount, if any, shown on line 25 . . . . . . | **33**
34 Subtract line 33 from line 32. If zero or less, enter zero . . . . . | **34**
35 Add lines 31 and 34 . . . . | **35**
36 Subtract line 35 from line 30. If zero or less, enter zero. This is your **long-term capital loss carryover from 1989 to 1990** . . . . | **36**

Part V   Complete This Part Only If You Elect Out of the Installment Method and Report a Note or Other Obligation at Less Than Full Face Value

37 Check here if you elect out of the installment method . . . . ▶ ☐
38 Enter the face amount of the note or other obligation . . . . ▶ ....
39 Enter the percentage of valuation of the note or other obligation . . . . ▶

Part VI   Reconcile Forms 1099-B for Bartering Transactions
(Complete this part if you received one or more Form(s) 1099-B or an equivalent substitute statement(s) reporting bartering income.) | Amount of bartering income from Form 1099-B or equivalent statement reported on form or schedule

40 Form 1040, line 22 . . . . | **40**
41 Schedule C (Form 1040) . . . . | **41**
42 Schedule D (Form 1040) . . . . | **42**
43 Schedule E (Form 1040) . . . . | **43**
44 Schedule F (Form 1040) . . . . | **44**
45 Other form (identify) (if not taxable, indicate reason—attach additional sheets if necessary) ▶ ....

....

.... | **45**

46 Total (add lines 40 through 45) . . . . | **46**

Note: The amount on line 46 should be the same as the total bartering income on all Forms 1099-B and equivalent statements received.

Continuation Sheet for Schedule D
(Form 1040)

▶ See Instructions for Schedule D (Form 1040).

▶ Attach to Schedule D If you need more space to list transactions.

OMB No. 1545-0074

1989

Attachment
Sequence No. **12B**

Name(s) shown on Form 1040

Your social security number

Part I Short-Term Capital Gains and Losses—Assets Held One Year or Less

(a) Description of property (Example, 100 shares 7% preferred of "Z" Co.)	(b) Date acquired (Mo., day, yr.)	(c) Date sold (Mo., day, yr.)	(d) Sales price (see Instructions)	(e) Cost or other basis (see Instructions)	(f) LOSS If (e) is more than (d), subtract (d) from (e)	(g) GAIN If (d) is more than (e), subtract (e) from (d)
2a Stocks, Bonds, and Other Securities (Include all Form 1099-B transactions. See Instructions.)						

2b Totals (add columns (d), (f), and (g)). Enter here and on Schedule D (Form 1040), line 2b. . . . . . **2b▶**

Proof as of June 30

Name(s) shown on Form 1040. (Do not enter name and social security number if shown on other side.) | Your social security number

| Part II | Long-Term Capital Gains and Losses—Assets Held More Than One Year |

(a) Description of property (Example, 100 shares 7% preferred of "Z" Co.)	(b) Date acquired (Mo., day, yr.)	(c) Date sold (Mo., day, yr.)	(d) Sales price (see Instructions)	(e) Cost or other basis (see Instructions)	(f) LOSS If (e) is more than (d), subtract (d) from (e)	(g) GAIN If (d) is more than (e), subtract (e) from (d)

9a Stocks, Bonds, and Other Securities (Include all Form 1099-B transactions. See Instructions.)

9b Totals (add columns (d), (f), and (g)). Enter here and on Schedule D (Form 1040), line 9b . . . . . . **9b▶**

SCHEDULE E
(Form 1040)

Department of the Treasury
Internal Revenue Service   (4)

Supplemental Income and Loss

(From rents, royalties, partnerships, estates, trusts, REMICs, etc.)
▶ Attach to Form 1040 or Form 1041.
▶ See Instructions for Schedule E (Form 1040).

OMB No. 1545-0074

1989

Attachment
Sequence No. **13**

Name(s) shown on return

Your social security number

Part I   Income or Loss From Rentals and Royalties   Caution: *Your rental loss may be limited. See Instructions.*

1 Show the kind and location of **rental property:**

A ....

B ....

C ....

2 For each rental property listed on line 1, did you or your family use it for personal purposes for more than the greater of 14 days or 10% of the total days rented at fair rental value during the tax year?

	Yes	No
A		
B		
C		

3 For each **rental real estate property** listed on line 1, did you actively participate in its operation during the tax year? (See Instructions.)

A		
B		
C		

Rental and Royalty Income:		Properties			D Totals
		A	B	C	(Add columns A, B, and C)
4 Rents received	**4**				**4**
5 Royalties received	**5**				**5**
Rental and Royalty Expenses:					
6 Advertising	**6**				
7 Auto and travel	**7**				
8 Cleaning and maintenance	**8**				
9 Commissions	**9**				
10 Insurance	**10**				
11 Legal and other professional fees	**11**				
12 Mortgage interest paid to banks, etc. (see Instructions)	**12**				**12**
13 Other interest	**13**				
14 Repairs	**14**				
15 Supplies	**15**				
16 Taxes	**16**				
17 Utilities (see Instructions)	**17**				
18 Wages and salaries	**18**				
19 Other (list) ▶	**19**				
20 Add lines 6 through 19	**20**				**20**
21 Depreciation expense or depletion (see Instructions)	**21**				**21**
22 Total expenses. Add lines 20 and 21	**22**				
23 Income or (loss) from rental or royalty properties. Subtract line 22 from line 4 (rents) or line 5 (royalties). If the result is a (loss), see Instructions to find out if you must file **Form 6198**	**23**				
24 Deductible rental loss. **Caution:** *Your rental loss on line 23 may be limited. See Instructions to find out if you must file **Form 8582***	**24**	( )(	)(	)	

25 Income. Add rental and royalty income from line 23. Enter the total income here **25**

26 Losses. Add royalty losses from line 23 and rental losses from line 24. Enter the total losses here . . . **26** ( )

27 Combine amounts on lines 25 and 26. Enter the net income or (loss) here **27**

28 Net farm rental income or (loss) from Form 4835. (Also complete line 43 on page 2.) **28**

29 Total rental and royalty income or (loss). Combine amounts on lines 27 and 28. Enter the result here. If Parts II, III, and IV on page 2 do not apply to you, enter the amount from line 29 on Form 1040, line 18. Otherwise, include the amount from line 29 in the total on line 42 on page 2 . . . . **29**

For Paperwork Reduction Act Notice, see Form 1040 Instructions.

Schedule E (Form 1040) 1989

Name(s) shown on return. (Do not enter name and social security number if shown on other side.)	Your social security number

Note: *If you report amounts from farming or fishing on Schedule E, you must include your gross income from those activities on line 43 below.*

Part II   Income or Loss From Partnerships and S Corporations

If you report a loss from an at-risk activity, you MUST check either column **(e)** or **(f)** to describe your investment in the activity. See Instructions.
If you check column **(f)**, you must attach **Form 6198.**

30	(a) Name	(b) Enter P for partnership; S for S corporation	(c) Check if foreign partnership	(d) Employer identification number	Investment At Risk? (e) All is at risk	(f) Some is not at risk
A						
B						
C						
D						
E						

	Passive Income and Loss		Nonpassive Income and Loss		
	(g) Passive loss allowed from Form 8582	(h) Passive income from Schedule K-1	(i) Nonpassive loss from Schedule K-1	(j) Section 179 deduction (see Instructions for limits)	(k) Nonpassive income from Schedule K-1
A					
B					
C					
D					
E					
31a Totals					
b Totals					

32	Add amounts in columns (h) and (k) of line 31a. Enter the total income here	32	
33	Add amounts in columns (g), (i), and (j) of line 31b. Enter the total here	33	( )
34	Total partnership and S corporation income or (loss). Combine amounts on lines 32 and 33. Enter the result here and include in the total on line 42 below	34	

Part III   Income or Loss From Estates and Trusts

35	(a) Name	(b) Employer identification number
A		
B		
C		

	Passive Income and Loss		Nonpassive Income and Loss	
	(c) Passive deduction or loss allowed from Form 8582	(d) Passive income from Schedule K-1	(e) Deduction or loss from Schedule K-1	(f) Other income from Schedule K-1
A				
B				
C				
36a Totals				
b Totals				

37	Add amounts in columns (d) and (f) of line 36a. Enter the total income here	37	
38	Add amounts in columns (c) and (e) of line 36b. Enter the total here	38	( )
39	Total estate and trust income or (loss). Combine amounts on lines 37 and 38. Enter the result here and include in the total on line 42 below	39	

Part IV   Income or Loss From Real Estate Mortgage Investment Conduits (REMICs)—Residual Holder

40	(a) Name	(b) Employer identification number	(c) Excess inclusion from Schedules Q, line 2c (see Instructions)	(d) Taxable income (net loss) from Schedules Q, line 1b	(e) Income from Schedules Q, line 3b

41	Combine amounts in columns (d) and (e) only. Enter the result here and include in the total on line 42 below	41	

Part V   Summary of Parts I Through IV

42	TOTAL income or (loss). Combine amounts on lines 29, 34, 39, and 41. Enter the result here and on Form 1040, line 18 . . . . ▶	42	

Part VI   Reconciliation of Farming and Fishing Income

43	Farmers and fishermen: Enter your **gross** farming and fishing income reported in Parts I, II, and III (see Instructions)	43		

Note: if you sold real estate in 1989, you will receive a Form 1099-S reporting the gross amount for which you sold the property. A 1099-S transaction is reported on Form 2119 in the case of a personal residence, on Form 4797 or Form 6252 in the case of rental or investment property. From there, follow the rules pertaining to those specific forms.

Report the gain from Form 2119 on **line 3** or **line 10** of Schedule D if you do not expect to replace the residence within the allowable twenty-four-month period.

Gains from installment sales are reported on **line 4** if short term or **line 11** if long term. Use Form 6252 for the underlying computation of the amount of gain.

Use **line 5** or **line 12** to report gains or losses from partnerships, S-corporations, or trusts (fiduciaries). You receive reports of your gain or loss from any of these organizations on a Schedule K-1.

Line 13 is used to report capital-gain distributions on mutual or stock funds. These are, by definition, long-term gains.

If you as an artist sell business property during the year, you must calculate the gain or loss from the sale (taking into account the adjusted basis of the property) on Form 4797. From that form, enter any gain on **line 14** of Schedule D. Any loss is reported directly on line 15 of Form 1040.

If you have a capital loss carryover from a previous year, report it on **line 6** if it is a short-term loss and on **line 15** if it is a long-term loss.

Add up your short-term gain (or loss) on **line 7**; add up your long-term gain (or loss) on **line 16**. Combine the columns on line 7 to give you an overall net short-term gain (or loss) on **line 8**; combine the columns on line 16 to give you an overall net long-term gain (or loss) on **line 17**. Combine lines 8 and 17 to determine your combined gain (or loss) for 1989 on **line 18.**

Transfer any gain shown on line 18 to line 13 on the front of the 1989 Form 1040. If you show a loss on **line 18,** you must complete **line 19.** Any capital loss (other than losses on business property) is limited to $3,000 for most tax filers (to $1,500 for a married person filing a separate return). Any losses that exceed that limit must be carried over to the next tax year. Use Part IV to compute your carryover figures.

Note that if line 37 of your 1989 Form 1040 is already zero, you are eligible to carry over any loss you show on Schedule D. This is a change from the 1988 tax forms.

Schedule E

Use Schedule E if you own rental property or oil wells, are a partner or owner of an S-corporation, have income from estates or trusts, or own a Real Estate Mortgage Investment Conduit (REMICs came into existence after limited partnerships lost some of their sparkle).

If you are an author who receives royalties, royalty income must be reported on Schedule C. The "royalties" referred to in the subtitle of this schedule are royalties from oil and mineral exploration.

Use Part I to report income from rental property (commercial or residential housing or other real property) and royalties from oil and gas exploration companies or mines. Allowable expenses parallel those used by a sole proprietor. You must calculate depreciation expense separately, using Form 4562.

If you show a loss in this (or any other) sections of Schedule E, you must complete Form 8582 to determine which part of that loss is deductible this year and which part must be deferred. Form 8582 is complicated. If you need it to file your return correctly, it is probably inappropriate for you to do your own tax return.

What limits a loss? If you are not materially participating in running a rental property business, you must complete Form 8582 to determine how much of the loss you can deduct in 1989. Even if you materially participate in the rental business (which means you screen potential tenants, make repairs, set rents, or otherwise provide for the management of the rental units) *and* you purchased your properties before October 22, 1986, your losses are limited in 1989 to $25,000 plus 20 percent of the loss exceeding $25,000.

If you have properties purchased both before and after October 22, 1986, you must use Form 8582 to calculate your allowable loss. If you have properties purchased only after October 22, 1986, you must use Form 8582 to calculate the amount deferred to the first year you show a profit—or to the date of sale, whichever comes sooner.

Use Part II if you have income from a partnership or an S-corporation. Again, losses are limited, depending on level of participation (material or not) and whether the investment is active or passive. Use Form 8582 to determine how much (if any) of a loss you can use in 1989.

A further word of caution: If you are a member of a limited partnership with real estate holdings in several locales, be aware of the need to allocate income and deductions among the individual properties. A gain from a property in one location cannot offset a loss from a property in another.

Especially as the current-year deduction for losses is phased out (it drops from 20 percent for pre-October 22, 1986 acquisitions in 1989, to 10 percent in 1990, to nothing in 1991 and beyond), you must keep records (separate from the tax return) of amounts disallowed for each property in a specific year. Disallowed losses can be applied either in the first year a specific property shows a gain, or in the year of sale, whichever comes sooner.

Part III is comparatively straightforward. While you are asked again to segregate passive losses and passive income (generally from rental property owned by the estate or trust), most entries from Form K-1 will show income and hence escape the requirements of Form 8582.

Use Part IV only if you are an investor in a Real Estate Mortgage Investment Conduit, a particular form of limited partnership.

Part V summarizes your gains and losses from the previous four parts. Report the overall gain or loss from all Schedule E activities on line 18 of Form 1040.

9

Putting It All Together

The preceding pages have outlined for you, in some detail, the major forms you might use in putting together your 1989 federal tax return. But knowing the mechanics is one thing; putting it all together is another. How do you start?

The first step is to gather the information you'll need. This includes your personal receipts along with books from your business. You'll need your mileage log, utility bills, and telephone bills. If your phone or utility company hasn't provided a 1989 total for you (probably on the January bill), haul out your calculator and add it up yourself. You'll also need your copy of last year's tax returns.

Next you'll need a set of 1989 tax forms. Some taxpayers will be sent booklets containing the major forms, while many taxpayers will receive only a card with their IRS tax label and instructions on how to order forms (a change from last year). If you need additional forms, you should determine this early on and call the IRS or visit a district IRS office. If you rely on the mails, allow at least four weeks to receive forms.

As a sole proprietor, you should start with Schedule C. Complete the preliminary questions at the top of the schedule, enter your income, and start entering the figures. When you reach the depreciation expense, break away to last year's return to identify any depreciable items that must be brought forward to this year's Form 4562. Check the depreciation schedules in the instructions so you use the correct depreciation percentages for property you purchased in 1989.

When you've completed Schedule C and know your profit or loss for the year, transfer the figure on line 30 to line 12 on the front of Form 1040 so you don't forget to do it. Then set aside Form 4562 and Schedule C while you complete Schedule SE.

After calculating your Social Security tax liability for 1989, enter that figure on line 48 on the back of Form 1040. Set aside the completed Schedule SE and turn to the "personal" side of your 1989 tax return.

If you are involved in a partnership (limited or not) or have trust income or received a distribution from an estate or have rental income, complete Schedule E. Once these calculations are complete, enter the total combined gain or loss on line 18 on the front of Form 1040.

Schedule D is complicated, so complete it next. You need to use this if you sold stocks or bonds during 1989 or if you sold shares in a mutual fund. In any of these transactions you received a notice of the sale proceeds via a Form 1099-B from the selling agent. This form may have come as part of your monthly statement for the last month of the year, so look at that last statement carefully and don't miss the reporting.

To determine gains and losses from sales of securities, you need to know when you bought them and how much you paid for them. In the case of shares of a mutual fund, you also need to know how many taxable distributions you reported on previous years' tax returns. These distributions were reinvested. To avoid paying tax on them again, you need to add the taxable distributions reported in earlier years to the basis (amount you paid for the shares) to determine a per-share cost at the time of sale.

If you cannot find copies of prior years' returns, you may need to write the IRS for copies. Use Form 4506, but keep in mind that during the tax season it takes a minimum of eight weeks to receive copies of previous years' tax returns.

Once you've sorted out your capital gains and losses, enter the overall gain (or loss) on line 13 on the front of Form 1040.

After Schedules D and E, turn to Schedule B and enter your taxable interest and dividends received in 1989. Taxable amounts are reported to you on Form 1099-INT or Form 1099-DIV forms. You may also receive a bank statement with that number printed on it, or you may receive a substitute form from a brokerage house as part of your last statement of the year. Be sure you double check to see you have included all interest and dividends from:

—Savings accounts

—Checking accounts

—Brokerage houses

—Interest from relatives

—Interest on contracts for deed.

Nothing triggers an audit faster than unreported income.

Enter your taxable interest on line 8a on the front of Form 1040 and taxable dividends on line 9. Remember that you need to report your nontaxable interest on line 8b on the front of Form 1040 because it plays a role in determining whether or not you're subject to the alternative minimum tax.

After all this, Schedule A should be easy. This is where you calculate your allowable deductions for medical expenses, taxes, interest, contributions, casualty losses or thefts, and miscellaneous deductions. Total itemized deductions are entered on line 34 on the back of Form 1040.

Believe it or not, you've almost finished your 1989 tax return. Peel off the label on the tax packet or card sent to you and affix it in the address section at the top of Form 1040. Complete the identifying information at the top of the form. Enter the Social Security number for any child in your household over the age of two. Work through the rest of Form 1040 by reading each line to see if it pertains to you. Use the tax tables in the instructions to determine your 1989 income tax. Enter the amount of federal tax withheld from your paycheck (from Form W-2) along with payments made via quarterly estimated tax payments. Are you ahead or in the red? Do they owe you or do you owe them?

No matter, at this point. Put away the return, including all the schedules and forms you've completed, for several days. Once it (and you) have cooled off, look at it again. Double check for errors in arithmetic. Make sure you haven't overlooked any income or obvious deductions. Copy it, and file the copy in a place you can find it. Sign and send the original to the IRS, making sure you have enough postage on the envelope. Congratulate yourself on a job well done.

10

State Returns

Vagaries and Variances

The differences among state tax returns make it impossible for any one book to deal with them all. Some general observations, however, can be helpful.

Among the items to watch out for are items that differ on the state level from the federal level. While many states, in the wake of the 1986 Tax Reform Act, moved to bring state tax codes into compliance with the federal code, local lobbies and interest groups preserved a number of peculiarities.

One major area of difference between federal tax law and state tax laws has been depreciation. Generally, where a state has opted for its own rules on depreciation, less is allowed on the state return than on the federal return. Usually you need to file a separate schedule for the state to calculate the adjustment.

A second area of difference is personal itemized deductions. No state allows a deduction for state or local income taxes (line 5 of Schedule A). Some states allow the deduction of moving expenses only if you are moving into that state. On the plus side, some states provide additional personal itemized deductions for adoption expenses or tuition payments.

Third, states sometimes have different rules from the IRS on what constitutes a legitimate business deduction. The same applies to income reported on Schedule E. Where there are differences between state and federal tax law, you will see printed on the state form a notice to attach the state version of a particular schedule. On the state version of the schedule, you'll see where the state law varies from federal law.

Almost all states now have some kind of voluntary check-off for a special interest: wildlife preservation, the homeless, political candidates, or scholarship funds, to name a few. In most cases, amounts contributed to these causes increase your tax liability.

Some states still allow a deduction or credit for contributions to political candidates or political campaigns; some allow a full deduction for medical expenses. On the down side, more and more states are imposing their own early-withdrawal penalties on pension or IRA funds withdrawn before the taxpayer is 59½ years old.

The federal government requires that you pay 90 percent of your current year's tax liability, or face a penalty. You can escape that penalty by filing Form 2210 and meeting one of the tests exempting you from the penalty. Some states do not allow you that much latitude. New York, for example, requires you to be overpaid or face penalty.

Not only do you face new problems with state returns, but some localities require you to file a tax return. New York City has a tax form for all sole proprietors operating within the city limits, whether or not they reside there.

Of course, you may live in a state that has no income tax. Lucky, lucky, lucky. Unless, of course, you're a sole proprietor who works in multiple states. That means you need to file state returns for each state in which you make enough income on which you could be taxed. Let's take the example of a folk singer from Minnesota who works in Iowa, Montana, Colorado, Maine, and Illinois. That taxpayer will file six state tax returns. The same holds true for a portrait artist who travels from one Renaissance festival to another.

Do these people pay double, triple, or even sextuple tax? No. Each state has a form for nonresidents. Using the form, you calculate tax only on the amount you earned in that particular state. In your state of residence, you either exempt the other state income or receive a credit for the taxes you pay those other states. In no case are you taxed in multiple instances on the same income, although if you live in a low tax (or no income tax) state, you may find yourself receiving a credit that's less than the amount you pay the other state.

Sometimes you'll find you received a Form 1099-MISC from a company in a particular state, but because of expenses you did not make a profit on that particular gig. Do you still need to file a state tax return for that state? Yes. The state revenue authorities do not know the entire amount isn't taxable. They, like the federal government, want as much as they can get.

How do you allocate income and expenses among various states? The easiest way is to take a portion of expenses that matches that state's percentage of gross income. So, if Iowa represents 10 percent of your self-employment income, then Iowa is allocated 10 percent of your expenses, whether or not you spent that money in Iowa. A second method is to keep separate books on each gig for each state. This is cumbersome, however, and may not make an appreciable difference in the end.

Filing multiple state returns is tedious and time-consuming. If you need tax forms from a particular state, call the state revenue department, in the state capital, and request the long tax form plus the schedule for nonresidents who earned income in that state. Leave at least a week to receive the forms. Better yet, make it part of your New Year's resolutions to call, during the first week of January, all the states in which you worked in 1989. That way you'll have plenty of time to calculate your various state taxes.

A similar problem faces the taxpayer who moves to another state during the year. That person must file state tax returns for both states, unless no income was earned in one of the states or one of the states does not have a state income tax.

Special Reporting Requirements

The federal government requires myriad reports detailing the income people receive. An employer issues an employee a W-2 (if the employer has withheld income tax or Social Security tax, regardless of the gross amount paid) or an independent contractor a Form 1099-MISC (if payments for the year exceed $600).

The original Form W-2 or Form 1099-MISC is sent to the federal government (the former to the Social Security Administration, the latter to the IRS). In addition, some states require that you send them copies of the forms you file with the federal government. Others require that you complete their version of the federal form and attach a copy of the federal form to it.

To determine what your local reporting requirements are, contact your state revenue department. Tell them what business you're in and what federal reports you think you're required to file. They should be able to tell you quickly what the state reporting requirements are. A caveat: Be sure to keep a written record of that call in case you receive incomplete advice!

You may also need to file city or county tax reports. If you live in a large metropolitan area you may have a separate tax authority that expects reports. Call the local revenue department to determine what your reporting responsibilities are.

Remember that when it comes to dealing with state and local authorities, what you do not know can hurt you!

Sales Tax

Sales tax is a thorn in the side of any business that operates in a state with a sales tax. Most states now do. If there is a federal sales tax, which seems increasingly likely, every business owner will face additional recordkeeping and reporting requirements.

Sales tax is levied as a percentage of the cost of the item purchased and is paid by the purchaser. The seller, or vendor, collects the tax and then, at intervals determined by the taxing authority, turns that money over to that authority.

The amount of sales tax a state charges is set by state law. Cities and in some cases counties may levy additional sales taxes. Wherever there are one or more sales-taxing levels, it's important for the sole proprietor to devise a system for assessing, collecting, and keeping money collected for sales tax.

If you operate a business and your goods or services are subject to sales tax, make it a practice to know the local or state laws pertaining to you. Know when changes are made. If you collect an insufficient amount, you will pay the tax out of your own money. Never use funds collected as sales tax for your own operating expenses.

Does this mean you need to keep a separate account for sales taxes you collect? No. In the first place, if you collect very much, the state or local tax authority will require you to send it to them frequently, before it adds up. Second, you should make it a practice to file the required reports and pass on the tax collected more frequently than the law requires. Minimum compliance eases the paperwork burden but may pose too great a temptation to borrow against funds earmarked (and owned) by others. Bypass that temptation by filing early and sending the money as you collect it.

The process of learning what state or local laws pertain to the products or services you sell starts when you open your business. You may need a state sales tax identification number. If you operate under a business name, you may be required to register that name. Offices to call regarding your responsibilities include the state and local revenue departments along with the secretary of state's office. Always keep a record of your contacts and your understanding of what you are told in case of trouble further down the line.

11

Examples

Reprinted on the following pages are four "typical" taxpayer scenarios. Each scenario has a worksheet on which relevant tax information is summarized, followed by the actual returns as they might be prepared for 1989.

Based on the information in this chapter, you should be able to figure out how and why expenses listed on the worksheet end up looking different on the tax return itself.

Example 1. Married Filing Jointly; One Is Self- Employed.

Bob Luce and Sally Bradford are married. They have three children: Bernie, age six; Michelle, age four; and baby Helen, born in 1988. Bob is a sculptor, Sally is an engineer for a defense contractor.

To prepare their 1989 tax return, they gathered the records to support this information:

Bob's business
    Income = $26,400

    Expenses:
        supplies $9,658
        small tools   110
        dues and publications   80
        professional conferences   360
        state license fee   25
        business meals   66
        entertainment   20
        office supplies   85
        postage   88
        freight   641
        independent contractors   300
        auto use:
            business miles = 6,936
            commuting miles (@ 14 per round-trip) = 4,862
            total miles for 1989 = 16,214

Sally's employee expenses
        magazines related to work $ 34
        business lunches   66
        repairs to equipment   80
        conference fees (reimbursed)   340
        state license (reimbursed)   60

Personal deductions
        Home mortgage interest $6,625
        property taxes   1,976
        automobile licenses (2)   168

charitable contributions	960
church	120
medical costs: glasses	180
insurance	425
prescriptions	66
credit card interest: 68 + 36 + 2 + 326	
automobile loan interest (Sally's car): 968	
child-care expenses	4,840

*   *   *

Bob and Sally's 1989 tax return includes Form 1040, Schedule A, Schedule C, Schedule SE, Form 2106, Form 2441, and Form 4562.

● **Comments**

Complete Bob's Schedule C first. Since he has no inventory, complete the questions at the top of Schedule C, along with Part I and Part II. Bob had business equipment depreciated in a previous year, so he had to look at his 1988 tax return to see what he brought forward to 1989. Since there's only one item, Bob can identify it right on the Form 4562 instead of keeping a separate record.

Sally's professional expenses must be itemized on Form 2106 because she is claiming a larger deduction than the mount her employer reimbursed. Because the reimbursement is not included on her W-2 form, she must identify it on Form 2106. Excess deductions, then, are transferred to line 20 of Schedule A.

Because Bernie and Michelle are older than two, their Social Security numbers must be listed on the front of Form 1040. Next year, Helen's number will also need to be included.

Example 2. Married Filing Jointly; Both Are Self-Employed.

John and Mary Grace Stewart are married. Both are self-employed. John is a carpenter, Mary Grace paints portraits. To prepare their 1989 tax return, they gathered the records as follows:

John's business
   Income = $36,925

Expenses:	
lumber and supplies	$6,846
nails, screws, small hardware	645
small tools	1,015
equipment (band saw, 11/10)	375
work clothing	68
independent contractors	9,425
licenses, bonds	480
yellow pages listing	740
business telephone	900
equipment repairs	120
auto use:	

      business miles = 11,019
      commuting miles (@ 2 per round-trip) = 860
      total miles for 1989 = 14,112

Mary Grace's business
    Income = $2,472

    Expenses:
paints and brushes	$ 476
framing	900
conference registration fees	60
office and postage	32
business lunches	46
home office deduction: 25%	1,200
utilities: 25%	54

        auto use:
            business miles = 462
            commuting miles (@ 3 per roundtrip) = 147
            total miles for 1989 = 14,112

Personal deductions
medical insurance	$ 960
state tax paid in 1989	410
interest paid on credit cards	16
contributions to nonprofit organizations	495

    IRA contributions: $2,000 for John, $2,000 for Mary Grace

*   *   *

John and Mary Grace's 1989 tax return includes Form 1040, two Schedules C, two Schedules SE, and Form 4562.

● Comments
Begin with Schedule C. John's and Mary Grace's business activities are reported on separate Schedules C. (Even if they worked together in the same business, two Schedules C would be required.) John uses Part III of Schedule C, even though he has no inventory. Supplies he purchases to use in his work and payments to independent contractors he hires are listed in that section. This reserves the supplies line on Schedule C for other supplies he buys for his business that are not attributable to a specific job.

More important is his ability to track cost of goods as a percentage of gross revenues from year to year. Note that John filed 6 1099-MISC forms to document payments to six of the nine independent contractors he hired during the year. The other three were paid less than $600 during 1989. John's profit is transferred to his Schedule SE.

Mary Grace has a loss. But since that loss is caused by her deducting office in the home costs, that deduction is limited to the amount that causes her not to have a loss—in other words, her bottom line must be adjusted to zero. That figure is her net profit for the year and is transferred to her Schedule SE.

On line 12 on the front of Form 1040, John's profit is added to Mary Grace's profit. On line 48 on the back of Form 1040, only John's FICA tax is listed because only John needs to pay Social Security tax for 1989.

John and Mary Grace have one automobile, which both of them use for work and pleasure. They can use one Form 4562 and change the column headings to identify John's use and Mary Grace's use. Of course, both kept odometer readings (shown on the worksheet).

Form 4562 — Depreciation and Amortization

Form 4562

Department of the Treasury
Internal Revenue Service (4)

Depreciation and Amortization

▶ See separate instructions.
▶ Attach this form to your return.

OMB No. 1545-0172

1989

Attachment Sequence No. 67

Name(s) as shown on return: ROBERT LUCE + SALLY BRADFORD

Business or activity to which this form relates: SCHEDULE C

Identifying number: 567 77 8341

Part I Depreciation (Use Part III for automobiles, certain other vehicles, computers, and property used for entertainment, recreation, or amusement.)

Section A.—Election To Expense Depreciable Assets (Section 179)

1 Maximum dollar limitation	1	$10,000
2 Total cost of section 179 property placed in service during the tax year (see instructions)	2	
3 Threshold cost of section 179 property before reduction in limitation	3	$200,000
4 Reduction in limitation (Subtract line 3 from line 2, but do not enter less than -0-.)	4	
5 Dollar limitation for tax year (Subtract line 4 from line 1, but do not enter less than -0-.)	5	

6	(a) Description of property	(b) Date placed in service	(c) Cost	(d) Elected cost

7 Listed property—Enter amount from line 28	7	
8 Tentative deduction (Enter the lesser of: (a) line 6 plus line 7; or (b) line 5.)	8	
9 Taxable income limitation (Enter the lesser of: (a) Taxable income; or (b) line 5) (see instructions)	9	
10 Carryover of disallowed deduction from 1988 (see instructions)	10	
11 Section 179 expense deduction (Enter the lesser of: (a) line 8 plus line 10; or (b) line 9.)	11	
12 Carryover of disallowed deduction to 1990 (Add lines 8 and 10, less line 11.)	▶ 12	

Section B.—MACRS Depreciation

(a) Classification of property	(b) Date placed in service	(c) Basis for depreciation (Business use only—see instructions)	(d) Recovery period	(e) Convention	(f) Method	(g) Depreciation deduction
13 General Depreciation System (GDS) (see instructions): For assets placed in service ONLY during tax year beginning in 1989						
a 3-year property						
b 5-year property						
c 7-year property						
d 10-year property						
e 15-year property						
f 20-year property						
g Residential rental property			27.5 yrs.	MM	S/L	
			27.5 yrs.	MM	S/L	
h Nonresidential real property			31.5 yrs.	MM	S/L	
			31.5 yrs.	MM	S/L	
14 Alternative Depreciation System (ADS) (see instructions): For assets placed in service ONLY during tax year beginning in 1989						
a Class life					S/L	
b 12-year			12 yrs.		S/L	
c 40-year			40 yrs.	MM	S/L	

15 Listed property—Enter amount from line 27	15	
16 GDS and ADS deductions for assets placed in service before 1989 (see instructions)	16	

Section C.—ACRS and/or Other Depreciation

17 Property subject to section 168(f)(1) election (see instructions)	17	
18 ACRS and/or other depreciation (see instructions) EQUIPMENT (IRS) 5-YR ACRS 2010	18	548.

Section D.—Summary

19 Total (Add deductions on line 11 and lines 13 through 18.) Enter here and on the appropriate line of your return (Partnerships and S corporations—see instructions.)	19	20	548.

20 For assets shown above and placed in service during the current year, enter the portion of the basis attributable to section 263A costs (see instructions).

For Paperwork Reduction Act Notice, see page 1 of the separate instructions.

Form **4562** (1989)

Bob's Schedule C

Schedule C (Form 1040)

SCHEDULE C (Form 1040)

Department of the Treasury
Internal Revenue Service (4)

Profit or Loss From Business
(Sole Proprietorship)

Partnerships, Joint Ventures, Etc., Must File Form 1065.
▶ Attach to Form 1040 or Form 1041. ▶ See Instructions for Schedule C (Form 1040).

OMB No. 1545-0074

1989

Attachment Sequence No. 09

Name of proprietor: ROBERT LUCE

Social security number (SSN): 567 77 8341

A Principal business or profession, including product or service (see instructions): FINE ARTS: SCULPTURE

B Principal business code (from page 2) ▶ 8 8 8 8

C Business name and address ▶ dba DESIGN INTERIORS 14010 LAKE CHARLES RD., MINNETONKA, MN 55367

D Employer ID number (Not SSN)

E Method(s) used to value closing inventory: (1) ☐ Cost (2) ☐ Lower of cost or market (3) ☐ Other (attach explanation) (4) ☒ Does not apply (if checked, skip line G)

F Accounting method: (1) ☒ Cash (2) ☐ Accrual (3) ☐ Other (specify) ▶

G Was there any change in determining quantities, costs, or valuations between opening and closing inventory? (If "Yes," attach explanation.) ☐ Yes ☒ No

H Are you deducting expenses for business use of your home? (If "Yes," see instructions for limitations.) ☐ Yes ☒ No

I Did you "materially participate" in the operation of this business during 1989? (If "No," see instructions for limitations on losses.) ☒ Yes ☐ No

J If this schedule includes a loss, credit, deduction, income, or other tax benefit relating to a tax shelter required to be registered, check here. ▶ ☐

Part I Income

1 Gross receipts or sales	1	26,400	00
2 Returns and allowances	2		0
3 Subtract line 2 from line 1. Enter the result here	3	26,400	00
4 Cost of goods sold and/or operations (from line 39 on page 2)	4		0
5 Subtract line 4 from line 3 and enter the gross profit here	5	26,400	00
6 Other income, including Federal and state gasoline or fuel tax credit or refund (see instructions)	6		0
7 Add lines 5 and 6. This is your **gross income** ▶	7	26,400	00

Part II Expenses

8 Advertising	8			22 Repairs	22		
9 Bad debts from sales or services (see Instructions)	9			23 Supplies (not included in Part III)	23	9,658	00
10 Car and truck expenses	10	1,769	00	24 Taxes	24		
11 Commissions	11	300	00	25 Travel, meals, and entertainment:			
12 Depletion	12			a Travel	25a		
13 Depreciation and section 179 deduction from Form 4562 (not included in Part III)	13	548	00	b Meals and entertainment		86	00
14 Employee benefit programs (other than on line 20)	14			c Enter 20% of line 25b subject to limitations (see instructions)		17	
15 Freight (not included in Part III)	15	641	00	d Subtract line 25c from line 25b	25d		
16 Insurance (other than health)	16			26 Utilities (see Instructions)	26		
17 Interest:				27 Wages (less jobs credit)	27		
a Mortgage (paid to banks, etc.)	17a			28 Other expenses (list type and amount):			
b Other	17b			DUES + PUBS = 80			
18 Legal and professional services	18			SMALL TOOLS = 110			
19 Office expense	19	173	00	CONFS/CONT. ED = 360			
20 Pension and profit-sharing plans	20			LICENSE = 25			
21 Rent or lease:							
a Machinery and equipment	21a				28	575	00
b Other business property	21b						

29 Add amounts in columns for lines 8 through 28. These are your total expenses ▶	29	13,733	00
30 Net profit or (loss). Subtract line 29 from line 7. If a profit, enter here and on Form 1040, line 12, and on Schedule SE, line 2. If a loss, you MUST go on to line 31. (Fiduciaries, see instructions).	30	12,667	00

31 If you have a loss, you MUST check the box that describes your investment in this activity (see instructions). If you checked 31a, enter the loss on Form 1040, line 12, and Schedule SE, line 2. If you checked 31b, you MUST attach Form 6198.

31a ☐ All investment is at risk.
31b ☐ Some investment is not at risk.

For Paperwork Reduction Act Notice, see Form 1040 Instructions.

Schedule C (Form 1040) 1989

Luce and Bradford's Form 4562 (front)

Form 4562 (1989)

Part II — Amortization

(a) Description of property	(b) Date amortization begins	(c) Cost or other basis	(d) Code section	(e) Amortization period or percentage	(f) Amortization for this year

21 Amortization for property placed in service only during tax year beginning in 1989

22 Amortization for property placed in service before 1989 22

23 Total. Enter here and on "Other Deductions" or "Other Expenses" line of your return . . . 23

Part III — Listed Property.—Automobiles, Certain Other Vehicles, Computers, and Property Used for Entertainment, Recreation, or Amusement

If you are using the standard mileage rate or deducting vehicle lease expense, complete columns (a) through (d) of Section A, all of Section B, and Section C if applicable.

Section A.—Depreciation (Caution: See instructions for limitations for automobiles.)

24a Do you have evidence to support the business use claimed? ☒ Yes ☐ No 24b If "Yes," is the evidence written? ☒ Yes ☐ No

(a) Type of property (list vehicles first)	(b) Date placed in service	(c) Business use percentage (%)	(d) Cost or other basis (see instructions for leased property)	(e) Basis for depreciation — business use only	(f) Recovery period	(g) Method	(h) Depreciation deduction	(i) Elected section 179 cost
1984 DATSUN	1/1/85	42.8%	$7,000 ← STD. MILEAGE	DEDUCTION USED				
25 Property used more than 50% in a trade or business:					S/L			
					S/L			
26 Property used 50% or less in a trade or business:					S/L			
					S/L			

27 Total (Enter here and on line 15, page 1.) 27

28 Total (Enter here and on line 7, page 1.) 28

Section B.—Information Regarding Use of Vehicles—*If you deduct expenses for vehicles:*
- Always complete this section for vehicles used by a sole proprietor, partner, or other "more than 5% owner," or related person.
- If you provided vehicles to your employees, first answer the questions in Section C to see if you meet an exception to completing this section for those vehicles.

	(a) Vehicle 1		(b) Vehicle 2		(c) Vehicle 3		(d) Vehicle 4		(e) Vehicle 5		(f) Vehicle 6	
29 Total business miles driven during the year (DO NOT include commuting miles)	6,936		@25.5¢/mile = $1769									
30 Total commuting miles driven during the year	4,862											
31 Total other personal (noncommuting) miles driven	4,416											
32 Total miles driven during the year (Add lines 29 through 31)	16,214											
	Yes	No	Yes	No	Yes	No	Yes	No	Yes	No	Yes	No
33 Was the vehicle available for personal use during off-duty hours?												
34 Was the vehicle used primarily by a more than 5% owner or related person?												
35 Is another vehicle available for personal use?												

Section C.—Questions for Employers Who Provide Vehicles for Use by Their Employees
(Answer these questions to determine if you meet an exception to completing Section B. Note: Section B must always be completed for vehicles used by sole proprietors, partners, or other more than 5% owners or related persons.)

	Yes	No
36 Do you maintain a written policy statement that prohibits all personal use of vehicles, including commuting, by your employees?		
37 Do you maintain a written policy statement that prohibits personal use of vehicles, except commuting, by your employees? (See instructions for vehicles used by corporate officers, directors, or 1% or more owners.)		
38 Do you treat all use of vehicles by employees as personal use?		
39 Do you provide more than five vehicles to your employees, retain the information received from your employees concerning the use of the vehicles?		
40 Do you meet the requirements concerning qualified automobile demonstration use (see instructions)?		

Note: *If your answer to 36, 37, 38, 39, or 40 is "Yes," you need not complete Section B for the covered vehicles.*

Luce and Bradford's Form 4562 (back)

SCHEDULE SE (Form 1040)

Social Security Self-Employment Tax

OMB No. 1545-0074

Department of the Treasury
Internal Revenue Service (4)

► See Instructions for Schedule SE (Form 1040).
► Attach to Form 1040.

1989 Attachment Sequence No. 18

Name of person with self-employment income (as shown on social security card)	Social security number of person with self-employment income ►
ROBERT LUCE	567 : 77 : 834

Who Must File Schedule SE

You must file Schedule SE if:

- Your net earnings from self-employment were $400 or more (or you had wages of $100 or more from an electing church or church-controlled organization); AND
- Your wages (subject to social security or railroad retirement tax) were less than $48,000.

Exception. If your only self-employment income was from earnings as a minister, member of a religious order, or Christian Science practitioner, AND you filed Form 4361 and received IRS approval not to be taxed on those earnings, DO NOT file Schedule SE. Instead, write "Exempt—Form 4361" on Form 1040, line 48.

For more information about Schedule SE, see the Instructions.

Note: *Most people can use the short Schedule SE on this page. But, you may have to use the longer Schedule SE that is on the back.*

Who MUST Use the Long Schedule SE (Section B)

You must use Section B if ANY of the following applies:

- You choose the "optional method" to figure your self-employment tax (see Section B, Part II);
- You are a minister, member of a religious order, or Christian Science practitioner and you received IRS approval (from Form 4361) not to be taxed on your earnings from these sources, but you owe self-employment tax on other earnings;
- You were an employee of a church or church-controlled organization that chose by law not to pay employer social security taxes;
- You had tip income that is subject to social security tax, but you did not report those tips to your employer; OR
- You were a government employee with wages subject ONLY to the 1.45% Medicare part of the social security tax.

Section A—Short Schedule SE

(Read above to see if you must use the long Schedule SE on the back (Section B).)

1 Net farm profit or (loss) from Schedule F (Form 1040), line 36, and farm partnerships, Schedule K-1 (Form 1065), line 14a	1	
2 Net profit or (loss) from Schedule C (Form 1040), line 30, and Schedule K-1 (Form 1065), line 14a (other than farming). See the Instructions for other income to report	2	12,667 00
3 Add lines 1 and 2. Enter the total. If the total is less than $400, **do not** file this schedule; you **do not** owe self-employment tax ▲	3	12,667 00
4 The largest amount of combined wages and self-employment earnings subject to social security or railroad retirement tax (tier 1) for 1989 is	4	$48,000 00
5 Total social security wages and tips (from Form(s) W-2) and railroad retirement compensation (tier 1)	5	0
6 Subtract line 5 from line 4. Enter the result. If the result is zero or less, stop here; you **do not** owe self-employment tax ▲	6	48,000 00
7 Enter the **smaller** of line 3 or line 6	7	12,667 00
8 Rate of tax	8	× .1302
9 Self-employment tax. If line 7 is $48,000, enter $6,249.60. Otherwise, multiply the amount on line 7 by the decimal amount on line 8 and enter the result. Also enter this amount on Form 1040, line 48	9	1,649 00

For Paperwork Reduction Act Notice, see Form 1040 Instructions. Schedule SE (Form 1040) 1989

Bob's Schedule SE

Form 2106 — Employee Business Expenses

Department of the Treasury
Internal Revenue Service

▶ See separate Instructions.
▶ Attach to Form 1040.

Your name: **SALLY BRADFORD**
Social security number: **434 22 1444**
Occupation in which expenses were incurred: **ENGINEER**

Part I — Employee Business Expenses

STEP 1 — Enter Your Expenses

		Column A Other Than Meals and Entertainment	Column B Meals and Entertainment
1	Vehicle expense from Part II, line 28 or line 35		
2	Parking fees, tolls, and local transportation, including train, bus, etc.		
3	Travel expense while away from home, including lodging, airplane, car rental, etc. **Do not** include meals and entertainment		
4	Business expenses not included on lines 1 through 3. **Do not** include meals and entertainment	580 00	
5	Meals and entertainment expenses. (See Instructions.)		
6	Add lines 1 through 5 and enter the total expenses here.	580 00	—

Note: *If you were not reimbursed for any expenses in Step 1, skip lines 7–9 and enter the amount from line 6 on line 10.*

STEP 2 — Enter Amounts Your Employer Gave You For Expenses Listed In STEP 1. (See the Instructions for lines 7 and 8.)

7	Enter amounts your employer gave you that were not reported to you on Form W-2 (see Instructions)	400 00	
8	Enter amounts your employer gave you that were reported to you in Box 16 of Form W-2 (see Instructions)	—	
9	Add the amounts on lines 7 and 8. Enter the total here	400 00	—

STEP 3 — Figure Expenses To Deduct on Schedule A (Form 1040)

10	Subtract line 9 from line 6	180 00	—
	Note: *If both columns of line 10 are zero, stop here. If Column A is less than zero, report the amount as income. See the Instructions for how to report.*	180	
11	Enter 20% (.20) of line 10, Column B	—	
12	Subtract line 11 from line 10	180 00	180 00
13	Add the amounts on line 12 of both columns and enter the total here. Also enter the total on Schedule A (Form 1040), line 20. (Qualified performing artists and handicapped employees, see Instructions for special rules on where to enter the total.) ▶ 13		180 00

PROOF of June 30

For Paperwork Reduction Act Notice, see Instructions.

Form 2106 (1989)

Luce and Bradford's Form 2106 for Sally's business expenses

SCHEDULES A&B (Form 1040) — Schedule A—Itemized Deductions

(Schedule B is on back)

Department of the Treasury
Internal Revenue Service (4)

▶ Attach to Form 1040. ▶ See Instructions for Schedules A and B (Form 1040).

Name(s) shown on Form 1040: **ROBERT LUCE + SALLY BRADFORD**
Your social security number: **567 77 8341**

Medical and Dental Expenses
(Do not include expenses reimbursed or paid by others.)
(See Instructions on page 23.)

1a	Prescription medicines and drugs, insulin, doctors, dentists, nurses, hospitals, medical insurance premiums you paid, etc.	491 00
b	Other. (List—include hearing aids, dentures, (eyeglasses), transportation and lodging, etc.) ▶ 180	180 00
2	Add the amounts on lines 1a and 1b. Enter the total here	671 00
3	Multiply the amount on Form 1040, line 32, by 7.5% (.075)	
4	Subtract line 3 from line 2. If zero or less, enter -0-. Total medical and dental	0

Taxes You Paid
(See Instructions on page 24.)

5	State and local income taxes	2,418 00
6	Real estate taxes	1,996 00
7	Other taxes. (List—include personal property taxes.) ▶ 2 AUTO LICENSES (LESS BASE RATE)	92 00
8	Add the amounts on lines 5 through 7. Enter the total here. **Total taxes**	4,486 00

Interest You Paid
(See Instructions on page 24.)

9a	Deductible home mortgage interest (from Form 1098) that you paid to financial institutions. Report deductible points on line 10.	6,625 00
b	Deductible home mortgage interest. (If paid to an individual, show that person's name and address.) ▶	
10	Deductible points. (See Instructions for special rules.)	
11	Deductible investment interest. (See page 25.)	
12a	Personal interest you paid. (See page 25.) 12a 1,400 00	
b	Multiply the amount on line 12a by 20% (.20). Enter the result 12b 280 00	
13	Add the amounts on lines 9a through 11, and 12b. Enter the total here. **Total interest** ▶	6,905 00

Gifts to Charity
(See Instructions on page 25.)

14	Contributions by cash or check. (If you gave $3,000 or more to any one organization, show to whom you gave and how much you gave.) ▶	1,080 00
15	Other than cash or check. (You must attach Form 8283 if over $500.)	
16	Carryover from prior year	
17	Add the amounts on lines 14 through 16. Enter the total here. **Total contributions** ▶	1,080 00

Casualty and Theft Losses

18	Casualty or theft loss(es) (attach Form 4684). (See page 26 of the Instructions.) ▶	0

Moving Expenses

19	Moving expenses (attach Form 3903 or 3903F). (See page 26 of the Instructions.) ▶	0

Job Expenses and Most Other Miscellaneous Deductions
(See page 26 for expenses to deduct here.)

20	Unreimbursed employee expenses—job travel, union dues, job education, etc. (You MUST attach Form 2106 in some cases. See Instructions.) ▶	180 00
21	Other expenses (investment, tax preparation, safe deposit box, etc.). List type and amount ▶	
22	Add the amounts on lines 20 and 21. Enter the total.	180 00
23	Multiply the amount on Form 1040, line 32, by 2% (.02). Enter the result here.	
24	Subtract line 23 from line 22. Enter the result. If zero or less, enter -0- ▶	

Other Miscellaneous Deductions

25	Other (from list on page 26 of Instructions). List type and amount ▶	

Total Itemized Deductions

26	Add the amounts on lines 4, 8, 13, 17, 18, 19, 24, and 25. Enter the total here. Then enter on Form 1040, line 34, the LARGER of this total or your standard deduction from page 17 of the Instructions	12,471 00

For Paperwork Reduction Act Notice, see Form 1040 Instructions.

Schedule A (Form 1040) 1989

Luce and Bradford's Schedule A

Form 2441 — Child and Dependent Care Expenses

Form **2441**

Department of the Treasury
Internal Revenue Service (4)

▶ Attach to Form 1040.
▶ See separate Instructions.

OMB No. 1545-0068
1989
Attachment Sequence No. 23

Name(s) shown on Form 1040: **Robert Luce + Sally Bradford**
Your social security number: **567 77 8341**

- If you are claiming the child and dependent care credit, complete Parts I and II below. But if you received employer-provided dependent care benefits, first complete Part III on the back.
- If you are not claiming the credit but you received employer-provided dependent care benefits, only complete Part I, below, and Part III on the back.

Part I — Persons or Organizations Who Provided the Care — You must complete this part. (See the Instructions. If you need more space, attach a statement.)

1	(a) Name	(b) Address (number, street, city, state, and ZIP code)	(c) Identification number (SSN or EIN)	(d) Amount paid (see Instructions)
	Kinder Karten	444 Idaho W. St. Paul, MN 55001	41-1560001	4,200 00
	Mila Mueller	35 W. 26th St. Minneapolis, MN 55405	452 66 1744	640 00

2 Add the amounts in column (d) of line 1 and enter the total .... | 2 | 4,840 00

Note: If you paid cash wages of $50 or more in a calendar quarter to an individual for services performed in your home, you must file an employment tax return. Get Form 942 for details.

Part II — Credit for Child and Dependent Care Expenses

3 Enter the number of qualifying persons who were cared for in 1989. (See the Instructions for the definition of qualifying persons.) **Caution:** To qualify, the person(s) must have shared the same home with you in 1989 .... ▶ | 3 | **2**

4 Enter the amount of qualified expenses you incurred and actually paid in 1989. Also see the Instructions if you received employer-provided dependent care benefits. See **What Are Qualified Expenses?** in the Instructions. **Do not enter more than $2,400 ($4,800 if you paid for the care of two or more qualifying persons)** | 4 | 4,800 00

5 Enter your earned income | 5 | 0

6 Subtract line 5 from line 4 and enter the result. If the result is zero or less, stop here; you cannot claim the credit | 6 | 4,800 00

7 You must enter your **earned income**. (See the Instructions for the definition of earned income.) | 7 | 12,667 00

8 If you are married filing a joint return, you **must** enter your spouse's earned income. (If your spouse was a full-time student or disabled, see the Instructions for the amount to enter.) | 8 | 46,500 00

9 If you are married filing a joint return, compare the amounts on lines 7 and 8. Enter the **smaller** of the two amounts here | 9 | 12,667 00

10
- If you are married filing a joint return, compare the amounts on lines 6 and 9. Enter the **smaller** of the two amounts here.
- All others, compare the amounts on lines 6 and 7. Enter the **smaller** of the two amounts here.
| 10 | 4,800 00

11 Enter the decimal amount from the table below that applies to the adjusted gross income on Form 1040, line 32.

If line 32 is:		Decimal amount is:	If line 32 is:		Decimal amount is:
Over—	But not over—		Over—	But not over—	
$0	–10,000	.30	$20,000	–22,000	.24
10,000	–12,000	.29	22,000	–24,000	.23
12,000	–14,000	.28	24,000	–26,000	.22
14,000	–16,000	.27	26,000	–28,000	.21
16,000	–18,000	.26	28,000		.20
18,000	–20,000	.25			

| 11 | × .20 |

12 Multiply the amount on line 10 by the decimal amount on line 11, and enter the result | 12 | 960 00

13 Multiply any child and dependent care expenses for 1988 that you paid in 1989 by the percentage that applies to the adjusted gross income on your 1988 Form 1040, line 32, or Form 1040A, line 14. Enter the result. (You must complete Part I and attach a statement. See the Instructions.) | 13 | 0

14 Add the amounts on lines 12 and 13. See the Instructions for the amount of credit you can claim | 14 | 960 00

For Paperwork Reduction Act Notice, see separate Instructions.

Form **2441** (1989)

Luce and Bradford's Form 2441

Form 1040 — U.S. Individual Income Tax Return

Form **1040**

Department of the Treasury—Internal Revenue Service

U.S. Individual Income Tax Return **1989** (4)

For the year Jan.–Dec. 31, 1989, or other tax year beginning ____, 1989, ending ____, 19 ____ | OMB No. 1545-0074

Label (L A B E L H E R E)

Your first name and initial: **Robert** Last name: **Luce**
Your social security number: **567 77 8341**

If a joint return, spouse's first name and initial: **Sally Bradford** Last name: **Bradford**
Spouse's social security number: **434 22 1444**

Home address (number and street). (If a P.O. box, see page 7 of Instructions.): **123 Pleasant St.** Apt. no.

City, town or post office, state and ZIP code. (If a foreign address, see page 7.): **Minneapolis, MN 55423**

For Privacy Act and Paperwork Reduction Act Notice, see Instructions.

Presidential Election Campaign ▶
Do you want $1 to go to this fund? | Yes ☐ No ☐
If joint return, does your spouse want $1 to go to this fund? | Yes ☐ No ☐

Note: Checking "Yes" will not change your tax or reduce your refund.

Filing Status
1 ☐ Single
2 ☒ Married filing joint return (even if only one had income)
3 ☐ Married filing separate return. Enter spouse's social security no. above and full name here.
4 ☐ Head of household (with qualifying person). (See page 7 of Instructions.) If the qualifying person is your child but not your dependent, enter child's name here.
5 ☐ Qualifying widow(er) with dependent child (year spouse died ▶ 19 ____). (See page 7 of Instructions.)

Exemptions (See Instructions on page 8.)
6a ☒ Yourself — If someone (such as your parent) can claim you as a dependent on his or her tax return, do not check box 6a. But be sure to check the box on line 33b on page 2.
6b ☒ Spouse
Number of boxes checked on 6a and 6b: **2**

c Dependents:

(1) Name (first, initial, and last name)	(2) Check if under age 2	(3) If age 2 or older, dependent's social security number	(4) Relationship	(5) No. of months lived in your home in 1989
Bernie Luce		349 62 7854	Son	12
Michelle Luce	X	349 62 7858	Daughter	12
Helen Luce	X		Daughter	12

No. of your children on 6c who: • lived with you **3**

d If your child didn't live with you but is claimed as your dependent under a pre-1985 agreement, check here ▶ ☐

e Total number of exemptions claimed .... ▶ | **5**

Income
Please attach Copy B of your Forms W-2, W-2G, and W-2P here.

7 Wages, salaries, tips, etc. (attach Form(s) W-2) | 7 | 46,500 00
8a Taxable interest income (also attach Schedule B if over $400) | 8a | 64 00
8b Tax-exempt interest income (see page 10). DON'T include on line 8a | 8b |
9 Dividend income (also attach Schedule B if over $400) | 9 | 0
10 Taxable refunds of state and local income taxes, if any, from worksheet on page 11 of Instructions | 10 | 118 00
11 Alimony received | 11 |
12 Business income or (loss) (attach Schedule C) | 12 | 12,667 00
13 Capital gain or (loss) (attach Schedule D) | 13 |
14 Capital gain distributions not reported on line 13 (see page 11) | 14 |
15 Other gains or (losses) (attach Form 4797) | 15 |
16a Total IRA distributions | 16a | 16b Taxable amount (see page 11) | 16b |
17a Total pensions and annuities | 17a | 17b Taxable amount (see page 12) | 17b |
18 Rents, royalties, partnerships, estates, trusts, etc. (attach Schedule E) | 18 |
19 Farm income or (loss) (attach Schedule F) | 19 |
20 Unemployment compensation (insurance) (see page 13) | 20 |
21a Social security benefits | 21a | 21b Taxable amount (see page 13) | 21b |
22 Other income (list type and amount—see page 13) | 22 | 0
23 Add the amounts shown in the far right column for lines 7 through 22. This is your **total income** ▶ | 23 | **59,349 00**

Adjustments to Income (See Instructions on page 14.)
24 Your IRA deduction, from applicable worksheet on page 14 or 15 | 24 |
25 Spouse's IRA deduction, from applicable worksheet on page 14 or 15 | 25 |
26 Self-employed health insurance deduction, from worksheet on page 15 | 26 |
27 Keogh retirement plan and self-employed SEP deduction | 27 |
28 Penalty on early withdrawal of savings | 28 |
29 Alimony paid. a Recipient's last name ____ and b social security number ____ | 29 |
30 Add lines 24 through 29. These are your **total adjustments** ▶ | 30 | 0

Adjusted Gross Income
31 Subtract line 30 from line 23. This is your **adjusted gross income**. If this line is less than $19,340 and a child lived with you, see "Earned Income Credit" (line 58) on page 20 of the Instructions. If you want IRS to figure your tax, see page 16 of the Instructions | 31 | **59,349 00**

Luce and Bradford's Form 1040 (front)

Tax Computation	32	Amount from line 31 (adjusted gross income)	32	59,349 00
	33a	Check if: ☐ You were 65 or older ☐ Blind; ☐ Spouse was 65 or older ☐ Blind;		
		Add the number of boxes checked and enter the total here ▶ 33a ☐		
	b	If someone (such as your parent) can claim you as a dependent, check here ▶ 33b ☐		
	c	If you are married filing a separate return and your spouse itemizes deductions, or you are a dual-status alien, see page 16 and check here ▶ 33c ☐		
	34	Enter the larger of: • Your standard deduction (from page 17 of the Instructions), OR • Your itemized deductions (from Schedule A, line 26). If you itemize, attach Schedule A and check here ▶ ☐	34	12,471 00
	35	Subtract line 34 from line 32. Enter the result here	35	46,878 00
	36	Multiply $2,000 by the total number of exemptions claimed on line 6e	36	12,000 00
	37	Taxable income. Subtract line 36 from line 35. Enter the result (if less than zero, enter zero)	37	34,878 00
		Caution: If under age 14 and you have more than $1,000 of investment income, check here ▶ ☐ and see page 17 to see if you have to use Form 8615 to figure your tax.		
	38	Enter tax. Check if from a ☐ Tax Table, b ☐ Tax Rate Schedules, or c ☐ Form 8615 (If any is from Form(s) 8814, enter that amount here ▶ d _____)	38	6,303 00
	39	Additional taxes (see page 18). Check if from: a ☐ Form 4970 b ☐ Form 4972	39	0
	40	Add lines 38 and 39 ▶	40	6,303 00
Credits (See Instructions on page 18.)	41	Credit for child and dependent care expenses (attach Form 2441)	41	960 00
	42	Credit for the elderly or the disabled (attach Schedule R)	42	0
	43	Foreign tax credit (attach Form 1116)	43	
	44	General business credit. Check if from a ☐ Form 3800 or b ☐ Form (specify) _____	44	
	45	Credit for prior year minimum tax (attach Form 8801)	45	
	46	Add lines 41 through 45. Enter the total	46	960 00
	47	Subtract line 46 from line 40. Enter the result (if less than zero, enter zero) ▶	47	5,343 00
Other Taxes (Including Advance EIC Payments)	48	Self-employment tax (attach Schedule SE)	48	1,649 00
	49	Alternative minimum tax (attach Form 6251)	49	0
	50	Recapture taxes (see page 18). Check if from a ☐ Form 4255 b ☐ Form 8611	50	
	51	Social security tax on tip income not reported to employer (attach Form 4137)	51	
	52	Tax on an IRA or a qualified retirement plan (attach Form 5329)	52	
	53	Add lines 47 through 52. Enter the total ▶	53	6,992 00
Medicare Premium	54	Supplemental Medicare premium (attach Form 8808)	54	0
	55	Add lines 53 and 54. This is your total tax and any supplemental Medicare premium ▶	55	6,992 00
Payments Attach Forms W-2, W-2G, and W-2P to front	56	Federal income tax withheld (if any is from Form(s) 1099, check ▶ ☐)	56	6,421 00
	57	1989 estimated tax payments and amount applied from 1988 return	57	3,900 00
	58	Earned income credit (see page 20)	58	0
	59	Amount paid with Form 4868 (extension request)	59	
	60	Excess social security tax and RRTA tax withheld (see page 20)	60	
	61	Credit for Federal tax on fuels (attach Form 4136)	61	
	62	Regulated investment company credit (attach Form 2439)	62	
	63	Add lines 56 through 62. These are your total payments ▶	63	10,321 00
Refund or Amount You Owe	64	If line 63 is larger than line 55, enter amount OVERPAID	64	3,329 00
	65	Amount of line 64 to be REFUNDED TO YOU ▶	65	2,329 00
	66	Amount of line 64 to be APPLIED TO YOUR 1990 ESTIMATED TAX ▶ 66	1,000 00	
	67	If line 55 is larger than line 63, enter AMOUNT YOU OWE. Attach check or money order for full amount payable to "Internal Revenue Service." Write your social security number, daytime phone number, and "1989 Form 1040" on it	67	
	68	Penalty for underpayment of estimated tax (see page 21)	68	

Sign Here (Keep a copy of this return for your records.)

Under penalties of perjury, I declare that I have examined this return and accompanying schedules and statements, and to the best of my knowledge and belief, they are true, correct, and complete. Declaration of preparer (other than taxpayer) is based on all information of which preparer has any knowledge.

| Your signature _Robert Luce_ | Date 3/18/90 | Your occupation |
| Spouse's signature (if joint return, BOTH must sign) _Sally Bradford_ | Date 3/19/90 | Spouse's occupation |

Paid Preparer's Use Only

Preparer's signature ▶	Date	Check if self employed ☐	Preparer's social security no
Firm's name (or yours if self-employed) and address ▶		E.I. No	......
		ZIP code	

Luce and Bradford's Form 1040 (back)

SCHEDULE C (Form 1040)

Profit or Loss From Business
(Sole Proprietorship)

Partnerships, Joint Ventures, Etc., Must File Form 1065.

Department of the Treasury Internal Revenue Service (4) ▶ Attach to Form 1040 or Form 1041. ▶ See Instructions for Schedule C (Form 1040).

OMB No. 1545-0074

1989

Attachment Sequence No. 09

Name of proprietor JOHN STEWART

Social security number (SSN) 373 : 64 : 9573

A Principal business or profession, including product or service (see Instructions)
CONSTRUCTION: BUILDING TRADES: CARPENTER

B Principal business code (from page 2) ▶ 0 | 4 | 1 | 4

C Business name and address ▶ aba ... Ready Repairs Carpenter
1962 .. Wilben Ave. .. St. Paul

D Employer ID number (Not SSN)

E Method(s) used to value closing inventory: (1) ☐ Cost (2) ☐ Lower of cost or market (3) ☐ Other (attach explanation)

F Accounting method: (1) ☐ Cash (2) ☒ Accrual (3) ☐ Other (specify) ▶

G Was there any change in determining quantities, costs, or valuations between opening and closing inventory? (If "Yes," attach explanation.) | Yes | No ☒

H Are you deducting expenses for business use of your home? (If "Yes," see Instructions for limitations.) ▶ ☐

I Did you "materially participate" in the operation of this business during 1989? (If "No," see Instructions for limitations on losses.)

J If this schedule includes a loss, credit, deduction, income, or other tax benefit relating to a tax shelter required to be registered, check here . . . ▶ ☐
If you checked this box, you MUST attach Form 8271.

Part I Income

1 Gross receipts or sales	1	36,925	00
2 Returns and allowances	2		0
3 Subtract line 2 from line 1. Enter the result here	3	36,925	00
4 Cost of goods sold and/or operations (from line 39 on page 2)	4	16,751	00
5 Subtract line 4 from line 3 and enter the **gross profit** here	5	20,174	00
6 Other income, including Federal and state gasoline or fuel tax credit or refund (see Instructions)	6		0
7 Add lines 5 and 6. This is your **gross income** ▶	7	20,174	00

Part II Expenses

8 Advertising	8		
9 Bad debts from sales or services (see Instructions)	9		
10 Car and truck expenses	10	3,810	00
11 Commissions	11		
12 Depletion	12		
13 Depreciation and section 179 deduction from Form 4562 (not included in Part III)	13		
14 Employee benefit programs (other than on line 20)	14		
15 Freight (not included in Part III)	15		
16 Insurance (other than health)	16		
17 Interest:			
a Mortgage (paid to banks, etc.)	17a		
b Other	17b		
18 Legal and professional services	18		
19 Office expense	19		
20 Pension and profit-sharing plans	20		
21 Rent or lease:			
a Machinery and equipment	21a		
b Other business property	21b		
22 Repairs	22	120	00
23 Supplies (not included in Part III)	23	2,103	00
24 Taxes	24		
25 Travel, meals, and entertainment:			
a Travel	25a		
b Meals and entertainment			
c Enter 20% of line 25b subject to limitations (see Instructions)			
d Subtract line 25c from line 25b	25d		
26 Utilities (see Instructions)	26	1,640	00
27 Wages (less jobs credit)	27		
28 Other expenses (list type and amount):			

29 Add amounts in columns for lines 8 through 28. These are your total expenses	▶	29	6,673	00
30 **Net profit or (loss).** Subtract line 29 from line 7. If a profit, enter here and on Form 1040, line 12, and on Schedule SE, line 2. If a loss, you MUST go on to line 31. (Fiduciaries, see Instructions).		30	13,501	00

31 If you have a loss, you MUST check the box that describes your investment in this activity (see Instructions).
If you checked 31a, enter the loss on Form 1040, line 12, and Schedule SE, line 2.
If you checked 31b, you MUST attach Form 6198.

31a ☐ All investment is at risk.
31b ☐ Some investment is not at risk.

For Paperwork Reduction Act Notice, see Form 1040 Instructions.

Schedule C (Form 1040) 1989

John's Schedule C

Schedule C (Form 1040) 1989   J. STEWART   373 64 9573   Page 2

Part III Cost of Goods Sold and/or Operations (See Instructions.)

32 Inventory at beginning of year. (If different from last year's closing inventory, attach explanation.)	32		0
33 Purchases less cost of items withdrawn for personal use	33	6,846	00
34 Cost of labor. (Do not include salary paid to yourself.) 6 - 1099s ISSUED	34	9,425	00
35 Materials and supplies LICENSES + BONDS	35	480	00
36 Other costs	36		0
37 Add lines 32 through 36	37	16,751	00
38 Inventory at end of year	38		0
39 Cost of goods sold and/or operations. Subtract line 38 from line 37. Enter the result here and on page 1, line 4	39	16,751	00

Part IV Principal Business or Professional Activity Codes

Locate the major business category that best describes your activity (for example, Retail Trade, Services, etc.). Within the major category, select the activity code that most closely identifies the business or profession that is the principal source of your sales or receipts. Enter this 4-digit code on page 1, line B. (Note: If your principal source of income is from farming activities, you should file Schedule F (Form 1040), Farm Income and Expenses.)

Construction

Code
0018 Operative builders (for own account)

General contractors
0034 Residential building
0059 Nonresidential building
0075 Highway and street construction
3889 Other heavy construction (pipe laying, bridge construction, etc.)

Building trade contractors, including repairs
0232 Plumbing, heating, air conditioning
0257 Painting and paper hanging
0273 Electrical work
0299 Masonry, dry wall, stone, tile
0414 Carpentering and flooring
0430 Roofing, siding, and sheet metal
0455 Concrete work
0885 Other building trade contractors (excavation, glazing, etc.)

Manufacturing, Including Printing and Publishing
0638 Food products and beverages
0653 Textile mill products
0679 Apparel and other textile products
0695 Leather, footwear, handbags, etc.
0810 Furniture and fixtures
0836 Lumber and other wood products
0877 Paper and allied products
1032 Printing and publishing
1057 Primary metal industries
1073 Fabricated metal products
1099 Machinery and machine shops
1115 Electric and electronic equipment
1883 Other manufacturing industries

Mining and Mineral Extraction
1511 Metal mining
1537 Coal mining
1719 Oil and gas
1719 Quarrying and nonmetallic mining

Agricultural Services, Forestry, Fishing
1933 Crop services
1958 Veterinary services, including pets
1990 Livestock breeding
1974 Other animal services
2113 Farm labor and management services
2212 Horticulture and landscaping
2238 Forestry, except logging
0836 Logging
2246 Commercial fishing
2469 Hunting and trapping

Wholesale Trade—Selling Goods to Other Businesses, Etc.
Durable goods, including machinery, equipment, wood, metals, etc.
2618 Selling for your own account
2634 Agent or broker for other firms—more than 50% of gross sales on commission
Nondurable goods, including food, fiber, chemicals, etc.
2659 Selling for your own account

2675 Agent or broker for other firms—more than 50% of gross sales on commission

Retail Trade—Selling Goods to Individuals and Households
3012 Selling door-to-door, by telephone or party plan, or from mobile unit
3038 Catalog or mail order
3053 Vending machine selling

Selling From Showroom, Store, or Other Fixed Location
Food, beverages, and drugs
3079 Eating places (meals or snacks)
3086 Catering services
3095 Drinking places (alcoholic beverages)
3210 Grocery stores (general line)
0612 Bakeries selling at retail
3236 Other food stores (meat, produce, candy, etc.)
3251 Liquor stores
3277 Drug stores

Automotive and service stations
3319 New car dealers (franchised)
3335 Used car dealers
3517 Other automotive dealers (motorcycles, recreational vehicles, etc.)
3533 Tires, accessories, and parts
3558 Gasoline service stations

General merchandise, apparel, and household
3715 Variety stores
3731 Other general merchandise stores
3756 Shoe stores
3772 Men's and boys' clothing stores
3913 Women's ready-to-wear stores
3921 Women's accessory and specialty stores and furriers
3939 Family clothing stores
3954 Other apparel and accessory stores
3970 Furniture stores
3996 TV, audio, and electronics
3988 Computer and software stores
4119 Household appliance dealers
4317 Other home furnishings stores (china, floor coverings, etc.)
4333 Music and record stores

Building, hardware, and garden supply
4416 Building materials dealers
4432 Paint, glass, and wallpaper stores
4457 Hardware stores
4473 Nurseries and garden supply stores

Used merchandise and antique stores (except motor vehicle parts)
4614
4630 Gift, novelty, and souvenir shops
4655 Florists
4671 Jewelry stores
4697 Sporting goods and bicycle shops
4812 Boat dealers
4838 Hobby, toy, and game shops
4853 Camera and photo supply stores
4879 Optical goods stores
4895 Luggage and leather goods stores
5033 Book stores, excluding newsstands
5058 Stationery stores
5074 Fabric and needlework stores
5090 Mobile home dealers
5884 Fuel dealers (except gasoline)
Other retail stores

Finance, Insurance, Real Estate, and Related Services
5520 Real estate agents or brokers
5579 Real estate property managers
5710 Subdividers and developers, except cemeteries
5538 Operators and lessors of buildings, including residential
5553 Operators and lessors of other real property
5702 Insurance agents or brokers
5744 Other insurance services
6064 Security brokers and dealers
6080 Commodity contracts brokers and dealers, and security and commodity exchanges
6130 Investment advisors and services
6155 Credit institutions and mortgage bankers
5777 Title abstract offices
Other finance and real estate

Transportation, Communications, Public Utilities, and Related Services
6114 Taxicabs
6312 Bus and limousine passenger transportation
6361 Other highway passenger transportation
6338 Trucking (except trash collection)
6395 Courier or package delivery services
6510 Trash collection without own dump
6536 Public warehousing
6551 Water transportation
6619 Air transportation
6635 Travel agents and tour operators
6650 Other transportation services
6676 Communication services
6692 Utilities, including dumps, snowplowing, road cleaning, etc.

Services (Personal, Professional, and Business Services)
Hotels and other lodging places
7096 Hotels, motels, and tourist homes
7211 Rooming and boarding houses
7237 Camps and camping parks

Laundry and cleaning services
7419 Coin-operated laundries and dry cleaning
7435 Other laundry, dry cleaning, and garment services
7450 Carpet and upholstery cleaning
7476 Janitorial and related services (building, house, and window cleaning)

Business and/or personal services
7617 Legal services (or lawyer)
7633 Income tax preparation
7658 Accounting and bookkeeping
7682 Engineering services
7708 Architectural services
7245 Surveying services
7260 Management services
7286 Consulting services
7716 Advertising, except direct mail
7732 Employment agencies and personnel supply
7799 Consumer credit reporting and collection services

7856 Mailing, reproduction, commercial art and photography, and stenographic services
7872 Computer programming, processing, data preparation, and related services
7922 Computer repair, maintenance, and leasing
7773 Equipment rental and leasing (except computer or automotive)
7914 Investigative and protective services
7880 Other business services

Personal services
8110 Beauty shops (or beautician)
8318 Barber shop (or barber)
8334 Photographic portrait studios
8532 Funeral services and crematories
8714 Child day care
8730 Teaching or tutoring
8755 Counseling (except health practitioners)
8771 Ministers and chaplains
6882 Other personal services

Automotive rental or leasing, without driver
8813
8839 Parking, except valet
8953 Automotive repairs, general and specialized
8896 Other automotive services (wash, towing, etc.)

Miscellaneous repair, except computers
9019 TV and audio equipment repair
9035 Other electrical equipment repair
9050 Reupholstery and furniture repair
2881 Other equipment repair

Medical and health services
9217 Offices and clinics of medical doctors (MDs)
9233 Offices and clinics of dentists
9258 Osteopathic physicians and surgeons
9241 Podiatrists
9274 Chiropractors
9290 Optometrists
9431 Registered and practical nurses
9431 Other health practitioners
9456 Medical and dental laboratories
9472 Nursing and personal care facilities
9886 Other health services

Amusement and recreational services
8557 Physical 'fitness facilities
9597 Motion picture and video production
9688 Motion picture and tape distribution and allied services
9613 Motion picture theaters
9639 Bowling centers
9670 Professional sports and racing, including promoters and managers
9696 Theatrical performers, musicians, agents, producers, and related services
9811 Other amusement and recreational services

8888 Unable to classify

John's Schedule C (back)

SCHEDULE SE (Form 1040)

Social Security Self-Employment Tax

Department of the Treasury
Internal Revenue Service (4)

► See Instructions for Schedule SE (Form 1040).
► Attach to Form 1040.

1989
Attachment Sequence No. 18

Name of person with self-employment income (as shown on social security card): **JOHN STEWART**

Social security number of person with self-employment income ► **373 : 64 : 9523**

Who Must File Schedule SE

You must file Schedule SE if:

- Your net earnings from self-employment were $400 or more (or you had wages of $100 or more from an electing church or church-controlled organization); AND
- Your wages (subject to social security or railroad retirement tax) were less than $48,000.

Exception. If your only self-employment income was from earnings as a minister, member of a religious order, or Christian Science practitioner, AND you filed **Form 4361** and received IRS approval not to be taxed on those earnings, DO NOT file Schedule SE. Instead, write "Exempt–Form 4361" on Form 1040, line 48.

For more information about Schedule SE, see the Instructions.

Note: *Most people can use the short Schedule SE on this page. But, you may have to use the longer Schedule SE that is on the back.*

Who MUST Use the Long Schedule SE (Section B)

You must use Section B if ANY of the following applies:

- You choose the "optional method" to figure your self-employment tax (see Section B, Part II);
- You are a minister, member of a religious order, or Christian Science practitioner and you received IRS approval (from **Form 4361**) not to be taxed on your earnings from these sources, but you owe self-employment tax on other earnings;
- You were an employee of a church or church-controlled organization that chose by law not to pay employer social security taxes;
- You had tip income that is subject to social security tax, but you did not report those tips to your employer; OR
- You were a government employee with wages subject ONLY to the 1.45% Medicare part of the social security tax.

Section A—Short Schedule SE

(Read above to see if you must use the long Schedule SE on the back (Section B).)

1	Net farm profit or (loss) from Schedule F (Form 1040), line 36, and farm partnerships, Schedule K-1 (Form 1065), line 14a	1	
2	Net profit or (loss) from Schedule C (Form 1040), line 30, and Schedule K-1 (Form 1065), line 14a (other than farming). See the Instructions for other income to report	2	13,501 00
3	Add lines 1 and 2. Enter the total. If the total is less than $400, **do not** file this schedule; you **do not** owe self-employment tax	3	13,501 00
4	The largest amount of combined wages and self-employment earnings subject to social security or railroad retirement tax (tier 1) for 1989 is	4	$48,000 00
5	Total social security wages and tips (from Form(s) W-2) and railroad retirement compensation (tier 1)	5	
6	Subtract line 5 from line 4. Enter the result. If the result is zero or less, stop here; you **do not** owe self-employment tax	6	
7	Enter the **smaller** of line 3 or line 6	7	13,501 00
8	Rate of tax	8	x .1302
9	**Self-employment tax.** If line 7 is $48,000, enter $6,249.60. Otherwise, multiply the amount on line 7 by the decimal amount on line 8 and enter the result. Also enter this amount on Form 1040, line 48	9	1,758 00

For Paperwork Reduction Act Notice, see Form 1040 Instructions.   Schedule SE (Form 1040) 1989

John's Schedule SE

SCHEDULE C (Form 1040)

Profit or Loss From Business
(Sole Proprietorship)

Department of the Treasury
Internal Revenue Service (4)

Partnerships, Joint Ventures, Etc., Must File Form 1065.
► Attach to Form 1040 or Form 1041. ► See Instructions for Schedule C (Form 1040).

1989
Attachment Sequence No. 09

Name of proprietor: **MARY GRACE STEWART**

Social security number (SSN): **215 : 43 : 6593**

A Principal business or profession, including product or service (see Instructions) ► **FINE ARTS : PORTRAITURE**

B Principal business code (from page 2) ► **8888**

C Business name and address ► **MARY GRACE STEWART** **1962 WILSON AVE · ST. PAUL**

D Employer ID number (Not SSN)

E Method(s) used to value closing inventory: (1) ☐ Cost (2) ☐ Lower of cost or market (3) ☐ Other (attach explanation) (4) ☒ Does not apply (if checked, skip line G)

F Accounting method: (1) ☒ Cash (2) ☐ Accrual (3) ☐ Other (specify) ►

G Was there any change in determining quantities, costs, or valuations between opening and closing inventory? (If "Yes," attach explanation.) Yes ☐ No ☒

H Are you deducting expenses for business use of your home? (If "Yes," see Instructions for limitations.) ☐ ☒

I Did you "materially participate" in the operation of this business during 1989? (If "No," see Instructions for limitations on losses.)

J If this schedule includes a loss, credit, deduction, income, or other tax benefit relating to a tax shelter required to be registered, check here. ►☐
If you checked this box, you MUST attach **Form 8271**.

Part I Income

1	Gross receipts or sales	1	2,492 00
2	Returns and allowances	2	0
3	Subtract line 2 from line 1. Enter the result here	3	2,492 00
4	Cost of goods sold and/or operations (from line 39 on page 2)	4	0
5	Subtract line 4 from line 3 and enter the **gross profit** here	5	2,492 00
6	Other income, including Federal and state gasoline or fuel tax credit or refund (see Instructions)	6	0
7	Add lines 5 and 6. This is your **gross income** ►	7	2,492 00

Part II Expenses

8	Advertising	8	
9	Bad debts from sales or services (see Instructions)	9	
10	Car and truck expenses	10	118 00
11	Commissions	11	
12	Depletion	12	
13	Depreciation and section 179 deduction from **Form 4562** (not included in Part III)	13	
14	Employee benefit programs (other than on line 20)	14	
15	Freight (not included in Part III)	15	
16	Insurance (other than health)	16	
17	Interest:		
a	Mortgage (paid to banks, etc.)	17a	
b	Other	17b	
18	Legal and professional services	18	
19	Office expense	19	32 00
20	Pension and profit-sharing plans	20	
21	a Machinery and equipment (25%)	21a	1,200 00
	b Other business property (25%)	21b	= 849
22	Repairs	22	
23	Supplies (not included in Part III)	23	1,376 00
24	Taxes	24	
25	Travel, meals, and entertainment:		
a	Travel	25a	
b	Meals and entertainment	46 00	
	c Enter 20% of line 25b subject to limitations (see Instructions)	9 00	
	d Subtract line 25c from line 25b	25d	37 00
26	Utilities (see Instructions) (25%)	26	54 00
27	Wages (less jobs credit)	27	
28	Other expenses (list type and amount): **CONFS / CONT. ED. = 60.**		
		28	60 00
29	Add amounts in columns for lines 8 through 28. These are your **total expenses** ►	29	2,877 00 2,472
30	**Net profit or (loss).** Subtract line 29 from line 7. If a profit, enter here and on Form 1040, line 12, and on Schedule SE, line 2. If a loss, you MUST go on to line 31. (Fiduciaries, see Instructions.)	30	0
31	If you have a loss, you MUST check the box that describes your investment in this activity (see Instructions).	31a ☐ All investment is at risk.
	If you checked 31a, enter the loss on Form 1040, line 12, and Schedule SE, line 2.	31b ☐ Some investment is not at risk.
	If you checked 31b, you MUST attach **Form 6198**.	

For Paperwork Reduction Act Notice, see Form 1040 Instructions.   Schedule C (Form 1040) 1989

Mary Grace's Schedule C

STEWART
373 64 9573

Page 2

Part II Amortization

(a) Description of property	(b) Date amortization begins	(c) Cost or other basis	(d) Code section	(e) Amortization period or percentage	(f) Amortization for this year

21 Amortization of property placed in service only during tax year beginning in 1989

22 Amortization for property placed in service before 1989 . . . . | 22 |

23 Total. Enter here and on "Other Deductions" or "Other Expenses" line of your return | 23 |

Part III Listed Property.—Automobiles, Certain Other Vehicles, Computers, and Property Used for Entertainment, Recreation, or Amusement

If you are using the standard mileage rate or deducting vehicle lease expense, complete columns (a) through (d) of Section A, all of Section B, and Section C if applicable.

Section A.—Depreciation (Caution: See instructions for limitations for automobiles.)

24a Do you have evidence to support the business use claimed? ☐ Yes ☐ No 24b If "Yes," is the evidence written? ☐ Yes ☐ No

(a) Type of property (list vehicles first)	(b) Date placed in service	(c) Business use percentage (%)	(d) Cost or other basis (see instructions for leased property)	(e) Basis for depreciation — business use only	(f) Recovery period	(g) Method	(h) Depreciation deduction	(i) Elected section 179 cost
1982 DATSUN	1983	81.4	$9,600	—	STD. MILEAGE RATE USED			
					S/L			
					S/L			
					S/L			

25 Property used more than 50% in a trade or business:

26 Property used 50% or less in a trade or business:

27 Total (Enter here and on line 15, page 1.) . . . . | 27 |

28 Total (Enter here and on line 7, page 1.) . . . . | 28 |

Section B.—Information Regarding Use of Vehicles—If you deduct expenses for vehicles:

- Always complete this section for vehicles used by a sole proprietor, partner, or other "more than 5% owner," or related person.
- If you provided vehicles to your employees, first answer the questions in Section C to see if you meet an exception to completing this section for those vehicles.

	Vehicle 1 JOHN		Vehicle 2 MARY GRACE		Vehicle 3		Vehicle 4		Vehicle 5		Vehicle 6	
29 Total business miles driven during the year (DO NOT include commuting miles)	11,019		462		@ 25.5¢ = 2,810 FOR JOHN							
30 Total commuting miles driven during the year	860		147		+ 118 FOR MARY GRACE							
31 Total other personal (noncommuting) miles driven	1,624←											
32 Total miles driven during the year (Add lines 29 through 31)	14,112←											
	Yes	No	Yes	No	Yes	No	Yes	No	Yes	No	Yes	No
33 Was the vehicle available for personal use during off-duty hours?												
34 Was the vehicle used primarily by a more than 5% owner or related person?												
35 Is another vehicle available for personal use?												

Section C.—Questions for Employers Who Provide Vehicles for Use by Their Employees

(Answer these questions to determine if you meet an exception to completing Section B. **Note:** Section B must always be completed for vehicles used by sole proprietors, partners, or other more than 5% owners or related persons.)

	Yes	No
36 Do you maintain a written policy statement that prohibits all personal use of vehicles, including commuting, by your employees?		
37 Do you maintain a written policy statement that prohibits personal use of vehicles, except commuting, by your employees? (See instructions for vehicles used by corporate officers, directors, or 1% or more owners.)		
38 Do you treat all use of vehicles by employees as personal use?		
39 Do you provide more than five vehicles to your employees and retain the information received from your employees concerning the use of the vehicles?		
40 Do you meet the requirements concerning qualified automobile demonstration use (see instructions)?		

Note: If your answer to 36, 37, 38, 39, or 40 is "Yes," you need not complete Section B for the covered vehicles.

Stewarts' Form 4562 (back)

Social Security Self-Employment Tax

▶ See Instructions for Schedule SE (Form 1040).
▶ Attach to Form 1040.

OMB No. 1545-0074

1989

Attachment Sequence No. 18

Name of person with self-employment income (as shown on social security card) MARY GRACE STEWART

Social security number of person with self-employment income ▶ 215 : 43 : 6573

Who Must File Schedule SE

You must file Schedule SE if:

- Your net earnings from self-employment were $400 or more (or you had wages of $100 or more from an electing church or church-controlled organization); AND
- Your wages (subject to social security or railroad retirement tax) were less than $48,000.

Exception. If your only self-employment income was from earnings as a minister, member of a religious order, or Christian Science practitioner, AND you filed **Form 4361** and received IRS approval not to be taxed on those earnings, DO NOT file Schedule SE. Instead, write "Exempt–Form 4361" on Form 1040, line 48.

For more information about Schedule SE, see the Instructions.

Note: Most people can use the short Schedule SE on this page. But, you may have to use the longer Schedule SE that is on the back.

Who MUST Use the Long Schedule SE (Section B)

You must use Section B if ANY of the following applies:

- You choose the "optional method" to figure your self-employment tax (see Section B, Part II);
- You are a minister, member of a religious order, or Christian Science practitioner and you received IRS approval (from **Form 4361**) not to be taxed on your earnings from these sources, but you owe self-employment tax on other earnings;
- You were an employee of a church or church-controlled organization that chose by law not to pay employer social security taxes;
- You had tip income that is subject to social security tax, but you did not report those tips to your employer; OR
- You were a government employee with wages subject ONLY to the 1.45% Medicare part of the social security tax.

Section A—Short Schedule SE
(Read above to see if you must use the long Schedule SE on the back (Section B).)

1 Net farm profit or (loss) from Schedule F (Form 1040), line 36, and farm partnerships, Schedule K-1 (Form 1065), line 14a	1	
2 Net profit or (loss) from Schedule C (Form 1040), line 30, and Schedule K-1 (Form 1065), line 14a (other than farming). See the instructions for other income to report	2	0
3 Add lines 1 and 2. Enter the total. If the total is less than $400, **do not** file this schedule; you **do not** owe self-employment tax	3	0
4 The largest amount of combined wages and self-employment earnings subject to social security or railroad retirement tax (tier 1) for 1989 is	4	$48,000 00
5 Total social security wages and tips (from Form(s) W-2) and railroad retirement compensation (tier 1)	5	
6 Subtract line 5 from line 4. Enter the result. If the result is zero or less, stop here; you **do not** owe self-employment tax	6	0
7 Enter the **smaller** of line 3 or line 6	7	0
8 Rate of tax	8	x .1302
9 **Self-employment tax.** If line 7 is $48,000, enter $6,249.60. Otherwise, multiply the amount on line 7 by the decimal amount on line 8 and enter the result. Also enter this amount on Form 1040, line 48	9	0

For Paperwork Reduction Act Notice, see Form 1040 Instructions.

Schedule SE (Form 1040) 1989

Mary Grace's Schedule SE

Form 1040 — U.S. Individual Income Tax Return (1989)

OMB No. 1545-0074

Stewars' Form 1040 (front)

Department of the Treasury—Internal Revenue Service
For the year Jan.–Dec. 31, 1989, or other tax year beginning _____ 1989, ending _____ 19__

Label
Your first name and initial: **JOHN** — Last name: **STEWART**
If a joint return, spouse's first name and initial: **MARY GRACE** — Last name: **STEWART**
Home address (number and street): **1962 WILBEN AVE.**
City, town or post office, state, and ZIP code: **ST. PAUL, MN 55106**

Your social security number: **373 64 9573**
Spouse's social security number: **215 43 6593**

For Privacy Act and Paperwork Reduction Act Notice, see Instructions.

Presidential Election Campaign
Do you want $1 to go to this fund? — Yes / **No**
If joint return, does your spouse want $1 to go to this fund? — Yes / **No**
Note: Checking "Yes" will not change your tax or reduce your refund.

Filing Status (Check only one box)
1 Single
2 ⊠ Married filing joint return (even if only one had income)
3 Married filing separate return.
4 Head of household (with qualifying person).
5 Qualifying widow(er) with dependent child (year spouse died ▶ 19__)

Exemptions
6a ⊠ Yourself
6b ⊠ Spouse
No. of boxes checked on 6a and 6b ▶ **2**
No. of your children on 6c who: lived with you __ ; didn't live with you __
No. of other dependents on 6c __
Add numbers entered on lines above ▶ **2**

Income (Please attach Copy B of your Forms W-2, W-2G, and W-2P here.)
Line	Description	Amount
7	Wages, salaries, tips, etc.	13,501 00
8a	Taxable interest income	
8b	Tax-exempt interest income	
9	Dividend income	
10	Taxable refunds of state and local income taxes	
11	Alimony received	
12	Business income or (loss)	
13	Capital gain or (loss)	
14	Capital gain distributions not reported on line 13	
15	Other gains or (losses)	
16a	Total IRA distributions / 16b Taxable amount	
17a	Total pensions and annuities / 17b Taxable amount	
18	Rents, royalties, partnerships, estates, trusts, etc.	
19	Farm income or (loss)	
20	Unemployment compensation (insurance)	
21a	Social security benefits / 21b Taxable amount	
22	Other income	2,000 00
23	Add the amounts shown in the far right column for lines 7 through 22. This is your total income ▶	13,501 00

Adjustments to Income
Line	Description	Amount
24	Your IRA deduction	2,000 00
25	Spouse's IRA deduction	
26	Self-employed health insurance deduction	240 00
27	Keogh retirement plan and self-employed SEP deduction	
28	Penalty on early withdrawal of savings	
29	Alimony paid	
30	Add lines 24 through 29. These are your total adjustments ▶	2,240 00

Adjusted Gross Income
| 31 | Subtract line 30 from line 23. This is your adjusted gross income. | 11,261 00 |

Stewars' Form 1040 (back)

Form 1040 (1989) — Page 2
STEWART 373 64 9573

Tax Computation
32	Amount from line 31 (adjusted gross income)	11,261 00
33a	Check if: Blind; Spouse was 65 or older; Blind	
33c	If you are married filing a separate return and your spouse itemizes deductions, check here	
34	Enter the larger of your standard deduction or your itemized deductions	5,200 00
35	Subtract line 34 from line 32	6,061 00
36	Multiply $2,000 by the total number of exemptions claimed on line 6e	4,000 00
37	Taxable income. Subtract line 36 from line 35	2,061 00
38	Enter tax	309 00
39	Additional taxes	
40	Add lines 38 and 39	309 00

Credits
41	Credit for child and dependent care expenses	
42	Credit for the elderly or the disabled	
43	Foreign tax credit	
44	General business credit	
45	Credit for prior year minimum tax	
46	Add lines 41 through 45	
47	Subtract line 46 from line 40	309 00

Other Taxes
Line	Description	Amount
48	Self-employment tax	1,258 00
49	Alternative minimum tax	
50	Recapture taxes	
51	Social security tax on tip income not reported to employer	
52	Tax on an IRA or a qualified retirement plan	
53	Add lines 47 through 52	2,166 00

Medicare Premium
| 54 | Supplemental Medicare premium | |
| 55 | Add lines 53 and 54. This is your total tax and any supplemental Medicare premium | 2,166 00 |

Payments
Line	Description	Amount
56	Federal income tax withheld	
57	1989 estimated tax payments and amount applied from 1988 return	2,000 00
58	Earned income credit	
59	Amount paid with Form 4868 (extension request)	
60	Excess social security tax and RRTA tax withheld	
61	Credit for Federal tax on fuels	
62	Regulated investment company credit	
63	Add lines 56 through 62. These are your total payments ▶	2,000 00

Refund or Amount You Owe
64	If line 63 is larger than line 55, enter amount OVERPAID	
65	Amount of line 64 to be REFUNDED TO YOU	
66	Amount of line 64 to be APPLIED TO YOUR 1990 ESTIMATED TAX ▶	
67	If line 55 is larger than line 63, enter AMOUNT YOU OWE	166 00
68	Penalty for underpayment of estimated tax	

Sign Here
Your signature: [JOHN'S SIGNATURE]
Spouse's signature (if joint return, BOTH must sign): [MARY GRACE'S SIGNATURE]

Paid Preparer's Use Only

Note that John and Mary Grace contributed almost $500 to charities in 1989. Because their itemized personal deductions do not exceed the standard deduction ($5,100), they do not itemize personal deductions and thus do not include Schedule A with their finished tax return.

John's IRA contribution is deductible because neither he nor Mary Grace are covered by a pension plan and because he has earned income. Mary Grace's contribution is nondeductible, because she is working but shows no profit. (Had she not been working, $250 of her $2,000 would have been deductible as a spousal contribution.)

Faced with a nondeductible IRA, Mary Grace can withdraw it prior to April 15, 1990 or the date they file their tax return, whichever is earlier. Or she can file Form 8606, "Nondeductible IRA Contributions," with the return and continue to let the money earn tax-deferred dividends.

Example 3. Single; Self-Employed and Regular Income

Jeffrey Pierce is an actor. To pay the bills, he's also an occasional waiter. In early January he receives a W-2 from his employer and completes his December records on his acting career. His income and expenses look like this:

W-2s from waiting tables = $6,249

Self-employment income from acting = 4,216

Expenses:
costumes	146
cast party	25
props	6
make-up	16
grooming	26

Personal deductions:
charitable contributions	20

*   *   *

Jeffrey's 1989 tax return consists of Form 1040, Schedule C, and Schedule SE.

● Comments

Jeffrey doesn't owns an automobile, so he has no auto expenses to report on Form 4562.

Because he owes the IRS more than $500, he may be liable for a penalty because he underpaid his estimated tax payments. He needs to order Form 2210 from his district IRS office to determine whether or not he's eligible for an exemption from the penalty. If not, he'll use that same Form 2210 to calculate the amount of the penalty, which he needs to pay with his completed return.

Example of Safe Harbor Election for Filmmaker

Cecily D. Mill is a filmmaker who generates most of her income by hiring out to work on other people's film projects. During 1989 she began her own short subject. At the close of 1988, her books showed the following totals:

Income = $26,488

Expenses:
rent on studio	$2,100
utilities	480

Jeffrey's Schedule C

SCHEDULE C (Form 1040)

Department of the Treasury
Internal Revenue Service (4)

Profit or Loss From Business
(Sole Proprietorship)

► Partnerships, Joint Ventures, Etc., Must File Form 1065.
► Attach to Form 1040 or Form 1041.   ► See Instructions for Schedule C (Form 1040).

OMB No. 1545-0074

1989

Attachment
Sequence No. 09

Name of proprietor **JEFFREY PIERCE**   Social security number (SSN) **456 : 23 : 4285**

A Principal business or profession, including product or service (see Instructions) **SERVICES : AMUSEMENT REC. ACTOR**   B Principal business code (from page 2) ► **9 8 1 1**

C Business name and address ► **JEFFREY PIERCE   STILLWATER MN**   D Employer ID number (Not SSN)
2 SHADY LANE

E Method(s) used to value closing inventory: (1) ☐ Cost (2) ☐ Lower of cost or market (3) ☐ Other (attach explanation)

F Accounting method: (1) ☒ Cash (2) ☐ Accrual (3) ☐ Other (specify) ►

G Was there any change in determining quantities, costs, or valuations between opening and closing inventory? (If "Yes," attach explanation.) Yes / No ☒ No

H Are you deducting expenses for business use of your home? (If "Yes," see Instructions for limitations.)

I Did you "materially participate" in the operation of this business during 1989? (If "No," see Instructions for limitations on losses.)

J If this schedule includes a loss, credit, deduction, income, or other tax benefit relating to a tax shelter required to be registered, check here . . ► ☐
If you checked this box, you MUST attach Form 8271.

Part I Income

1 Gross receipts or sales . . .	1	4,216 00
2 Returns and allowances . . .	2	—
3 Subtract line 2 from line 1. Enter the result here	3	4,216 —
4 Cost of goods sold and/or operations (from line 39 on page 2)	4	4,216 —
5 Subtract line 4 from line 3 and enter the **gross profit** here	5	0
6 Other income, including Federal and state gasoline or fuel tax credit or refund (see Instructions)	6	
7 Add lines 5 and 6. This is your **gross income** . . ►	7	4,216 00

Part II Expenses

8 Advertising . . .	8	
9 Bad debts from sales or services (see Instructions)	9	
10 Car and truck expenses . .	10	
11 Commissions . . .	11	
12 Depletion . . .	12	
13 Depreciation and section 179 deduction from Form 4562 (not included in Part III)	13	
14 Employee benefit programs (other than on line 20)	14	
15 Freight (not included in Part III)	15	
16 Insurance (other than health)	16	
17 Interest:		
a Mortgage (paid to banks, etc.)	17a	
b Other . . .	17b	
18 Legal and professional services	18	
19 Office expense . . .	19	
20 Pension and profit-sharing plans	20	
21 Rent or lease:		
a Machinery and equipment	21a	
b Other business property	21b	
22 Repairs . . .	22	
23 Supplies (not included in Part III)	23	168 00
24 Taxes . . .	24	
25 Travel, meals, and entertainment:		
a Travel . . .	25a	
b Meals and entertainment		25 00
c Enter 20% of line 25b subject to limitations (see Instructions)		5
d Subtract line 25c from line 25b	25d	20 00
26 Utilities (see Instructions)	26	
27 Wages (less jobs credit)	27	
28 Other expenses (list type and amount):		
	28	
29 Add amounts in columns for lines 8 through 28. These are your **total expenses** . . . ►	29	188 00
30 **Net profit or (loss).** Subtract line 29 from line 7. If a profit, enter here and on Form 1040, line 12, and on Schedule SE, line 2. If a loss, you MUST go on to line 31 (Fiduciaries, see Instructions).	30	4,028 00

31 If you have a loss, you MUST check the box that describes your investment in this activity (see Instructions).
If you checked 31a, enter the loss on Form 1040, line 12, and Schedule SE, line 2.
If you checked 31b, you MUST attach Form 6198.
31a ☐ All investment is at risk.
31b ☐ Some investment is not at risk.

For Paperwork Reduction Act Notice, see Form 1040 Instructions.   Schedule C (Form 1040) 1989

Jeffrey's Schedule SE

SCHEDULE SE (Form 1040)

Department of the Treasury
Internal Revenue Service (4)

Social Security Self-Employment Tax

► See Instructions for Schedule SE (Form 1040).
► Attach to Form 1040.

OMB No. 1545-0074

1989

Attachment
Sequence No. 18

Name of person with self-employment income (as shown on social security card) **JEFFREY PIERCE**   Social security number of person with self-employment income ► **456 : 23 : 4285**

Who Must File Schedule SE

You must file Schedule SE if:

● Your net earnings from self-employment were $400 or more (or you had wages of $100 or more from an electing church or church-controlled organization); AND

● Your wages (subject to social security or railroad retirement tax) were less than $48,000.

Exception. If your only self-employment income was from earnings as a minister, member of a religious order, or Christian Science practitioner, AND you filed Form 4361 and received IRS approval not to be taxed on those earnings, DO NOT file Schedule SE. Instead, write "Exempt–Form 4361" on Form 1040, line 48.

For more information about Schedule SE, see the Instructions.

Note: *Most people can use the short Schedule SE on this page. But, you may have to use the longer Schedule SE that is on the back.*

Who MUST Use the Long Schedule SE (Section B)

You must use Section B if ANY of the following applies:

● You choose the "optional method" to figure your self-employment tax (see Section B, Part II);

● You are a minister, member of a religious order, or Christian Science practitioner and you received IRS approval (from Form 4361) not to be taxed on your earnings from these sources, but you owe self-employment tax on other earnings;

● You were an employee of a church or church-controlled organization that chose by law not to pay employer social security taxes;

● You had tip income that is subject to social security tax, but you did not report those tips to your employer; OR

● You were a government employee with wages subject ONLY to the 1.45% Medicare part of the social security tax.

Section A—Short Schedule SE
(Read above to see if you must use the long Schedule SE on the back (Section B).)

1 Net farm profit or (loss) from Schedule F (Form 1040), line 36, and farm partnerships, Schedule K-1 (Form 1065), line 14a	1	
2 Net profit or (loss) from Schedule C (Form 1040C), line 30, and Schedule K-1 (Form 1065), line 14a (other than farming). See the Instructions for other income to report	2	4,028 00
3 Add lines 1 and 2. Enter the total. If the total is less than $400, **do not** file this schedule; you **do not** owe self-employment tax . . . ►	3	4,028 00
4 The largest amount of combined wages and self-employment earnings subject to social security or railroad retirement tax (tier 1) for 1989 is	4	$48,000 00
5 Total social security wages and tips (from Form(s) W 2) and railroad retirement compensation (tier 1)	5	6,249 00
6 Subtract line 5 from line 4. Enter the result. If the result is zero or less, stop here; you **do not** owe self-employment tax . . . ►	6	41,751 00
7 Enter the **smaller** of line 3 or line 6	7	4,028 00
8 Rate of tax . . .	8	× .1302
9 **Self-employment tax.** If line 7 is $48,000, enter $6,249.60. Otherwise, multiply the amount on line 7 by the decimal amount on line 8 and enter the result. Also enter this amount on Form 1040, line 48	9	524 00

For Paperwork Reduction Act Notice, see Form 1040 Instructions.   Schedule SE (Form 1040) 1989

Jeffrey's Form 1040 (front)

Form **1040** Department of the Treasury—Internal Revenue Service
U.S. Individual Income Tax Return **1989** (4)

For the year Jan.–Dec. 31, 1989, or other tax year beginning , 1989, ending , 19

OMB No. 1545-0074

Label (Use IRS label. Otherwise, please print or type.)

Your first name and initial: JEFFREY — Last name: PIERCE

Your social security number: 456 23 4285

Home address (number and street). (If a P.O. box, see page 7 of instructions.): 2 SHADY LANE — Apt. no.

City, town or post office, state and ZIP code. (If a foreign address, see page 7.): STILLWATER, MN 55082

For Privacy Act and Paperwork Reduction Act Notice, see Instructions.

Presidential Election Campaign ▶ Do you want $1 to go to this fund? — Yes ☒ No — Note: Checking "Yes" will not change your tax or reduce your refund.
If joint return, does your spouse want $1 to go to this fund? — Yes / No

Filing Status (Check only one box.)
1 ☒ Single
2 ☐ Married filing joint return (even if only one had income)
3 ☐ Married filing separate return. Enter spouse's social security no. above and full name here.
4 ☐ Head of household (with qualifying person). (See page 7 of instructions.) If the qualifying person is your child but not your dependent, enter child's name here.
5 ☐ Qualifying widow(er) with dependent child (year spouse died ▶ 19). (See page 7 of instructions.)

Exemptions (See Instructions on page 8.)
6a ☒ Yourself — If someone (such as your parent) can claim you as a dependent on his or her tax return, do not check box 6a. But be sure to check the box on line 33b on page 2.
b ☐ Spouse

No. of boxes checked on 6a and 6b: 1
No. of your children on 6c who: lived with you / didn't live with you due to divorce or separation (see page 9)
No. of other dependents on 6c
Add numbers entered on lines above: 1

c Dependents:
(1) Name (first, initial, and last name)
(2) Check if under age 2
(3) If age 2 or older, dependent's social security number
(4) Relationship
(5) No. of months lived in your home in 1989

d If your child didn't live with you but is claimed as your dependent under a pre-1985 agreement, check here ▶ ☐
e Total number of exemptions claimed — 7

Income (Please attach Copy B of your Forms W-2, W-2G, and W-2P here. If you do not have a W-2, see page 6 of Instructions.)
7 Wages, salaries, tips, etc. (attach Form(s) W-2) — 6,249 00
8a Taxable interest income (also attach Schedule B if over $400) — 8a
b Tax-exempt interest income (see page 10). DON'T include on line 8a — 8b
9 Dividend income (also attach Schedule B if over $400) — 9
10 Taxable refunds of state and local income taxes, if any, from worksheet on page 11 of Instructions — 10
11 Alimony received — 11
12 Business income or (loss) (attach Schedule C) — 12 — 4,028 00
13 Capital gain or (loss) (attach Schedule D) — 13 — 0
14 Capital gain distributions not reported on line 13 (see page 11) — 14
15 Other gains or (losses) (attach Form 4797) — 15
16a Total IRA distributions — 16a — 16b Taxable amount (see page 11) — 16b
17a Total pensions and annuities — 17a — 17b Taxable amount (see page 12) — 17b
18 Rents, royalties, partnerships, estates, trusts, etc. (attach Schedule E) — 18
19 Farm income or (loss) (attach Schedule F) — 19
20 Unemployment compensation (insurance) (see page 13) — 20
21a Social security benefits. — 21a — 21b Taxable amount (see page 13) — 21b
22 Other income (list type and amount—see page 13) — 22
23 Add the amounts shown in the far right column for lines 7 through 22. This is your total income ▶ 23 — 0

Adjustments to Income (See Instructions on page 14.)
24 Your IRA deduction, from applicable worksheet on page 14 or 15 — 24
25 Spouse's IRA deduction, from applicable worksheet on page 14 or 15 — 25
26 Self-employed health insurance deduction, from worksheet on page 15 — 26
27 Keogh retirement plan and self-employed SEP deduction — 27
28 Penalty on early withdrawal of savings — 28
29 Alimony paid. a Recipient's last name and b social security number. — 29
30 Add lines 24 through 29. These are your total adjustments ▶ 30 — 0

Adjusted Gross Income
31 Subtract line 30 from line 23. This is your adjusted gross income. If this line is less than $19,340 and a child lived with you, see "Earned Income Credit" (line 58) on page 20 of the instructions. If you want IRS to figure your tax, see page 16 of the instructions ▶ 31 — 10,277 00

Jeffrey's Form 1040 (back)

PIERCE 456 23 4285 — Form 1040 (1989) Page 2

Tax Computation
32 Amount from line 31 (adjusted gross income) — 32 — 10,277 00
33a Check if: ☐ You were 65 or older ☐ Blind; ☐ Spouse was 65 or older ☐ Blind. Add the number of boxes checked and enter the total here. ▶ 33a
b If someone (such as your parent) can claim you as a dependent, check here. ▶ 33b ☐
c If you are married filing a separate return and your spouse itemizes deductions, or you are a dual-status alien, see page 16 and check here. ▶ 33c ☐
34 Enter the larger of:
• Your standard deduction (from page 17 of the Instructions), OR
• Your itemized deductions (from Schedule A, line 26).
If you itemize, attach Schedule A and check here. ▶ ☐
Subtract line 34 from line 32. Enter the result here — 34 — 3,100 00
35 Subtract line 34 from line 32. Enter the result here — 35 — 7,177 00
36 Multiply $2,000 by the total number of exemptions claimed on line 6e — 36 — 2,000 00
37 Taxable income. Subtract line 36 from line 35. Enter the result (if less than zero, enter zero) — 37 — 5,177 00
Caution: If under age 14 and you have more than $1,000 of investment income, check here ▶ ☐ and see page 17 to see if you have to use Form 8615 to figure your tax.
38 Enter tax. Check if from: a ☒ Tax Table, b ☐ Tax Rate Schedules, or c ☐ Form 8615 — 38 — 797 00
39 Additional taxes. Check if from: a ☐ Form 4970 b ☐ Form 4972 — 39 — 0
40 Add lines 38 and 39. Enter the total ▶ 40 — 797 00

Credits (See Instructions on page 18.)
41 Credit for child and dependent care expenses (attach Form 2441) — 41
42 Credit for the elderly or the disabled (attach Schedule R) — 42
43 Foreign tax credit (attach Form 1116) — 43
44 General business credit. Check if from: a ☐ Form 3800 or b ☐ Form (specify) — 44
45 Credit for prior year minimum tax (attach Form 8801) — 45
46 Add lines 41 through 45. Enter the total — 46 — 0
47 Subtract line 46 from line 40. Enter the result (if less than zero, enter zero) — 47 — 797 00

Other Taxes (Including Advance EIC Payments)
48 Self-employment tax (attach Schedule SE) — 48 — 524 00
49 Alternative minimum tax (attach Form 6251) — 49
50 Recapture taxes (see page 18). Check if from: a ☐ Form 4255 b ☐ Form 8611 — 50
51 Social security tax on tip income not reported to employer (attach Form 4137) — 51
52 Tax on an IRA or a qualified retirement plan (attach Form 5329) — 52
53 Add lines 47 through 52. Enter the total ▶ 53 — 1,301 00

Medicare Premium
54 Supplemental Medicare premium (attach Form 8808) — 54
55 Add lines 53 and 54. This is your total tax and any supplemental Medicare premium ▶ 55 — 1,301 00

Payments (Attach Forms W-2, W-2G, and W-2P to front.)
56 Federal income tax withheld (if any is from Form(s) 1099, check ▶ ☐) — 56 — 937 00
57 1989 estimated tax payments and amount applied from 1988 return — 57 — 148 00
58 Earned income credit (see page 20) — 58
59 Amount paid with Form 4868 (extension request) — 59
60 Excess social security tax and RRTA tax withheld (see page 20) — 60
61 Credit for Federal tax on fuels (attach Form 4136) — 61
62 Regulated investment company credit (attach Form 2439) — 62
63 Add lines 56 through 62. These are your total payments ▶ 63 — 1,085 00

Refund or Amount You Owe
64 If line 63 is larger than line 55, enter amount OVERPAID — 64
65 Amount of line 64 to be REFUNDED TO YOU — 65
66 Amount of line 64 to be APPLIED TO YOUR 1990 ESTIMATED TAX ▶ 66
67 If line 55 is larger than line 63, enter AMOUNT YOU OWE. Attach check or money order for full amount payable to "Internal Revenue Service." Write your social security number, daytime phone number, and "1989 Form 1040" on it — 67 — 216 00
68 Penalty for underpayment of estimated tax (see page 21) — 68

Sign Here (Keep a copy of this return for your records.)
Under penalties of perjury, I declare that I have examined this return and accompanying schedules and statements, and to the best of my knowledge and belief, they are true, correct, and complete. Declaration of preparer (other than taxpayer) is based on all information of which preparer has any knowledge.
Your signature: JEFFREY'S SIGNATURE — Date — Your occupation
Spouse's signature (if joint return, BOTH must sign) — Date — Spouse's occupation

Paid Preparer's Use Only
Preparer's signature — Date — Check if self-employed ☐ — Preparer's social security no
Firm's name (or yours if self-employed) and address — E.I. No — ZIP code

studio telephone	416
other business long distance	35
dues and publications	44
office expense	211
films, video rentals	197
motion picture camera (6/2)	8,990
repairs	88
film supplies	940
payments to independent contractors	550

Personal income:
 interest on savings account = $87

Other personal items:
 charitable contributions = $110
 payments to federal estimated tax = $3,600

● Comments

In past years, Cecily would have been able to fully deduct her filmmaking expenses. Since she was paid on a project basis, she could argue successfully that she was following the rules on capitalizing expenses by deducting them only when the project was paid for. As a "hired gun," her income always exceeded her expenses for a particular job. This year, however, she was faced with two options: Keep separate books on each project in order to allocate expenses among them as she incurred them, or make the safe harbor election and deduct 50 percent of her 1989 expenses in 1989 and carry over the remainder to 1990 and to 1991.

She didn't keep separate books and thus must make the safe harbor election. This results in an artificially high tax liability for 1989. Fortunately, she paid via estimated taxes an amount slightly greater than her 1988 tax liability. While she must cough up a large sum of money by April 15, 1990, at least a penalty for underpaying taxes won't be added, unless she fails to complete Form 2210 and attach it to her finished return.

Note that the IRS has not yet issued regulations as to how it wants to see the safe harbor election identified. The method suggested here is clear and describes the key points in making the election, which should suffice until explicit directions are issued.

Schedule C Form

SCHEDULE C (Form 1040)

Department of the Treasury — Internal Revenue Service (4)

3-YEAR SAFE HARBOR "ELECTION" PER IR NOTICE 88-62

OMB No. 1545-0074

1989

Attachment Sequence No. 09

Profit or Loss From Business
(Sole Proprietorship)
Partnerships, Joint Ventures, Etc., Must File Form 1065.
▶ Attach to Form 1040 or Form 1041. ▶ See Instructions for Schedule C (Form 1040).

Name of proprietor — **CECILY D. MILL**

Social security number (SSN) **222 33 4444**

A Principal business or profession, including product or service (see instructions) — **SERVICES: AMUSE/REC: CECILY D. MILL, FILMMAKER**

B Principal business code (from page 2) ▶ **9 6 5 4**

C Business name and address ▶ **HOLLYWOOD BLDG #204 · ST. PAUL, MN 5510;**

D Employer ID number (Not SSN)

E Method(s) used to value closing inventory: (1) ☐ Cost (2) ☐ Lower of cost or market (3) ☐ Other (attach explanation)

F Accounting method: (1) ☐ Cost (2) ☒ Cash (3) ☐ Accrual (4) ☒ Other (specify) ▶ **Does not apply (if checked, skip line G)**

G Was there any change in determining quantities, costs, or valuations between opening and closing inventory? (If "Yes," see Instructions for limitations.) — Yes ☐ No ☒

H Are you deducting expenses for business use of your home? (If "Yes," see Instructions for limitations.)

I Did you "materially participate" in the operation of this business during 1989? (If "No," see Instructions for limitations on losses.)

J If this schedule includes a loss, credit, deduction, income, or other tax benefit relating to a tax shelter required to be registered, check here. ▶ ☐

If you checked this box, you MUST attach Form 8271.

Part I Income

1 Gross receipts or sales	1	26,488 00
2 Returns and allowances	2	0
3 Subtract line 2 from line 1. Enter the result here	3	26,488 00
4 Cost of goods sold and/or operations (from line 39 on page 2)	4	0
5 Subtract line 4 from line 3 and enter the gross profit here	5	26,488 00
6 Other income, including Federal and state gasoline or fuel tax credit or refund (see Instructions)	6	0
7 Add lines 5 and 6. This is your **gross income** ▶	7	26,488 00

Part II Expenses

8 Advertising	8		
9 Bad debts from sales or services (see Instructions)	9		
10 Car and truck expenses	10	550	00
11 Commissions	11		
12 Depletion	12		
13 Depreciation and section 179 deduction from Form 4562 (not included in Part III)	13	899	00
14 Employee benefit programs (other than on line 20)	14		
15 Freight (not included in Part III)	15		
16 Insurance (other than health)	16		
17 Interest:			
a Mortgage (paid to banks, etc.)	17a		
b Other	17b		
18 Legal and professional services	18	211	00
19 Office expense	19		
20 Pension and profit-sharing plans	20		
21 Rent or lease:			
a Machinery and equipment	21a	199	00
b Other business property	21b	2,100	00
22 Repairs	22	88	00
23 Supplies (not included in Part III)	23	940	00
24 Taxes	24		
25 Travel, meals, and entertainment:			
a Travel	25a		
b Meals and entertainment			
c Enter 20% of line 25b subject to limitations (see Instructions)			
d Subtract line 25c from line 25b	25d		
26 Utilities (see Instructions)	26	931	00
27 Wages (less jobs credit)	27		
28 Other expenses (list type and amount): **DUES + PUB.S = 44** **Sec 263A ADJUSTMENT = (2980)** *	28	(2,936 00)	
29 Add amounts in columns for lines 8 through 28. These are your **total expenses** ▶	29	2980	00
30 **Net profit or (loss).** Subtract line 29 from line 7. If a profit, enter here and on Form 1040, line 12, and on Schedule SE, line 2. If a loss, you MUST go to line 31. (Fiduciaries, see Instructions.)	30	23,508	00

31 If you have a loss, you MUST check the box that describes your investment in this activity (see Instructions).
If you checked 31a, enter the loss on Form 1040, line 12, and Schedule SE, line 2.
If you checked 31b, you MUST attach Form 6198.

31a ☐ All investment is at risk.
31b ☐ Some investment is not at risk.

※ CARRYOVER TO 1990 = 1490
CARRYOVER TO 1991 = 1490

For Paperwork Reduction Act Notice, see Form 1040 Instructions. — Schedule C (Form 1040) 1989

Cecily's Schedule C

Form 4562 (back)

Form 4562 (1989) — Page 2

Part II Amortization

(a) Description of property	(b) Date amortization begins	(c) Amortizable amount	(d) Code section	(e) Amortization period or percentage	(f) Amortization for this year
21 Amortization for property placed in service only during tax year beginning in 1989					
22 Amortization for property placed in service before 1989					22
23 Total. Enter here and on "Other Deductions" or "Other Expenses" line of your return					23

Part III Listed Property.—Automobiles, Certain Other Vehicles, Computers, and Property Used for Entertainment, Recreation, or Amusement

If you are using the standard mileage rate or deducting vehicle lease expense, complete columns (a) through (c) of Section A, all of Section B, and Section C if applicable.

Section A.—Depreciation (Caution: See instructions for limitations for automobiles.)

24a Do you have evidence to support the business use claimed? ☒ Yes ☐ No 24b If "Yes," is the evidence written? ☒ Yes ☐ No

(a) Type of property (list vehicles first)	(b) Date placed in service	(c) Business use percentage (%)	(d) Cost or other basis	(e) Basis for depreciation — business use only	(f) Recovery period	(g) Method	(h) Depreciation deduction	(i) Elected section 179 cost
25 Property used more than 50% in a trade or business:								
S-YR REC (TV CAMERA)	**6/2/89**	**100%**	**8,990**	**8,990**	**5**	**MACRS/HY**	**899**	
26 Property used 50% or less in a trade or business:								
						S L		
						S L		
						S L		
27 Total (Enter here and on line 15, page 1)						27	899	
28 Total (Enter here and on line 7, page 1)								28 0

Section B.—Information Regarding Use of Vehicles—If you deduct expenses for vehicles.

• Always complete this section for vehicles used by a sole proprietor, partner, or other "more than 5% owner," or related person.
• If you provided vehicles to your employees, first answer the questions in Section C to see if you meet an exception to completing this section for those vehicles.

	(a) Vehicle 1		(b) Vehicle 2		(c) Vehicle 3		(d) Vehicle 4		(e) Vehicle 5		(f) Vehicle 6	
29 Total business miles driven during the year (DO NOT include commuting miles)												
30 Total commuting miles driven during the year												
31 Total other personal (noncommuting) miles driven												
32 Total miles driven during the year (Add lines 29 through 31)												
	Yes	No	Yes	No	Yes	No	Yes	No	Yes	No	Yes	No
33 Was the vehicle available for personal use during off-duty hours?												
34 Was the vehicle used primarily by a more than 5% owner or related person?												
35 Is another vehicle available for personal use?												

Section C.—Questions for Employers Who Provide Vehicles for Use by Their Employees

(Answer these questions to determine if you meet an exception to completing Section B Note: Section B must always be completed for vehicles used by sole proprietors, partners, or other more than 5% owners or related persons.)

	Yes	No
36 Do you maintain a written policy statement that prohibits all personal use of vehicles, including commuting by your employees?		
37 Do you maintain a written policy statement that prohibits personal use of vehicles, except commuting, by your employees? (See instructions for vehicles used by corporate officers, directors, or 1% or more owners.)		
38 Do you treat all use of vehicles by employees as personal use?		
39 Do you provide more than five vehicles to your employees and retain the information received from your employees concerning the use of the vehicles?		
40 Do you meet the requirements concerning qualified automobile demonstration use (see instructions)?		

Note: If your answer to 36, 37, 38, 39, or 40 is "Yes," you need not complete Section B for the covered vehicles.

Cecily's Form 4562 (back)

Schedule SE (Form 1040) — Social Security Self-Employment Tax

SCHEDULE SE
(Form 1040)
Department of the Treasury
Internal Revenue Service (4)
OMB No. 1545-0074
1989
Attachment Sequence No. 18

Social Security Self-Employment Tax

▶ See Instructions for Schedule SE (Form 1040).
▶ Attach to Form 1040.

Name of person with self-employment income (as shown on social security card)	Social security number of person with self-employment income ▶
CECILY D. MILL	222 : 33 : 4444

Who Must File Schedule SE

You must file Schedule SE if:

- Your net earnings from self-employment were $400 or more (or you had wages of $100 or more from an electing church or church-controlled organization); AND
- Your wages (subject to social security or railroad retirement tax) were less than $48,000.

Exception. If your only self-employment income was from earnings as a minister, member of a religious order, or Christian Science practitioner, AND you filed Form 4361 and received IRS approval not to be taxed on those earnings, DO NOT file Schedule SE. Instead, write "Exempt—Form 4361" on Form 1040, line 48.

For more information about Schedule SE, see the Instructions.

Note: *Most people can use the short Schedule SE on this page. But, you may have to use the longer Schedule SE that is on the back.*

Who MUST Use the Long Schedule SE (Section B)

You must use Section B if ANY of the following applies:

- You choose the "optional method" to figure your self-employment tax (see Section B, Part II);
- You are a minister, member of a religious order, or Christian Science practitioner and you received IRS approval (from Form 4361) not to be taxed on your earnings from these sources, but you owe self-employment tax on other earnings;
- You were an employee of a church or church-controlled organization that chose by law not to pay employer social security taxes;
- You had tip income that is subject to social security tax, but you did not report those tips to your employer; OR
- You were a government employee with wages subject ONLY to the 1.45% Medicare part of the social security tax.

Section A—Short Schedule SE
(Read above to see if you must use the long Schedule SE on the back (Section B).)

1	Net farm profit or (loss) from Schedule F (Form 1040), line 36, and farm partnerships, Schedule K-1 (Form 1065), line 14a	1	
2	Net profit or (loss) from Schedule C (Form 1040), line 30, and Schedule K-1 (Form 1065), line 14a (other than farming) See the Instructions for other income to report	2	23,508 00
3	Add lines 1 and 2. Enter the total. If the total is less than $400, do not file this schedule; you do not owe self-employment tax	3	23,508 00
4	The largest amount of combined wages and self-employment earnings subject to social security or railroad retirement tax (tier 1) for 1989 is	4	$48,000 00
5	Total social security wages and tips (from Form(s) W-2) and railroad retirement compensation (tier 1)	5	0
6	Subtract line 5 from line 4. Enter the result. If the result is zero or less, stop here; you do not owe self-employment tax	6	48,000 00
7	Enter the smaller of line 3 or line 6	7	23,508 00
8	Rate of tax	8	x .1302
9	Self-employment tax. If line 7 is $48,000, enter $6,249.60. Otherwise, multiply the amount on line 7 by the decimal amount on line 8 and enter the result. Also enter this amount on Form 1040, line 48	9	3,061 00

For Paperwork Reduction Act Notice, see Form 1040 Instructions.   Schedule SE (Form 1040) 1989

Cecily's Schedule SE

Form 4562 — Depreciation and Amortization

Form 4562
Department of the Treasury
Internal Revenue Service   (4)
OMB No. 1545-0172
1989
Attachment Sequence No. 67

Depreciation and Amortization

▶ See separate instructions.
▶ Attach this form to your return.

Name(s) as shown on return	Identifying number
CECILY D. MILL	222 33 4444

Business or activity to which this form relates   SCHEDULE C

Part I Depreciation (*Use Part III for automobiles, certain other vehicles, computers, and property used for entertainment, recreation, or amusement.*)

Section A.—Election To Expense Depreciable Assets (Section 179)

1 Maximum dollar limitation	1	$10,000
2 Total cost of section 179 property placed in service during the tax year (see instructions)	2	
3 Threshold cost of section 179 property before reduction in limitation	3	$200,000
4 Reduction in limitation (Subtract line 3 from line 2, but do not enter less than -0-.)	4	
5 Dollar limitation for tax year (Subtract line 4 from line 1, but do not enter less than -0-.)	5	

6	(a) Description of property	(b) Date placed in service	(c) Cost	(d) Elected cost

7 Listed property—Enter amount from line 28	7	
8 Tentative deduction (Enter the lesser of : (a) line 6 plus line 7, or (b) line 5.)	8	
9 Taxable income limitation (Enter the lesser of : (a) Taxable income, or (b) line 5) (see instructions).	9	
10 Carryover of disallowed deduction from 1988 (see instructions)	10	
11 Section 179 expense deduction (Enter the lesser of : (a) line 8 plus line 10, or (b) line 9) . ▶	11	
12 Carryover of disallowed deduction to 1990 (Add lines 8 and 10, less line 11.) . ▶	12	

Section B.—MACRS Depreciation

(a) Classification of property	(b) Date placed in service	(c) Basis for depreciation (Business use only—see instructions)	(d) Recovery period	(e) Convention	(f) Method	(g) Depreciation deduction
13 General Depreciation System (GDS) (see instructions) *For assets placed in service ONLY during tax year beginning in 1989*						
a 3-year property						
b 5-year property						
c 7-year property						
d 10-year property						
e 15-year property						
f 20-year property						
g Residential rental property			27.5 yrs.	MM	S/L	
			27.5 yrs.	MM	S/L	
h Nonresidential real property			31.5 yrs.	MM	S/L	
			31.5 yrs.	MM	S/L	
14 Alternative Depreciation System (ADS) (see instructions) *For assets placed in service ONLY during tax year beginning in 1989*						
a Class life					S/L	
b 12-year			12 yrs.		S/L	
c 40-year			40 yrs.	MM	S/L	

Section C.—ACRS and/or Other Depreciation

15 Listed property—Enter amount from line 27	15	899.
16 GDS and ADS deductions for assets placed in service before 1989 (see instructions)	16	
17 Property subject to section 168(f)(1) election (see instructions)	17	
18 ACRS and/or other depreciation (see instructions)	18	

Section D.—Summary

19 Total (Add deductions on line 11 and lines 13 through 18.) Enter here and on the appropriate line of your return (Partnerships and S corporations—see instructions.)	19	899.
20 For assets shown above and placed in service during the current year, enter the portion of the basis attributable to section 263A costs (see instructions.)	20	8990.

For Paperwork Reduction Act Notice, see page 1 of the separate instructions.   Form 4562 (1989)

Cecily's Form 4562 (front)

Cecily's Form 1040 (front)

For the year Jan.–Dec. 31, 1989, or other tax year beginning _____, 1989, ending _____

Label
Use IRS label. Otherwise, please print or type.

Your first name and initial: CECILY D.   Last name: MILL
If a joint return, spouse's first name and initial _____ Last name _____
Home address (number and street). (If a P.O. box, see page 7 of Instructions.) Apt. no. 99 PAISLEY LANE
City, town or post office, state and ZIP code. (If a foreign address, see page 7.) NIRVANA, MN 56111

Your social security number: 222 : 33 : 4444
Spouse's social security number: _____

For Privacy Act and Paperwork Reduction Act Notice, see Instructions.

Presidential Election Campaign ▶
Do you want $1 to go to this fund? Yes ☐ No ☐
Note: Checking "Yes" will not change your tax or reduce your refund.
If joint return, does your spouse want $1 to go to this fund? Yes ☐ No ☐

Filing Status
Check only one box.
1. ☒ Single
2. ☐ Married filing joint return (even if only one had income)
3. ☐ Married filing separate return. Enter spouse's social security no. above and full name here.
4. ☐ Head of household (with qualifying person). (See page 7 of Instructions.) If the qualifying person is your child but not your dependent, enter child's name here.
5. ☐ Qualifying widow(er) with dependent child (year spouse died ▶ 19). (See page 7 of Instructions.)

Exemptions
(See Instructions on page 8.)
If more than 6 dependents, see Instructions on page 8.

6a ☒ Yourself If someone (such as your parent) can claim you as a dependent on his or her tax return, do not check box 6a. But be sure to check the box on line 33b on page 2.
b ☐ Spouse
c Dependents:
(1) Name (first, initial, and last name) | (2) Check if under age 2 | (3) If age 2 or older, dependent's social security number | (4) Relationship | (5) No. of months lived in your home in 1989

d If your child didn't live with you but is claimed as your dependent under a pre-1985 agreement, check here ☐
e Total number of exemptions claimed

No. of boxes checked on 6a and 6b: 1
No. of your children on 6c who:
• lived with you
• didn't live with you due to divorce or separation (see page 9)
No. of other dependents on 6c
Add numbers entered on lines above ▶

Income
Please attach Copy B of your Forms W-2, W-2G, and W-2P here.
If you do not have a W-2, see page 6 of Instructions.
Please attach check or money order here.

7 Wages, salaries, tips, etc. (attach Form(s) W-2) | 7 |
8a Taxable interest income (also attach Schedule B if over $400) | 8a | 87 00
b Tax-exempt interest income (see page 10). DON'T include on line 8a | 8b |
9 Dividend income (also attach Schedule B if over $400) | 9 | 0
10 Taxable refunds of state and local income taxes, if any, from worksheet on page 11 of Instructions | 10 |
11 Alimony received | 11 |
12 Business income or (loss) (attach Schedule C) | 12 | 23,508 00
13 Capital gain or (loss) (attach Schedule D) | 13 | 0
14 Capital gain distributions not reported on line 13 (see page 11) | 14 |
15 Other gains or (losses) (attach Form 4797) | 15 |
16a Total IRA distributions 16a _____ | 16b Taxable amount (see page 11) | 16b |
17a Total pensions and annuities 17a _____ | 17b Taxable amount (see page 12) | 17b |
18 Rents, royalties, partnerships, estates, trusts, etc. (attach Schedule E) | 18 |
19 Farm income or (loss) (attach Schedule F) | 19 |
20 Unemployment compensation (insurance) (see page 13) | 20 |
21a Social security benefits. 21a _____ | 21b Taxable amount (see page 13) | 21b |
22 Other income (list type and amount—see page 13) | 22 | 0
23 Add the amounts shown in the far right column for lines 7 through 22. This is your total income ▶ | 23 | 23,595 00

Adjustments to Income
(See Instructions on page 14.)
24 Your IRA deduction, from applicable worksheet on page 14 or 15 | 24 |
25 Spouse's IRA deduction, from applicable worksheet on page 14 or 15 | 25 |
26 Self-employed health insurance deduction, from worksheet on page 15 | 26 |
27 Keogh retirement plan and self-employed SEP deduction | 27 |
28 Penalty on early withdrawal of savings | 28 |
29 Alimony paid. a Recipient's last name _____ and b social security number _____ | 29 |
30 Add lines 24 through 29. These are your total adjustments | 30 | 0

Adjusted Gross Income
31 Subtract line 30 from line 23. This is your adjusted gross income. If this line is less than $19,340 and a child lived with you, see "Earned Income Credit" (line 58) on page 20 of the Instructions. If you want IRS to figure your tax, see page 16 of the Instructions. ▶ | 31 | 23,595 00

Cecily's Form 1040 (back)

MILL
222 33 4444 Form 1040 (1989) Page 2

32 Amount from line 31 (adjusted gross income) | 32 | 23,595 00
33a Check if: ☐ You were 65 or older ☐ Blind; ☐ Spouse was 65 or older ☐ Blind.
Add the number of boxes checked and enter the total here ▶ 33a _____
b If someone (such as your parent) can claim you as a dependent, check here ▶ 33b ☐
c If you are married filing a separate return and your spouse itemizes deductions, or you are a dual-status alien, see page 16 and check here ▶ 33c ☐

34 Enter the {
Your standard deduction (from page 17 of the Instructions), OR
Your itemized deductions (from Schedule A, line 26)
} larger of:
If you itemize, attach Schedule A and check here ▶ ☐ | 34 | 3,100 00

35 Subtract line 34 from line 32. Enter the result here | 35 | 20,495 00
36 Multiply $2,000 by the total number of exemptions claimed on line 6e | 36 | 2,000 00
37 Taxable income. Subtract line 36 from line 35. Enter the result (if less than zero, enter zero) | 37 | 18,495 00

Tax Computation
(See page 17 of the Instructions.)

38 Enter tax. Check if from a ☐ Tax Table, b ☐ Tax Rate Schedules, or c ☐ Form 8615 | 38 | 2,774 00
39 Additional taxes (see page 18). Check if from a ☐ Form 4970 b ☐ Form 4972 | 39 | 0
40 Add lines 38 and 39. Enter the total ▶ | 40 | 2,774 00

Credits
(See Instructions on page 18.)
41 Credit for child and dependent care expenses (attach Form 2441) | 41 | 0
42 Credit for the elderly or the disabled (attach Schedule R) | 42 |
43 Foreign tax credit (attach Form 1116) | 43 |
44 General business credit. Check if from a ☐ Form 3800 or b ☐ Form (specify) | 44 |
45 Credit for prior year minimum tax (attach Form 8801) | 45 |
46 Add lines 41 through 45 | 46 | 0
47 Subtract line 46 from line 40. Enter the result (if less than zero, enter zero) ▶ | 47 | 2,774 00

Other Taxes
(Including Advance EIC Payments)
48 Self-employment tax (attach Schedule SE) | 48 | 3,061 00
49 Alternative minimum tax (attach Form 6251) | 49 |
50 Recapture taxes (see page 18). Check if from a ☐ Form 4255 b ☐ Form 8611 | 50 |
51 Social security tax on tip income not reported to employer (attach Form 4137) | 51 |
52 Tax on an IRA or a qualified retirement plan (attach Form 5329) | 52 |
53 Add lines 47 through 52. Enter the total ▶ | 53 | 5,835 00

Payments
Attach Forms W-2, W-2G, and W-2P to front.
54 Supplemental Medicare premium (attach Form 8808) | 54 |
55 Add lines 53 and 54. This is your total tax and any supplemental Medicare premium ▶ | 55 | 5,835 00
56 Federal income tax withheld (if any is from Form(s) 1099, check ▶ ☐) | 56 | 0
57 1989 estimated tax payments and amount applied from 1988 return | 57 | 3,600 00
58 Earned income credit (see page 20) | 58 | 0
59 Amount paid with Form 4868 (extension request) | 59 |
60 Excess social security tax and RRTA tax withheld (see page 20) | 60 |
61 Credit for Federal tax on fuels (attach Form 4136) | 61 |
62 Regulated investment company credit (attach Form 2439) | 62 |
63 Add lines 56 through 62. These are your total payments ▶ | 63 | 3,600 00

Refund or Amount You Owe
64 If line 63 is larger than line 55, enter amount OVERPAID | 64 |
65 Amount of line 64 to be REFUNDED TO YOU | 65 |
66 Amount of line 64 to be APPLIED TO YOUR 1990 ESTIMATED TAX ▶ 66 _____
67 If line 55 is larger than line 63, enter AMOUNT YOU OWE. Attach check or money order for full amount payable to Internal Revenue Service. Write your social security number, daytime phone number and "1989 Form 1040" on it. | 67 | 2,235 00
68 Penalty for underpayment of estimated tax (see page 21) 68 _____ | | -0-

Sign Here
Keep a copy of this return for your records.
Under penalties of perjury, I declare that I have examined this return and accompanying schedules and statements, and to the best of my knowledge and belief, they are true, correct, and complete. Declaration of preparer (other than taxpayer) is based on all information of which preparer has any knowledge.
Your signature: Cecily D. Mill Date: 4/16/90 Your occupation: _____
Spouse's signature (if joint return, BOTH must sign) Date Spouse's occupation

Paid Preparer's Use Only
Preparer's signature _____ Date _____ Check if self-employed ☐ Preparer's social security no.
Firm's name (or yours if self-employed) and address _____ E.I. No. _____ ZIP code _____

PART III
Appendices

Glossary of Terms

Accrual System
A system of accounting requiring income to be recognized (entered in the books) when a bill or invoice is sent and allowing expenses to be recognized when a bill for them is received. Bad debts are possible only with the accrual system of accounting.

Adjusted Gross Income
The sum of your income for the year after subtracting allowable adjustments (retirement-plan contributions, alimony payments, 25 percent of health insurance costs, employee business expenses, a penalty assessed by a bank on early withdrawal of savings); line 26 of 1989 Form 1040.

Amortization
A method of writing off costs over a period of years (generally no fewer than five). Differs from depreciation, which decreases the value of an asset for each year it's in service. Examples of expenses commonly amortized are start-up expenses and reorganization expenses.

Audit
Also known as "examination of return." A review by the Internal Revenue Service of your tax return for a particular year. Generally you are notified of an intention to audit within one year of filing a return. The audit may be done without further information from you, or the IRS may require that you provide documentation by mail (mail audit) or in person (office audit, if held in a local IRS office, or field audit, if held in your home or place of business).

Bad Debt
For use only with the accrual system of accounting. A bad debt occurs when a payment owed you and already recognized as income proves to be uncollectible.

Example: Bill Sweeney billed Karin Nelson $60 for pottery sent to her the previous week. The invoice date is the date on which $60 is entered as income into Bill's books. Two months and four telephone calls later, Bill learns that Karin's gone out of business and will not be paying him. Bill now has a bad debt.

He records this in his income books as a bad debt, probably in the miscellaneous category. On his tax return, all bad debts are listed on line 9 of Schedule C, in the expense section.

Notice that a bad debt only cancels out income previously reported. There is no "loss," even though Bill has suffered the actual loss of some materials and his time and craftsmanship. For tax purposes, the materials have already been written off as expenses, while Bill's time is not money and never shows up in the books. Moral of the story: Collect on those bills! Better yet, get your customers to pay on receipt of merchandise.

Barter

Trading your goods or services for another person's goods or services. To the IRS, the fair market value of the goods you receive through barter is unreported income. Since you're already writing off as deductions materials and supplies used in the goods you barter, barter becomes a fraudulent attempt to under-report income.

Recommendation: Do not barter. It's not allowed by the IRS and it's unprofessional. If you want something, pay for it; if the goods or the service you offer are valuable, sell them.

Basis

A tax term meaning your current investment in an asset. Basis changes throughout the life of an asset. When you, for example, purchase a new piece of equipment, basis equals purchase price. As that equipment is depreciated, the amount of depreciation reduces the basis. When an asset is fully depreciated, your basis in it is zero.

Basis is used to calculate the gain or loss from disposition (sale) of an asset.

Capital Gain (Loss)

The difference between basis and sale price of a capital asset used in business. If your basis in an asset is lower than the amount you receive for it when you sell it, you have a capital gain. If your basis is higher than the sale price, you have a capital loss. Sale of any capital asset used in business results in either a capital gain or a capital loss.

Capital Purchase/Capital Expenditure

Purchase of an item costing more than $500. Any capital purchase must be tracked individually on your tax return, in contrast to noncapital purchases such as office supplies, art supplies, or perhaps small equipment, which are written off under one of the expense categories on Schedule C. A capital purchase must be either immediately expensed or else depreciated.

Disposing of a capital purchase results in a capital gain or a capital loss and is calculated on Form 4797.

Cash System

A system of accounting under which income is recognized (entered in the books) when it is received and expenses are recognized when paid. You cannot use the cash method of accounting if you have an inventory that materially affects how you report income and expenses. A guideline: If you regularly have on hand raw materials and unfinished goods the value of which (cost or current market value, whichever is lower) exceeds 10 percent of your usual annual gross revenues, you must keep track of that inventory and use the accrual system of accounting.

Recommendation: Keep your inventory low. Goods sitting around your studio cannot earn money for you. Stick with the cash system of accounting as long as it meets IRS requirements because it's easier and because you aren't paying tax on money you haven't yet received.

Commuting

First trip out of your home each day and last trip back.

Credits

Items allowed by law to offset a tax liability, dollar for dollar. Some popular credits: child care credit, foreign tax credit.

Depreciation

A method of spreading the cost of an asset over its useful life. Each year, the asset loses a portion of its value (it's depreciated) until the cost of the asset is used up. At that time, the total depreciation taken on the asset will equal its original cost and its basis to you will be zero.

The useful life of an asset is determined by the IRS. IRS Publication 534, "Depreciation," lists many kinds of assets and the useful life assigned to each.

For 1989, automobiles, computers, and film and video equipment are assigned a five-year life. The depreciation method to be used is the double-declining balance (DDB) method (MACRS). Assets have either a shortened life (for use with the MACRS system) or a regular life (for use with the asset depreciation range [ADR] life system). Assets purchased in 1989 should use the MACRS useful life, provided the assets are used more than 50 percent for business. Enter automobiles, computers, and film and video equipment (including cameras) in the "listed property" section of Form 4562.

In theory, the double-declining balance method divides the cost of the business asset by its expected life and then, in the first year, doubles that amount of allowable depreciation. In the second year, the cost of the asset less the first year's depreciation, divided by the expected life, gives regular depreciation. Multiply regular depreciation times two to give you the double-declining balance amount.

In the third year, subtract depreciation of the first two years from the cost, then divide by the life and double the figure that results. Continue this way until there is no balance left, which means the asset is fully depreciated. You never claim depreciation expense that exceeds your cost or basis in the asset. That's how, in theory, the double-declining balance method of depreciating an asset works. Reality, however, is a bit different because of midyear and quarter-year conventions adopted by the IRS.

The midyear convention forces you to add a year of life to any asset you depreciate. The assumption is that you purchased the asset in the middle of the year, regardless of when you actually purchased it. The midyear convention requires you to use only a half-year of depreciation the first year and the last year you own the asset; the other years are full years.

TABLE I

3-YEAR PROPERTY

| | | Mid-Quarter Convention | | | |
Year	Half-Year Convention	First Quarter	Second Quarter	Third Quarter	Fourth Quarter
1	33.33%	58.33%	41.67%	25 %	8.33%
2	44.45	27.78	38.89	50	61.11
3	14.81	12.33	14.13	16.67	20.37
4	7.41	1.56	5.31	8.33	10.19

TABLE II

5-YEAR PROPERTY

| | | Mid-Quarter Convention | | | |
Year	Half-Year Convention	First Quarter	Second Quarter	Third Quarter	Fourth Quarter
1	20 %	35 %	25 %	15 %	5 %
2	32	26	30	34	38
3	19.2	15.6	18	20.4	22.8
4	11.52	11.01	11.37	12.24	13.68
5	11.52	11.01	11.37	11.30	10.94
6	5.76	1.38	4.26	7.06	9.58

TABLE III

7-YEAR PROPERTY

| | | Mid-Quarter Convention | | | |
Year	Half-Year Convention	First Quarter	Second Quarter	Third Quarter	Fourth Quarter
1	14.29%	25.01%	17.86%	10.72%	3.57%
2	24.50	21.43	23.48	25.52	27.56
3	17.49	15.31	16.77	18.22	19.68
4	12.50	10.93	11.97	13.02	14.06
5	8.92	8.74	8.87	9.29	10.04
6	8.92	8.74	8.87	8.85	8.73
7	8.92	8.74	8.87	8.85	8.73
8	4.46	1.10	3.31	5.53	7.63

TABLE IV

Accelerated depreciation tables for computing first-year depreciation for 31.5-year property placed in service in each month:

January	3.0423%
February	2.7778%
March	2.5132%
April	2.2487%
May	1.9841%
June	1.7196%
July	1.4550%
August	1.1905%
September	0.9259%
October	0.6614%
November	0.3968%
December	0.1323%

TABLE V

Accelerated depreciation tables for computing first-year depreciation for 27.5-year property placed in service in each month:

January	3.4848%
February	3.1818%
March	2.8788%
April	2.5758%
May	2.2727%
June	1.9697%
July	1.6667%
August	1.3636%
September	1.0606%
October	0.7576%
November	0.4545%
December	0.1515%

The plot thickens from here. If 40 percent of the total value of the assets purchased in 1989 falls in the last quarter of the year, you must use the midquarter convention. The percentages reprinted in the foregoing table apply to each class of property—three-year, five-year, seven-year, and so on—purchased in 1989 if that 40-percent rule applies.

This table is considerably easier to use than the IRS instructions for Form 4562 and will erase most uncertainties about depreciation, unless you purchased a luxury automobile for use in your business. If you purchase an automobile for business use in 1989 and the price of that automobile exceeds IRS guidelines on what constitutes luxury and what does not, your depreciation deduction is further limited.

First-year depreciation and Section 179 expense cannot exceed $2,560. If you use your vehicle less than 100 percent for business, that limit is $2,560 times your percentage business use. For 1990, the second year of depreciating that vehicle, the maximum limit increases to $4,100 (less, if business percentage use is less than 100 percent). In the third year, the maximum allowable depreciation amount is $2,450; in the fourth year and beyond, it is $1,475, until the automobile is fully depreciated.

Remember that your actual deduction is the maximum allowable amount times the business percentage use of your automobile, as substantiated by your daily mileage log. If your business use falls below 50 percent in any year, you must switch to the ADR life (seven years) and recapture the excess depreciation in prior years.

Any depreciable asset used less than 100 percent in business requires you to keep a daily log book of usage. This applies to automobiles, computers, and film and video equipment.

For assets placed into service prior to 1987, continue using the depreciation method and life you originally used, until the asset is fully depreciated. For assets purchased prior to 1981 but placed into service in a subsequent year, use the depreciation method least favorable to you. For example, a harp, purchased in 1983 for $3,000 and placed in service in 1989, would be depreciated under MACRS rules.

Note on home office: If you own your home, have an office in it, and deduct expenses for a home office on Schedule C (for example, a percent of mortgage interest, insurance, and utility payments), you must depreciate the same percentage of your home using the 31.5-year real property table in the Form 4562 instructions, unless

Claiming a home office or studio has tax consequences when you sell your residence because the tax on capital gains on the percentage attributable to business use falls due and cannot be deferred as can the capital gain on your residential portion.

Earned Income

Payments received for work performed or services rendered. Does not include prizes, fellowships, or awards. Alimony, however, is considered earned income for the purpose of calculating eligibility for an Individual Retirement Account (IRA).

Employee

A person who works for you at regular scheduled hours, on your premises, for more than seventeen weeks of the year. As an employee, that person is entitled to have you pay half her Social Security tax (FICA), and all of her workers' compensation and unemployment insurance and is, moreover, eligible for any retirement programs you have for the business you operate.

Employer Identification Number (EIN)

Also known as Federal Employer Identification Number (FEIN). It is required if you have employees or a Keogh plan.

You must have an EIN in order to file quarterly wage reports on income tax withholding and FICA taxes. Also required if you are a sole proprietor with a Keogh account. Apply for one on IRS Form SS-4. Do not apply for one if you do not have employees or a Keogh retirement plan.

Exempt Organization

A corporation that does not pay taxes on most corporate profits because it fits certain criteria. It is not enough for an organization or individual to incorporate under state law as a nonprofit entity. It must make a formal request for exempt status to the IRS to determine if it meets the legal criteria for exemption. If it does so within fifteen months of incorporation and meets the IRS criteria, the exemption from taxation is retroactive to the date of incorporation. If it does not, it is required to file a corporate tax return and to pay taxes on any profit shown.

An exempt organization may need to file an annual tax return (Form 990 or 990T). Consult a tax advisor.

Expenses

The costs of running a business, some of which are tax deductible.

Expensing

A decision to deduct the full cost of a capital purchase in one tax year, rather than to depreciate it. Also called a "Section 179 election to expense." Items totaling up to $10,000 can be expensed each year.

Fellowships

A fellowship or grant is a cash award to an individual from a nonprofit organization or exempt foundation, in recognition of that individual's professional contributions or promise.

A fellowship is fully taxable and should be reported on line 22 on the front of the 1989 Form 1040.

A fellowship is considered a prize or award, not earned income. Hence it is not subject to Social Security tax (FICA) and should not be reported as income on Schedule C. It cannot be included as earned income in calculating eligibility for an IRA, Simplified Employee Pension (SEP) Plan, or Keogh retirement plan contribution.

Filing

To file a tax return is to complete the forms and schedules needed to report your income and claim your deductions and to mail those forms and schedules to the IRS district office assigned to your area of residence by April 15 of the year following the close of the tax year.

Filing Deadlines

April 15 for an individual tax return. Quarterly estimated tax payments are due the fifteenth day of April, June, September, and January, unless the fifteenth falls on a Sunday or a holiday, in which case the due date is the next business day. Failure to file on time can result in penalties in addition to the interest due on underpaid tax liabilities.

March 15 for a corporate return. If the corporation has a fiscal year, the filing deadline is two and one-half months after the close of the fiscal year.

April 15 for a partnership return.

Note that the 1986 Tax Reform Act eliminated the use of fiscal years for almost all partnerships and S-corporations.

Filing extensions

File Form 4868 to request a four-month extension of the filing deadline. Form 4868 must be filed by April 15 (and signed by you and your spouse, if you are married) and must be accompanied by enough money to cover your tax liability. In other words, an extension is an extension on filing, not on paying. Requests for extensions beyond the four-month period must be accompanied by a written explanation of the further delay. If granted, the additional extension is valid for only two months.

If you are out of the country on April 15, an automatic two-month extension is given. When you file your tax return, use Form 4868 and note in upper right corner: "In (name of country) on April 15."

Fiscal Year

A twelve-month period that is different from a calendar year. Most taxpayers are calendar-year taxpayers. In the past, some partnerships and S-corporations were allowed to adopt a fiscal year. Under the Tax Reform Act of 1986, almost all partnerships and S-corporations adopted calendar-year reporting at some time during 1987.

401(k) and 403(b) Plans

Retirement plans through private [401(k)] or public [403(b)] employers that deposit pretax earnings in retirement savings that are tax deferred until you retire. Since these deposits are pretax dollars, your reportable wages (box 10 of your W-2) are lower than the total wages shown as paid to you on your wage stub and also in the W-2 box showing Social Security wages. This is one form of tax savings. Depending on your overall income, you may also be eligible for an IRA plan or a Keogh or SEP retirement contribution (the latter being based on your net profit from self-employment).

Grants

See "Fellowships."

Hobby

An activity pursued primarily for pleasure or relaxation, not for profit. Expenses incurred in running a hobby can be used to offset income generated by that hobby to the extent of that income. A hobby can never generate a tax loss to offset other income.

Income

All money—wages, prizes, awards, gambling winnings, stipends, alimony—you receive is considered income. Important exceptions are:
1. scholarships for undergraduates and tuition scholarships for graduate students
2. inheritances
3. legal judgments resulting from pain and suffering
4. child support.

Income Averaging

Repealed for 1987 and subsequent years.

Independent Contractor

A self-employed person who does not have income taxes or Social Security taxes withheld from gross pay prior to receiving it. An independent contractor pays his or her own Social Security and income taxes on all income received and has none of the benefits employees normally enjoy, such as unemployment insurance, workers' compensation protection, or health care benefits.

Independent contractors report their income and expenses on Schedule C. They must complete the long form (Form 1040) to file their federal income taxes.

Inventory

Finished goods or goods in progress when their cost in materials represents a major factor in the way a net profit is calculated.

Everyone in business has an inventory of some size. A writer has note pads and pencils; an artist has sketch pads, paints, and framing pieces. But these "inventories" are too insignificant to declare. Whether an inventory is declared for tax purposes depends on the size of the inventory and whether the cost of the inventory has a material impact on the way a profit or loss is figured.

As a general rule, if the cost of your inventory usually exceeds ten percent of your annual revenues, that inventory has an impact on how you report your profit and must be tracked.

Having a collection of reproductions or a stock of books will require you to keep track of and declare an inventory. The existence of several or even many one-of-a-kind works does not.

Individual Retirement Account (IRA)

All taxpayers with earned income are eligible to have an IRA and to make contributions to it. Any contributions to an IRA earn tax-deferred income. The deductibility of an IRA contribution in 1989 depends on your adjusted gross income (AGI) and whether or not you are covered by an employer-paid pension plan.

A single person can contribute up to $2,000 per year to an IRA account, provided that person has at least $2,000 in earned income. If that person has an AGI less than $25,000, the IRA is fully deductible from taxable income. If the AGI is between $25,000 and $35,000 and the person is covered by an employer-paid pension plan, the IRA contribution is only partly deductible. With an AGI above $35,000 and inclusion in a pension plan, no part of the IRA contribution is deductible, but earnings within the IRA account are tax deferred until withdrawal.

A married couple can contribute up to $4,000 per year to their IRA accounts ($2,000 each), provided each has earned income of at least $2,000. If one works and the other doesn't, the limit on the IRA contribution is $2,250 ($2,000 and $250, respectively). Deductibility of the IRA contribution again hinges on AGI and pension plan coverage. For a married couple with an AGI less than $40,000, the IRA contribution is fully deductible; between $40,000 and $50,000, partly deductible, if one or both are covered by a pension plan; over $50,000, not deductible at all unless neither spouse is covered by an employer-paid pension plan.

An IRA account is held in trust for you by a fiduciary institution, such as a bank or brokerage house. You cannot set aside money in a regular savings account, for example, and call it an IRA. Money invested in an IRA cannot be withdrawn until you have reached the age of 59½ years. Withdrawals prior to that time are considered to be premature and incur a penalty of 10 percent of the amount withdrawn. Withdrawals at any time are taxed as regular income.

Investment Tax Credit (ITC)

Repealed for most real property by the Tax Reform Act of 1986. Unused ITCs from previous years can continue to be rolled forward until used up. An ITC can offset only income tax, not Social Security tax.

Keoghs (H.R. 10)

Named for a congressman and the number of the bill he sponsored establishing this retirement account for self-employed people. A Keogh plan can be used in conjunction with or separate from an IRA.

A Keogh account must be opened prior to the end of the calendar year, although contributions to it can be made up until April 15 of the following year (or later, with an extension).

Keogh accounts are held in trust for the sole proprietor by a bank or brokerage house. The kind of account you have depends on your individual circumstances:

1. **Defined contribution.** One of two kinds:
   Profit sharing. Allows a contribution of up to 15 percent of net profit, prior to retirement account contribution considerations, per year, without imposing any minimum contribution requirements. (To calculate the maximum allowable contribution, multiply your net profit by

.13043 for the contribution equal to 15 percent of your net profit after the maximum contribution.) This kind of account is appropriate for individuals in the early stages of self-employment who cannot count on making enough profit to contribute regularly to a retirement account.

Defined contribution. Requires you to contribute a minimum percentage of net income per year. Maximum contribution with profit sharing and defined-contribution Keogh plans is 20 percent of net income, or $30,000 (whichever is less). Open a defined contribution Keogh account if your business is firmly established and you are within fifteen years of retirement.

2. **Defined benefit.** This plan requires you to accumulate a certain amount of money by a certain date in the retirement plan so that the plan will generate defined benefits of a certain dollar figure over your expected lifespan. This type of Keogh plan is appropriate for the older sole proprietor who is at the peak of her earnings potential and knows what she needs in monthly retirement income from this investment. Administrative costs are unreasonably high to establish this kind of plan for a single individual, and it makes sense only if you have many employees.

All Keogh retirement plans require the filing of an annual report (Form 5500C, 5500R, or 5500-EZ) by July 31 of the following year.

Limited Partnership

A partnership that has at least one general partner and one or more limited partners, but no more than thirty-five total partners. Only the general partner or partners are legally responsible for the debts and liabilities of the partnership. A limited partner shares in profits or losses but is limited in liability to the amount originally contributed to the partnership.

Marriage Penalty

Refers to the condition under previous tax law that levied higher taxes on married couples than on nonmarried couples (two single people) when both work. The penalty was a result of the progressive tax structure, which taxed higher earnings at a proportionately higher rate. Under the Tax Reform Act of 1986, a flatter tax structure virtually eliminates this penalty.

Mid-year Convention

A rule used in depreciating assets. It requires reducing first-year depreciation by half. If more than 40 percent of the cost of all assets purchased during the year falls in the final quarter of the year, you must use a quarter-year convention for each depreciable-asset group.

Net Operating Loss (NOL)

Calculated using Form 1045, an NOL usually arises from a severe downturn in business that causes losses to exceed all other sources of income. Calculate the potential NOL if adjusted gross income in any particular year is a negative number.

An NOL can be carried back three years to offset income taxes in any of those years, or you may elect to carry it forward for up to fifteen years, offsetting income tax in each year following the NOL year, until the NOL is used up. Your decision on where to apply the NOL must be made by the end of the calendar year following the NOL year.

NOLs that occur year after year may mean imminent bankruptcy of the business and/or individual involved.

Most state tax laws allow you to calculate an NOL, although state rules about items eligible for inclusion may differ from federal rules. Check with your state revenue department for forms and instructions.

Penalties

Charges levied when tax liabilities are not paid on time or when tax returns are not filed on time. The penalty for not paying your tax liability on time is 0.5 percent per month, up to 22.5 percent of the amount owed. The penalty for late filing is 4.5 percent per month, up to 25 percent of the amount owed. There is an exception. More than sixty days after the due date for the return, you will be assessed a penalty equal to $100 or the amount owed, whichever is less. The combined penalty for filing late and not paying on time is 47.5 percent of the amount owed.

In addition to these penalties, interest will accrue on the unpaid amount at the IRS interest rate in effect during the period of the unpaid liability.

Penalties are not deductible. Interest charges are, to the extent allowed on Schedule A.

Profit and Loss Statement (P&L)

Required by banks and mortgage companies to assess a sole proprietor's credit worthiness. A P&L contains the same type of information as that found on Schedule C.

Recapture

Recapture of investment tax credit (ITC). Most commonly occurs when business property used to gain an ITC is sold or returned to personal use. Depending on when the disposition occurs in the life of the property, some or all of the previously claimed or used ITC must be returned to the government. Use Form 4255 to calculate.

Receipts

Issued by a vendor, receipts are records verifying expenditures you make.

Refund

Not the same as a bad debt. A refund most often occurs after an overcharge or settlement of a disputed payment.

Example: John Smith sells the XYZ Corporation the layout for its annual report and bills the corporation $3,000. In thirty days, a check is sent to John for the full $3,000. Six weeks later the head of marketing for XYZ calls John. She tells him how much heat she received because he mixed up the bar graphs for the international and national sales groups, and she demands a refund of half the original fee. In the interest of good will, John agrees to a $1,000 refund.

In his books, John shows the $3,000 check as income, with a $1,000 refund entry in his miscellaneous expenses, identified as "Refund."

Self-Employment Income

Any money you earn from which Social Security tax is not withheld by the payer.

Self-employment income can be reported only on Schedule C. If you use a Schedule C, you must also use the long form (Form 1040), even if the bulk of your earnings are reported to you on W-2s.

Simplified Employee Pension (SEP) Plan

SEPs offer most of the advantages of Keogh plans without any annual reporting requirement. One significant difference is that SEPs, unlike Keoghs, cannot be pledged as collateral for loans.

Taxpayer Identification Number (TIN)

Your Social Security number. The TIN for a partnership or a corporation is its Federal Employer Identification Number, obtained by filing Form SS-4.

Underpayment of Tax

Failure to pay or overpay your federal tax liability in a given year. A penalty for underpayment of taxes results when you owe more than $500 to the federal government at the end of the tax year. This penalty is calculated on Form 2210.

The penalty for underpaying federal taxes can be significant. The moral is that you must file quarterly estimated tax payments (Form 1040-ES) if you expect to owe more than 10 percent of your total tax liability. Underpayment can result from untaxed income, self-employment income, or underwithholding at your place of employment. Make sure your W-4 does not overstate the withholding allowances to which you are entitled.

Uniform Gifts to Minors Act (UGMA)

Refers to a good estate-planning tool under which money can be given to a child in the child's name and held in trust until the child reaches the age of majority.

This is still a good way to establish a college fund for a child. Open an UGMA account at a bank or brokerage house in the name of a minor child, usually with a parent as trustee. The money put into the account is a gift and becomes the property of the child (trust beneficiary) when he or she reaches the age of majority (eighteen years, in most states). At that point, the money is the property of the child, no strings attached.

The trustee of an UGMA cannot pledge the UGMA as security for any loans the trustee may seek, nor may the trustee withdraw funds from the account for the basic living needs (food, clothing, education) of the trust beneficiary.

The earnings are taxed at the child's rate (usually zero) until annual earnings exceed $1,000, at which point the parents' highest tax rate is used.

Answers to Frequently Asked Tax Questions

Income

What is income? Is there any difference between earned income and regular income?

Income is wages, bartered goods, income you receive in exchange for products you sell or services you provide, distributions from partnerships or corporations, interest or dividends on a portfolio, capital gains on the sale of real property, distributions from pensions or profit-sharing plans, alimony, unemployment compensation, prizes or fellowships, gambling winnings, and fees paid for services such as honoraria or jury duty.

Most of what is considered regular income is earned income. Interest and dividends, by contrast, constitute unearned income because you presumably did nothing by the sweat of your brow to generate that income. (You may have worked to accumulate the investment in the first place, but the earnings on that investment come to you through the efforts of others.)

● **What income do I need to report on my 1989 tax return?**
All types of income listed above. Do not report inheritances, scholarships or tuition reimbursement, workers' compensation, the share you paid of pension distributions, child support payments, loans, credit-card advances, divorce settlements, lawsuit settlements for pain and suffering.

● **I'm self-employed on a part-time basis. When should I start declaring my business income on Schedule C?**
As soon as you begin receiving it. Under federal law you must declare all income you receive during a tax year.

● **I didn't make much money this year. Do I have to declare it?**
"Much money," in the eyes of the IRS, is anything over $1,000 in gross revenues. Your expenses may exceed that revenue, giving you a net loss for the year, but gross income over $1,000 requires you to file as a self-employed person.

● **Do I need to report cash I receive as a payment for goods (or services)?**
Yes.

● **How do I handle commissions I receive?**
If you received more than $600 during 1989 from a single payer, you probably also received a Form 1099-MISC. The amount on this form should be included in your gross revenues line on Schedule C. Even if you did not receive this form, the amount you were paid should be included in gross revenues on Schedule C. Should you ever want a loan (business or personal), your Schedule C activities will determine whether or not you are credit-worthy.

● **Where do I report royalties on a booklet (or a song or a book?)**
Royalties from a work you create are considered income from self-employment activities and are reportable only on Schedule C.

● **Is a fellowship taxable income?**
Yes. Fellowships awarded after August 16, 1986 are considered taxable to the recipient.

137

● **During the year I sold stock I inherited from my grandfather. How do I declare this when tax time rolls around?**

When you inherited the stock, a basis was assigned to it for the purpose of determining the amount of estate tax. Usually this basis is the same as the market value of the stock on the date the estate is settled. You should have been told the basis figure at the time you received the stock. If you did not receive this information or if you forgot what it was, contact the executor or executrix of the estate to determine the value at the time of the inheritance.

The amount you sold it for is identified on the "Sell" confirmation from the broker you used. All inherited property results, by definition, in long-term gains or losses, regardless of the length of time the beneficiary held the stock after inheriting it. Use Schedule D to calculate your capital gain.

● **Is my inheritance considered taxable income?**

No. Any taxes attributable to the estate were paid prior to the distribution made to you.

● **I sold a piece of equipment used in my business. Do I include this in my tax return for 1989?**

Yes. In prior years, you either depreciated or expensed that piece of equipment. Its sale forces you to report a gain or a loss on its disposition.

The depreciable basis of the equipment, less accumulated depreciation or the amount expensed, equals its basis at the time of sale. Sales price less basis gives you a profit (if the figure is positive) or a loss (if the figure is negative).

Use Form 4797 to calculate your gain or loss. Part I is used for assets owned less than six months; Part II for assets owned more than six months. Use Part III for real estate sales and gains on other property transactions.

On the sale of a house, you may also have recapture of excess depreciation if you used the ACRS method of depreciation.

On the sale of business property, you may have recapture of the investment tax credit if you sold it prior to the end of the useful life you declared for it in the year of purchase. Use Form 4255 to figure the recapture amount.

● **I sold my car in 1989. It wasn't a business vehicle—I just used the standard mileage deduction. Do I need to report anything about that sale?**

Yes. You need to use Form 4797 to determine the amount of your capital gain or loss. A car used in business is considered a piece of business equipment subject to the same requirements as a camera, a computer, or a videocassette recorder. When it's sold, you must calculate the gain or loss on that piece of equipment.

Begin by determining an overall business-use percentage for the car. To do that, add up the total miles driven on the car for all uses during the period you owned it. Add up the total number of business miles you used to claim a deduction. Divide the total business miles by total miles to give you the business-use percentage for that automobile. Multiply that percentage times the cost of the car to give you the business cost of the vehicle. Then multiply the sale price times that overall business use percentage to give you the business proceeds portion of the sale price.

You must then deduct depreciation from the vehicle's business cost. If you used the actual expense method of deducting automobile costs, the depreciation figure you use on Form 4797 is the total of the annual depreciation amounts you claimed in prior years. If you used the standard mileage deduction, you need to consult the tables in the Form 4797 instructions to determine what part of the standard mileage rate the IRS included for depreciation for each of the years you used the standard mileage rate. For example, in 1988 the standard mileage rate was twenty-four cents per mile, of which ten cents was allocated to depreciation. To calculate depreciation for 1988, multiply the number of 1988 business miles claimed by ten cents per mile.

Do the same (using the appropriate cents-per-mile figure) for each year you used the car for business and claimed a deduction for that use. Add up each year's depreciation figure to calculate total depreciation you claimed on the automobile.

Almost always, you sell an automobile for less than you paid for it. After taking into account depreciation claimed, however, you may end up with a taxable gain. Also note that the sale of an automobile may trigger recapture of excess depreciation and/or recapture of part of the investment tax credit.

Sale of an automobile is a tricky part of tax work. The IRS has records on your vehicle use dating back to the 1985 tax returns and will quiz you about the sale of any business property at an audit.

Deductions

● **How do I deduct the cost of using my car for business?**
To deduct the cost of using your automobile for business, you must first identify how many miles you drove for business, how many for commuting, and how many for personal use. The IRS requires you to keep a daily mileage log of these three categories. Practically, you should keep your business and commuting mileage by writing down odometer readings from point to point. Personal mileage will be anything left after those are subtracted from the total number of miles driven.

With a mileage log, you can at the end of the year calculate the number of miles driven, along with the number of miles driven for business use and for commuting.

If you purchased a car in 1989, the following information applies: The percentage of business use gives you practical information about whether to deduct actual expenses or claim the standard mileage deduction. If business use exceeds 50 percent and you own a luxury vehicle (defined as one costing more than $12,800) and you intend to use your car for the foreseeable future for more than 50 percent business driving, you should probably use the actual expense method of deducting automobile expenses. If business use is less than 50 percent or if you cannot reliably predict future business use, you should probably use the standard mileage deduction.

If you lease a vehicle, you must use the actual expense method of deducting expenses. If that leased vehicle is a luxury vehicle, you may have income imputed to you, depending on the value of the vehicle and the term of the lease. This imputed income is reported on the "other income" line of Schedule C and becomes part of your gross income subject to Social Security tax.

If you are continuing to use a car put into business service before 1989 and want to claim a deduction for business use of that car, the following applies: If you claimed business percentage of actual expenses in any prior year, you must continue to use the actual expense method of deduction. If you used the standard mileage rate, you have the option of continuing with that method or switching to the actual expense method. Once you opt for deducting actual expenses, however, you cannot return to using the standard mileage deduction.

General information for 1989:

Use Form 4562 to enter your usage profile and to calculate your allowable deduction, regardless of method.

In using the standard deduction for business use of your automobile, use 25.5 cents per business mile for the first 15,000 miles, and 11 cents per mile thereafter.

If you use the actual expense method for deducting automobile expenses, remember that once the auto is fully depreciated you can deduct expenses only at the eleven cents per mile rate or at the percentage-business-use rate times the actual expenses incurred.

If you chose the actual expense method in prior years and find that for 1989 your business use has slipped to less than 50 percent, you must depreciate the remaining car basis over seven years and calculate accelerated depreciation recovery amounts and possible recapture of investment tax credit.

● What is commuting mileage?

For a self-employed person or an employee, the IRS defines commuting mileage as the first trip out and the last trip home. Neither is deductible.

Even a self-employed person whose studio office is in the home has commuting mileage.

If you are a self-employed person who drives more than thirty-five miles to a job site or business appointment, even if this is the first trip of your business day, this is not considered commuting mileage. The thirty-five-mile radius of activity is an arbitrary distinction drawn by the IRS to define activities within the regular scope of business.

● I bought a car last year and ended up using it 66 percent for business. My accountant convinced me to use the actual expense method of deducting expenses. This year my business use will be only about 40 percent. How should I deduct my automobile costs?

Unfortunately, you were caught in a trap. Either you bought your accountant's explanation of how he could keep your taxes lower in 1988, or you didn't ask for and he didn't offer an explanation of the long-term consequences of this election.

For 1989 you must continue to use the actual expense method of deducting expenses (in your case, about 40 percent of the amounts spent on gas and oil, repairs and maintenance, insurance, license). Your depreciation deduction will be significantly cut. Determine the new basis of your automobile (the amount you paid for it less depreciation amounts taken in prior years) and then use seven-year MACRS tables.

You are also subject to recapture of excess depreciation taken by using five-year MACRS when your usage was greater than 50 percent. To calculate that recapture amount, determine the deduction, had you used seven-year MACRS instead of five-year MACRS, for each year you depreciated the car prior to 1989. This is the recapture amount you must list on the "other income" line of Schedule C.

Per your chagrin with your accountant: Make sure you understand the decisions that go into preparing your taxes. If your accountant isn't asking you about future usage, you may end up with a nice deduction this year and trouble next.

● Last year I used the standard mileage rate to deduct automobile expenses. This year I have had huge repair bills. Can I switch to the actual expense method? My business usage this year is over 70 percent.

Yes. But you must depreciate the vehicle using seven-year MACRS.

● My studio is in my home, but this year I have a net loss and cannot deduct that space. What is my daily commuting mileage?

If you are unable, for reasons of tax regulations, to claim office in the home but in reality operate from that space, you must nonetheless use the same commuting rules everyone else uses: First trip out each day and last trip home are considered commuting mileage and are not deductible as a business expense.

● How do I keep track of parking costs for business appointments?

Ask for and keep the receipt from a parking ramp. What about parking meters? In metropolitan areas, all parking meters contain an alpha-numeric code. Jot it down, along with the amount of money you put into the meter, for a reliable tax expense record. In a rural area, describe the approximate location and amount spent on parking.

● **I live in a downtown loft and deduct expenses for office in the home. Can I deduct the monthly parking fee I pay to put my car in the garage?**
No. You pay for the parking garage as a function of your living in a downtown area. You are incurring no additional expense because you also happen to be self-employed.

● **Should I lease or buy an auto?**
For your taxes it doesn't make a whole lot of difference. You need to keep a daily mileage log whether you own a car or lease it. With leasing, however, your only option for deducting automobile expenses is using the actual expense method.

As leasing has become more possible for the average person, the costs of leasing versus buying have evened out. A lease is generally easier to get into than a purchase, but you don't end up with an asset at the end of the payment schedule.

Car salespeople increasingly are using the strategy of trying to convince you a car payment is as necessary a part of your monthly budget as a house payment. This should be enough reason to disbelieve, but consider the rest of their pitch—as long as you have this monthly car payment until the end of time, you may as well drive something you like. Now you know you're sunk. What they want to sell you is a leased vehicle, such as a BMW or a Mercedes. You, too, can keep ahead of the neighbors.

A good guideline to follow is this: If you assume a monthly car payment is an item as necessary to your monthly budget as a rent or house payment, then by all means lease the car. If, however, you prefer to own assets and increase your net worth, buy the automobile.

● **Can I deduct for an office in my home?**
Only if you have a net profit from 1989 self-employment that exceeds the amount you want to deduct for home studio. If you have a loss, you cannot claim a home-office deduction, even if this is the only place you conduct business.

● **How much can I deduct for office in the home?**
Two methods of calculating costs associated with a home office are acceptable to the IRS. The first method involves using the square footage of your home. Figure out how many square feet are devoted exclusively to your business. Divide the business space by the total number of square feet and multiply the result by the actual expenses you have for your home.

The second method is to divide the number of rooms used exclusively for business use by the total number of rooms in your house (except for bathrooms), and then multiply the resulting percentage by the actual expenses you have for your house.

Actual expenses include rent and utilities for a renter; for a homeowner, property taxes, interest, insurance, utilities, depreciation, and fix-up expenses (but not those applying exclusively to nonbusiness areas of the house).

If you share the space with others, be sure to prorate the space first among the residents—one share each, whether adult or child—and then determine the business use of the space that is your share.

● **What studio expenses are deductible?**
Rent and utilities are deductible in the year paid. Leasehold improvements need to be depreciated over 31.5 years. If you terminate your lease prior to that time, the balance of the leasehold improvements costs are deductible in the year you move.

● **How do I deduct expenses for inventory items?**
You must keep track of an inventory if you have on hand, at regular intervals throughout

the year, raw materials whose value exceeds 10 percent of your average annual revenues. Your inventory then exceeds *de minimis* standards for the IRS and requires you to keep track of inventory and to keep your books using the accrual system of accounting.

To report your inventory, you must at the end of each year add up the cost of the raw materials you have in your possession. Count only the larger items (not pins and tacks, for example). Keep notes on how you added up the total costs so you'll be able to use the same method in future years.

Remember, the beginning inventory and inventory at end of year figures on Schedule C are dollar amounts, not numbers of items. To determine the dollar amounts, you must know how many items you have in inventory.

On the back of schedule C, report your year-end inventory cost in Part III. The inventory total from 1988, plus new raw materials purchased in 1989, labor, and supplies used in the product, less the remaining inventory on December 31 gives you your cost of goods sold in 1989. This is deducted from your gross revenues on the front of Schedule C.

Musicians provide a good example of how to track inventory. Let's say a musician cuts an album in 1989 and releases it on discs and on tapes. To make this album, certain costs were incurred: studio time, musicians' fees, design and layout costs, the manufacturing process itself. Each disc or tape is assigned a pro rata share of the costs incurred in manufacture, a cost that never changes.

From the original number of discs and tapes, promos are sent to radio stations and used for advertising. If there are no sales of either tapes or discs in 1989, then the only amount deducted is the number of discs sent out for promotional purposes multiplied by the per-disc cost plus the number of tapes sent out as promos multiplied by the per-tape cost. Inventory at end of year (a dollar figure) is the remaining number of discs multiplied by the per-disc cost plus the remaining number of tapes multiplied by the per-tape cost.

In 1990, the album sells out, and more discs and tapes are made. That second batch of discs and tapes has its own per-unit cost, based on total manufacturing costs. The per-unit cost of a tape or disc in a second release is always lower than the per-unit cost of a tape or disc in a first release because some of the start-up costs in making the album from scratch aren't there on a second release.

Beginning inventory for 1990 is the same figure used for 1989 inventory at end of year. Purchases is the manufacturing cost of the second release. Inventory at end of year is the number of discs and tapes from each release left over on December 31, 1990, multiplied by the per-unit cost for a disc or a tape from each release. Total costs less remaining inventory gives you your deduction for discs and albums sold or distributed for promos in 1990.

Using an inventory method means you deduct expenses only for what you use during the year, not for everything you purchase during the year.

● **What kinds of clothing costs are deductible?**
Clothing is deductible if it makes you stand out in a crowd when you walk down the main street of your town. A tuxedo could qualify as a business expense in the Midwest, but not in New York City.

Clothing costs are not deductible if the clothing can be converted to personal use. A dancer could deduct the cost of a leotard, but a painter could not deduct the cost of a smock.

● **How do I handle payments to independent contractors?**
If you pay a person more than $600 in 1989, you must file a Form 1099-MISC reporting the amount of that payment to the IRS. Partnerships and corporations are not independent contractors. Payments to individuals on which you do not withhold taxes are payments to

independent contractors and require you to issue a Form 1099-MISC by January 31, 1990 to that person, and to the IRS, if those payments are deductible business expenses to you.

If an individual uses a business name but is a sole proprietor, you must issue a Form 1099-MISC if you paid more than $600 during the year. Also, if the owner of the building where your studio is located is not a partnership or corporation, you must issue that owner a Form 1099-MISC, since rent payments are part of your business deductions.

Form 1099-MISC is a three-part form. The top part goes to the IRS. The second part is sent to the payee. You, as payer, keep the third part for your files.

Report payments to independent contractors as commissions in Part II of Schedule C or as cost of labor in Part III of Schedule C. If you send your landlord a Form 1099-MISC, this payment remains rent on Schedule C.

Failure to file a Form 1099-MISC within sixty days after the end of the year may result in a $50 fine. Be sure you issue all 1099s required, and do it in a timely fashion.

● I'm thinking about buying a computer. Should I?

If you need a computer in your business, buy it if you can afford it. If you use a computer for any kind of personal activity, you must keep a log book on daily usage. Report your tax treatment of the computer in the "listed" property section on the back of Form 4562.

● Can I deduct any time I contribute to a nonprofit organization? What about some sketches I did of costumes for a local theatre group? What are they worth?

Nothing. Time is not money to the IRS, so your contributions of time are not deductible contributions, regardless of how large or small your normal billing rate is. If you didn't bill for it, you never collected money. If you never collected money, the money is not in your taxable income. If it's not in your taxable income, you cannot deduct it.

If you bill the nonprofit organization for your time and are paid, you could turn around and contribute the money back to the organization. But then you have a "wash"—money comes in on Schedule C and is deducted on Schedule A. You may end up somewhat behind because the income on Schedule C will also be subject to Social Security tax and you may no longer be itemizing your personal deductions on Schedule A.

It's easier for everyone concerned if you simply donate your time and energies, to the degree you can, to an organization you support. Remember that your mileage is deductible, as are out-of-pocket expenses incurred in conjunction with nonprofit activities. If promotion describes a major part of your work for a nonprofit, consider the mileage as business miles and the out-of-pocket expenses as business expenses.

● What costs can I deduct for professional development?

The cost of seminars, conferences, and lessons are all deductible, provided they enhance your existing professional expertise. A course of study that prepares you to move to a new profession would be a personal (and therefore nondeductible) expense.

● I am researching a book on the Mayan Indians. How much of my travel and maintenance costs can I deduct?

None, unless you are an established authority in the field with other books already in print. Despite the repeal of capitalization provisions for authors, writing a book on speculation (without contract or monetary advance) is an activity the IRS will not underwrite.

If you are writing a book or article under these circumstances, keep track of your expenses to use against the time you do start to make money from the work.

For established writers in a given field, the rules on deductibility of expenses for a new work are less strict, since the argument can be made that the "new" book is really nothing more than a continuation of previous research (and published works) that enhances the author's status and earning power.

● **A state university is advertising study trips to see the art treasures of Italy. The informational brochure suggests the entire cost of the trip may be tax deductible. I am a painter and know this trip would enrich me and provide a broader base for my expertise. Can I take this trip as a business deduction?**
No. Rules on educational travel changed beginning with the 1987 tax year. Educators and professionals cannot deduct travel as a business expense unless the travel is the means of arriving at a conference or organized study segment, not simply an end, in and of itself.

One of the examples of prohibited travel explicitly cited in tax legislation is that of the college instructor of Italian who must return to Italy approximately every three years to update colloquial use and diction. While being current is necessary to teach the proper idiom, the instructor cannot take a tax deduction unless enrollment in a specific language program is the focus of the trip.

● **When I meet with my agent, we usually split the lunch tab. Can I deduct what I spend?**
No. What you describe is not a business meal. You may be discussing business items, but a business meal, by definition, implies you are picking up the entire bill as a necessary part of your business. According to the IRS, the situation you describe is for the mutual convenience of you and your agent; this makes it a nondeductible expense.

● **I'm attending a professional convention in San Francisco later this year. What business meal costs can I deduct?**
When you're away from your tax home overnight, all meals for the days you are gone are deductible expenses. At the time you file your income tax return, however, only 80 percent of the total amount spent can be used as a business deduction due to changes made by the 1986 Tax Reform Act.

● **I'm frequently rehearsing ten to twelve hours per day. If I stop on the way home for dinner, can I deduct this cost as a business meal? What about lunch if I go out with the rest of the cast? We all would waste a lot of time if we interrupted our work to go home and eat.**
Unfortunately, what you describe is not an allowable business meal. Sometimes it seems as though the IRS would rather you died of starvation, but the logic behind tax reform was to cut down on three-martini lunches or dinners. It has served to accomplish that, although Congress is still seriously discussing eliminating all entertainment and business-lunch expense deductions.

● **I'm a filmmaker who chose to capitalize expenses using the safe harbor method on my 1988 taxes. How do I identify the 25 percent carryover to 1989 from the 1988 return?**
Writing regulations to tell taxpayers how to implement capitalization provisions has created a bureaucratic nightmare for the IRS. Remember, the capitalization laws were made by Congress; the IRS is charged with devising systems to implement the laws.

To date, no specific examples of how to make the safe harbor election have been issued by the IRS. In the absence of a directive, then, the taxpayer must resort to logic and clear labeling. For example, any year you use the safe harbor election, write in block letters across the top of Schedule C: "Safe Harbor Election per IRC 88–62. Election made [identify the first tax year you used the method]."

In the "other expense" section of Schedule C, enter the disallowed amount for 1989 as a negative number; that is, put the number in brackets. The amount disallowed is 50 percent of the deductions you've claimed up to the point of calculating the disallowed portion. Label this "Sec. 263A disallowance*." At the bottom of the page, enter: "*carryover to 1990 = [half of the disallowed amount]; carryover to 1991 = [the other half of the disallowed amount]," being clear to enter numbers in the bracketed areas used in this example.

The filmmaker in this example has a carryforward deduction from the 1988 tax return. This number (amounting to half the disallowed portion on the 1988 tax return for 1988 expenses) is entered in the "other expenses" as a positive number (and hence a deduction). It is labeled: "Sec. 263A carryforward from 1988."

A filmmaker (or video artist) may have one entry for disallowances for the current tax year and a maximum of two carryforward entries per tax year.

● **I capitalized expenses in 1987 and 1988 using the project-basis method. Now I'm getting into independent work and shooting my own films. What are my options for 1989?**
For 1989 you can elect the safe harbor method for 1989 expenses. Your capitalized expenses from projects undertaken in earlier years will be deductible in 1989 only to the extent they generated income for you in 1989.

● **I elected the safe harbor method to deduct expenses on my 1987 taxes. I still haven't filed my 1988 tax return because I think I'm missing out on deductions—my tax bill seems too high for the amount of money I make. What can I do?**
Your tax liability is artificially high because you are reporting all your income in 1987 and 1988 but only part of your expenses (50 percent in 1987; 50 percent in 1988 plus 25 percent of the 1987 expenses carried over to 1988).

The tax return you filed for 1987 is undoubtedly the worst you'll file. You should start to see some relief with the 1988 return as you pick up the disallowed expenses from 1987. By the 1989 return, you should be on some kind of level playing field.

It's too late to rescind your election to use the safe harbor method of deducting expenses. It's a onetime, irrevocable election, at least until the next major tax reform.

Cutting Your Taxes

● **How can I cut my tax bill?**
Keep track of expenses and keep receipts. Know the current tax law. So-called tax shelters (with the exception of home ownership) are appropriate for only a small segment of the tax-paying public because of their level of risk and because the amount of capital tied up frequently loses more in income-generating opportunities than it gains in tax savings. If you're self-employed and show a healthy profit from year to year, consider a retirement account contribution (discussed in this section).

● **Can I still use income averaging?**
No. Income averaging was eliminated on the 1987 tax forms.

● **Is it beneficial for my spouse and me to file separate income tax returns?**
Generally, no. For married couples whose separate incomes are high (over $40,000 per year and up) and approximately equal, however, there may be some savings. The only way to determine the most beneficial filing status is to calculate the final tax liability both ways (married filing jointly and married filing separately). Be sure to take into account state laws about filing status and calculate your liabilities using both options.

● **I pay $250 per month in child support to my former spouse. Can I claim the child for whom I make these payments as an exemption on my tax return?**
For any divorce finalized after 1984 the custodial parent claims the exemption, unless the divorce decree stipulates something else and the custodial parent signs a waiver of the exemption. The waiver, on Form 8332, must be filed with your tax return.

For divorces finalized prior to 1985, most divorce decrees specify which parent is entitled to claim the exemption. If, however, that parent cannot meet the support test (requiring that parent to pay more than 50 percent of the maintenance costs for the child), neither parent is entitled to claim the exemption. If the pre-1985 divorce decree does not stipulate who is entitled to claim the exemption, the parent providing more than half the support of the child claims the exemption.

If the custodial parent provides less than half the support for the dependent and the divorce decree does not stipulate the noncustodial parent can claim the dependent, it is possible no one can take the exemption.

● Can I contribute to an IRA and cut my tax bill? How much can I contribute in 1989?
Contributing to an IRA is an excellent way of cutting taxes and providing for your retirement needs.

Anyone who has earned income is eligible for an IRA. For a married couple where one spouse has earned income, both are eligible for IRAs. For the single person, the maximum annual contribution is $2,000 or the amount of earned income, whichever is lower; for a married couple, the maximum annual contribution is $4,000, provided each spouse has at least $2,000 in earned income. For a married couple where one spouse earns income and the other does not, the maximum contribution is $2,250, with no more than $2,000 to either spouse's retirement account. If, however, one spouse is self-employed and has a net loss for the year, the maximum IRA contribution for that couple is $2,000.

Eligibility for IRA contributions is not the same as being able to deduct your IRA contributions. Deductibility is limited by coverage in a pension plan where you work and by adjusted gross income. For single people who are covered by a pension plan (definition: included in the plan, whether or not vested at present), the limits on deductibility phase in at $25,000. For every additional thousand dollars in adjusted gross income, $200 of the IRA contribution becomes nondeductible. At $35,000 in adjusted gross income, no contributions are tax deductible. For a married couple, those limits on adjusted gross income begin at $40,000. By $50,000 no IRA contribution is deductible.

These limits apply to anyone eligible for a pension plan where they work. For a married couple, if either is eligible for pension plan coverage, the limitations apply to both, unless they file their tax returns separately. It makes no difference whether or not you are contributing to the plan. If you belong to a group of employees who are not yet vested in the plan but are otherwise eligible for the plan, you are considered a "covered" employee, which will be designated on the Form W-2 you receive after the end of the year.

If you are solely self-employed, you are not covered by an employer-funded pension plan. But if you are self-employed and have a Keogh plan or an SEP, you are considered a "covered" employee and the limitations described above apply.

Your deductible IRA contribution is figured as a percentage of the contribution you make. Let's assume you want to contribute $2,000 to your 1989 IRA account. Of that, you calculated only $440 will be tax deductible (22 percent). Can you simply contribute $440 and claim all of it as your 1989 IRA contribution? No. Twenty-two percent of whatever you contribute is deductible (in this example), up to a $440 deduction on a contribution of $2,000.

The deductible portion of an IRA contribution is entered on lines 24 or 25 of Form 1040. The nondeductible portion is listed on Form 8606. A separate Form 8606 is required for each spouse.

Even if your IRA contribution is not deductible, it still represents a valuable strategy for building up your retirement nest egg, since all earnings on IRA accounts remain tax deferred until you begin to withdraw them.

You must keep careful records for all nondeductible IRA contributions. File Form 8606 with your tax return each year you make nondeductible contributions. In years when you do not make nondeductible contributions, keep a separate ledger to track the funds that have already been taxed. Then, when you begin to withdraw funds, you have a record of the deductible and nondeductible amounts contributed. Any withdrawal needs to be taken proportionately from all IRA accounts. The nondeductible portion of total contributions becomes the nontaxable portion of the current year withdrawal.

● Am I eligible for a SEP or a Keogh Plan?

As a self-employed person, you are eligible to open either an SEP (Simplified Employee Pension) plan or a Keogh Plan. Contributions to each depend on the size of your net profit. Of the two, more options for larger investments exist for the Keogh plan than the SEP offers, which makes the Keogh Plan more attractive to sole proprietors in their late thirties and forties and older.

● I have a Keogh plan retirement account. Besides making contributions, what can I do or not do with this plan?

First, the things you can do. Contributions are determined by the kind of plan you have: defined benefit or defined contribution. In a defined benefit plan, you lock yourself into a program of set annual contributions aimed at reaching a certain level by a certain year so that you can count on certain benefits for each year of your retirement. This kind of plan is appropriate for self-employed people who are fifty or older because they have a better idea of how much retirement income they need and have the revenue potential to generate the required contribution commitments. It is, however, not suitable for a sole proprietor because the administrative fees associated with a defined benefit plan are prohibitive for an individual.

A defined contribution plan allows you to (a) contribute anywhere from nothing to 15 percent of your net income, or (b) an amount no less than 15 percent and no more than 25 percent of your net income, depending on the plan you've established. In the case of the former, that 15 percent maximum is actually more like 13.043 percent of your net income because the IRS considers the contribution to have lowered your net profit. The 13.043 percent takes into account the adjustment.

As with all tax-deferred investments, you can watch earnings on your Keogh plan investments grow without taxation. Earnings will be taxed when you withdraw the money.

What you can't do with a Keogh account is withdraw money before you are 59½ without incurring a 10 percent penalty for early withdrawal, in addition to facing taxation on the principal withdrawn. If you have a defined contribution plan, you cannot fail to make the required payment. If you have the kind of defined contribution plan that requires a minimal 15 percent contribution and you fail to make that contribution, the plan can (and probably will) be terminated.

If you have a Keogh plan, you must register that plan each year with the IRS by filing a 5500 report. Sole proprietors who have no employees can file Form 5500-EZ. Sole proprietors who make no contribution for the year simply answer a few parts on Form 5500-EZ.

Keogh plans must be opened by December 31 of the year in which the contribution is to be claimed. Also, a Keogh plan owner must have a Federal Employer Identification Number (FEIN). If you have employees, you already have one of these. Otherwise, use Form SS-4 to apply for one.

● Can I have both a Keogh plan and a IRA?

Sure. The maximum contribution to the Keogh follows the guidelines listed above. Participating in a Keogh plan means you are covered by a pension plan where you work, so use the guidelines provided elsewhere on income limits for deductible IRA contributions.

● Can I have both a Keogh plan and a SEP?

Yes, but the total deductible contribution cannot exceed 20 percent of your net profit. Having either plan limits your eligibility for a deductible IRA contribution.

● **Should I open an IRA account or a Keogh account?**

Because the IRA is easier to administer, that should be your first stop in retirement plan shopping. When the $2,000 limit no longer suffices, open a SEP or Keogh plan.

Whether or not your IRA contribution is deductible, by the time you are forty years old you should set aside $2,000 per year in an IRA account. Without it, retirement will be financially uncertain.

● **My brother-in-law wants me to invest $10,000 in a limited real estate partnership in Florida. He says it will save me $2,800 per year in taxes. Shall I do it?**

Beware of any investment scheme that promises you a specific rate of return (unless it's something like a certificate of deposit) or a dollar figure in tax savings. In the scenario you describe, your entire investment would need to be deductible in the year you invest, plus you would need to be in the top tax bracket.

The offer you describe sounds phony. Look further into the management of the partnership, check with the Florida Better Business Bureau, and go slow. A good deal will always be around.

● **I own my home outright. Should I borrow against it to create a deduction? I don't really need the money.**

No, no, and no. The top tax bracket for 1989 is 33.5 percent. Presuming you are in the top bracket, that means that for every dollar you spend in interest, you'll save 33.5 cents on your federal tax return. Seems to me you've just given away 66.5 cents on the dollar. Moreover, if you own your home outright, thank your lucky stars and congratulate yourself on some good financial planning. Never jeopardize your home for the sake of squeezing a few bucks more out of your tax return or for the sake of a new venture. Keep that homestead safe!

● **I want to buy a new car. I know consumer interest is only partially deductible now, so I'm thinking of a second mortgage on my home. New car loans are carrying a 12 percent interest rate in town now, while I can get a second mortgage for only 10.5 percent. The choice seems clear to me. What do you think?**

I don't claim to have a lock on doomsday advice, but I don't think you should ever borrow against your home for a consumer product. Major surgery, yes; a college education for your child, yes. A new Subaru? No.

What you're doing is confusing tax savings with overall good, solid financial advice. Pay the higher interest rate and keep your home safe.

● **Should I buy equipment before the end of the year to lower my taxes?**

Only if you need the equipment. Certainly don't go into debt to buy equipment simply to avoid taxes; you'll dig yourself right into a cash-flow hole. Also, be aware of how much (or, in most instances, how little) the equipment will save you in taxes. Most artists are in a 20 percent bracket or lower. For every dollar they spend, they save twenty cents (or less) in taxes. Keep that in mind and buy equipment for business reasons, not for illusory tax savings.

● **Can I avoid paying Social Security taxes?**

No. Participation in the Social Security system is not voluntary. All earned income is subject to Social Security tax. Income from self-employment (sole proprietorship or partnership) is subject to FICA tax at the rate of 13.02 percent of your net profit.

● **How do I pay Social Security taxes on my income from self-employment?**

You pay Social Security taxes on net profit exceeding $400 in any given year. Social Security tax is paid as part of your total federal tax bill.

● **What happens to the money I pay for Social Security? Will I ever receive any benefits?**

Your Social security payments are credited to your account. It is advisable every three years to write the Social Security Administration to see if amounts you paid have been properly credited. Any errors made more than three years ago cannot be reversed.

Your contributions go toward creating credits, against which you will eventually draw benefits. You can obtain an estimate of the approximate dollar amount of those benefits in today's dollars by filing Form 7004 with the Social Security Administration (call your local office to order the form). In four to six weeks you'll receive a computerized summary of credits earned to date along with your projected benefits at retirement (62 years, 65 years, 70 years old).

For general retirement planning purposes, assuming you have been a full-time worker and participant in the Social Security system for thirty years before you retire, figure your monthly budget at 60 percent of your current budget (your home is paid for but medical and travel costs are higher), with Social Security providing only one-third of that amount.

• When am I eligible to claim the earned income credit?

You are eligible for an earned income credit if you have a dependent child for whom you claim an exemption on your tax return and who lives in your home, and you have less than $19,340 in adjusted gross income for 1989.

Look for the separate instructions in the tax instructions to determine the amount of credit you may receive. The earned income credit may result in a refund to you even if you paid no tax through withholding during the year.

• When do I pay my taxes?

Your tax return must be filed by April 15, 1990 (since this day falls on a Sunday, the due date is Monday, April 16) to avoid a late filing penalty. Payment is expected with the return. If you do not have the money, mail the return and the government will bill you. The bill will include penalty amounts calculated through the mailing date plus about ten days.

Mail your tax return on time, even if you do not have the money to pay the IRS. If your return is more than sixty days late, the late filing penalty is $100 or 100 percent of the tax due, whichever is less.

• Do I have to pay estimated taxes?

Yes. The rules on when tax payments must be made have become stricter in the past few years. For 1989, you must pay 90 percent of the actual tax liability or face a penalty for underpaying your taxes and interest on the amount underpaid. Moreover, you must make these payments in a "timely" fashion (that is, pay tax as you receive income). The IRS does give you a $500 "fudge" factor but for most self-employed people, this can easily be eaten up in Social Security taxes.

In 1989 you may be exempt from the penalty for underpaying your taxes if you paid an amount equal to your 1988 tax liability. File Form 2210 with your tax return if you end up owing the IRS more than $500. Form 2210 will tell you if you are considered exempt from that penalty for underpaying your taxes or exactly what that penalty amounts to.

• How do I calculate my estimated taxes?

Form 1040-ES contains instructions on how to figure your 1990 estimated taxes on the basis of your 1989 tax return. The central point is to estimate your prospective income accurately. Since most taxpayers earn approximately the same amount from year to year, this poses little difficulty for the average person. The self-employed person is not as fortunate. He must calculate his net profit at four points during the year—March 31, May 31, August 31, and December 31—and pay, by the fifteenth day of the month following, an amount sufficient to cover his accrued tax liability.

This is a chancey proposition, at best. A safer method is to divide your 1989 total tax liability (line 55 on the back of Form 1040) and divide that figure by four. Each quarter, pay one-fourth of your 1989 tax liability as your 1990 estimated tax payment.

When you file your 1990 tax return you will be underpaid or overpaid. If you have underpaid your 1990 taxes by more than $500, complete Form 2210. You will be exempt from any penalty for underpaying your taxes because you qualify for the exemption that requires a taxpayer to pay at least as much as his previous year's tax liability.

If you find you've overpaid for 1989, roll that money over toward your 1990 estimated tax payments. Then take the 1989 total tax liability and divide that figure by four. Subtract the overpayment from the first quarterly estimated payment. Make up any additional balance due by check and mail that quarterly payment by April 15, 1990 (or, in reality, April 16 because April 15 is on a Sunday). Make the other three required payments and repeat the procedure to exempt yourself from penalty outlined above.

Always be sure to put your Social Security number in the memo section of the check you send, along with the form number and quarter to which the payment is applied—for example, "2 Q 1040-ES." If you're married, enter the Social Security number of the person listed first on Form 1040, regardless of who is self-employed in the household.

● I'm going to be out of the country until May 1990. What can I do about filing my taxes?

If you can't file your 1989 tax return before you leave the country, you are eligible for an automatic extension until June 15. Attach Form 4868 to your completed return and note on it: "Taxpayer in [name of country] on April 15."

Remember that an extension to file a return is not an extension of time to pay the tax. You must be overpaid to use an extension. Underpayment will result in a penalty and interest.

Make sure you make a copy of Form 4868 to use with your state return as well.

● I'm going to be in the United States, but can't get my return done on time. Are there ways I can get an extension past April 15?

Yes. Use Form 4868 to request a four-month extension until August 15. This extension request is automatically granted unless you have an unpaid tax liability.

To file the extension, you need to calculate your probable tax liability for 1989. From that, subtract any payments you've made through withholding or estimated tax payments. If your liability is less than your payments, send the extension form to the IRS; if it is more, enclose a check with the extension form before you send it to the IRS.

Most states accept the federal Form 4868 in lieu of a state form requesting an extension. Make sure you make at least two copies of the original—one to go to the state, and one to file with your return.

● I need to file a state return for a state where I don't live. How can I get the forms?

Write or call the revenue department in that state's capital city and request a nonresident tax form along with instructions on how to complete the form. A written request usually takes two to three weeks to process; a telephone call will get faster results. Make sure you leave enough time to review the form before you must file it in case you need to request additional forms or schedules.

● What are my chances of being audited?

Less than 2 percent of all federal tax returns are audited. States seldom audit returns, relying instead on the IRS to uncover unreported income.

Self-employed people are more likely to be audited than are average taxpayers. The volume of paperwork a self-employed person has to process makes it more likely some information can be lost or ignored. Also, there are few reporting documents to verify the income generated by a self-employed individual. A third reason is that expenses can be padded more easily by the self-employed person than by someone's employee.

Audits tend to occur when income is unreported, when the information on a return is incomprehensible, or when expenses are excessive (as determined by comparisons with other taxpayers with similar profiles). If the problem is small, the IRS may take no action at all. Changes generating less than $50 in additional revenue are forgotten. If more than $50 is involved, the IRS may send you a letter spelling out its case and requesting the additional money. If the amount involved is significant and other problems appear on the return, the IRS may schedule an audit in one of their offices or in your place of business.

Noncompliant taxpayers stand a higher chance of being audited than do regular filers. If you haven't filed for several years, you may be contacted by the IRS because a computer check has turned up your whereabouts. The IRS will file a return for you, without any items that could benefit you, and send you the bill. That forces you to file on your own behalf or to risk having property seized or a lien placed on it. Repeated noncompliance risks imposition of a $500 per year punitive penalty, plus the regular penalty and interest charges for late filing.

● What happens at an audit?

An audit begins with the agent asking you background questions. One of these will be whether or not you belong to a barter or trade organization. You may also be asked about educational background, address and telephone numbers, or employment history. You are asked whether or not you have reported all income received in 1989 on your 1989 tax return.

The audit then proceeds with an examination of the items listed in the letter inviting you to the audit. Respond to the auditor's specific questions. Do not volunteer information. The auditor is in charge. Don't get into power plays over who is controlling the topic or pace of conversation.

The better prepared you are, the neater your records will be and the easier it will be for the auditor to examine the deductions you claimed. It's not to your advantage to toss the auditor your check register and tell her to try to find your telephone expense. If you made an entry on your tax return, you must be able to substantiate that entry.

Have canceled checks bundled together with receipts for each item being investigated. Your objective is to get out of that office with as little damage as possible. If the auditor adds up a bundle of checks and finds a discrepancy between the figure you have on your return and the total, be prepared to explain how and why that mistake happened. Be candid but don't go into too much detail. Blabbing or running on may result in more items being added to the audit list if the auditor suspects other problems.

If the auditor finds several discrepancies, you can bet she will run totals on all the packets you have and may request documentation on items not originally included in the audit list. An auditor can request the information, but if it was not included in the letter sent to you, you have the right to request time to gather those records and bring them in. Be firm in stating your case, reiterating if necessary that you prepared only those items identified in the IRS audit letter.

Most audits last one to one and a half hours. At the end of the audit, you usually know about any discrepancies the auditor has uncovered. If additional tax is owed, you are asked if you agree with the findings. Sometimes you are allowed to pay the undisputed amount on the spot; other times the auditor may need to check with a supervisor to see if the audit results are acceptable to the IRS.

If you do not agree with the findings, you have the option of requesting a second interview, with the same auditor, to bring in the records that will substantiate your case. If you disagree with the auditor's findings because of a different interpretation of the law, then you have the right to appeal to the office supervisor. Going to tax court to argue a point is a third course open to you, but since the minimum fee to file your dispute is $5,000, this is not generally viable for individuals.

Business Organizations

● **I'm currently a sole proprietor. At a recent seminar, a speaker promoted the advantages of incorporating. I'm still in the dark. Can you identify these advantages?**
The advantages to incorporating include some liability protection (less with an S-corporation than a standard or C-corporation), the ability to fund group health insurance plans, larger contribution potential for pension plans, and the deductibility of payroll taxes (FICA, Workers' Compensation, federal and state unemployment insurance).

The disadvantages for most one-person shops include:

—Quarterly filing of payroll taxes, plus unemployment taxes in most states

—The requirement that you have a payroll, even if you are the only employee. A corporate employee can't just draw funds from the corporation, as the sole proprietor can from her business

—Annual meeting of the board of directors

—Separate corporate bank accounts

—Use of the double-entry bookkeeping system

Failure to operate your incorporated business like a regular corporation can result in the IRS denying your status as a corporation. Such a ruling could be retroactive. Losses from an S-corporation, then, which you claimed on your individual income tax return, could be denied.

Generally, if you have a good business reason for incorporating, go ahead and do it. But be prepared to change many of your operating procedures. Never adopt a particular business organization form for tax purposes only.

● **What are the differences among a sole proprietorship, a partnership, and a corporation? What are the advantages of each?**
The grid on the following page identifies the relative advantages and disadvantages of each form.

● **Is there any advantage to being a C-corporation in contrast to being an S-corporation?**
A C-corporation, also known as a standard corporation, provides full protection of your personal assets should the corporation be sued. An S-corporation may provide some or total protection, depending on the way the S-corporation is used. If a business incorporated and operated a scam, its S-corporate election would probably not protect the owners of the corporation, especially if it were a closely held corporation.

C-corporations are subject to minimum corporate taxes, based on revenues, not on net profit.

Corporations become S-corporations by filing Form 2553 with the IRS. This form requires the unanimous approval of all shareholders because the profit or loss shown on the tax return of an S-corporation flows through the corporation to the individual owners, who report the profit or loss on Schedule E of their individual tax returns. A profit may not necessarily have provided any money to an individual owner, but this has no bearing on whether or not the owner pays tax on the reported income amount.

There are rules pertaining to the effective dates of the S-corporation election and the corporation's ability to change from S-corporation to standard corporation and back again. Consult an attorney or your tax advisor.

● **I'm researching the feasibility of starting my own business. What costs are deductible? What if I purchase an ongoing business?**
The costs of starting a business or acquiring an existing business must be amortized over a period of at least five years. Use Form 4562, Part II to calculate amortization. The amortiza-

	Sole proprietorship	Partnership	Corporation	S-Corporation
Owner/principal can draw out funds at will	Yes	Yes	No	No
Files its own tax return	No	Yes	Yes	Yes
Pays income taxes	No	No	Yes	No
Double-entry bookkeeping	No	Yes	Yes	Yes
Uses reimbursement forms	No	Recommended	Yes	Yes
Separate bank account	Recommended	Yes	Yes	Yes
Balance sheet	No	Yes	Yes	Yes
By-laws	No	Partnership agreement	Yes	Yes
Articles of incorporation	No	No	Yes	Yes
May have employees	Yes	Yes	Yes	Yes
Must have employees	No	No	Yes	Yes
Annual meeting to set objectives	Recommended	Recommended	Required	Required
Liability protection	No	No	Full	Conditional
Formal dissolution procedure	None	Final return	Final return plus dissolution docs plus state notice	Final return plus dissolution docs plus state notice

tion expense is then reported on the "other expense" line of the particular tax form being filed.

● **My business partner and I incorporated our business two years ago. Now he says he wants out. What do I do now?**
Find a buyer for his shares or dissolve the corporation. The latter involves substantial work, so don't choose it lightly. In addition to the tax work, however, many business decisions need to be made, including future use of the corporation's name, disposition of assets (including client lists), and future competition between you. It is hoped these issues are dealt with in your corporate bylaws. If not, and the breakup is less than friendly, you may be in for some difficult negotiations.

● **I've heard that you can draw money from an S-corporation, just as you would from a partnership or sole proprietorship, and simply pay taxes on that draw at the end of the year on your personal tax return. Is this true? If so, why don't more people do it?**
It is not true, though there are many people (including some attorneys) who think it still can be done. What's at issue here is a different stress on compliance, not a tax law change. And, since 1987, compliance has focused on conformity among closely held corporations.

A corporation, by its very nature, is a business entity with its own life that is separate and distinct from the lives of its employees. This is true even if the only employee is also the sole owner of the corporation's shares. The corporation has its own identifying numbers, conducts its own business, has its own tax return, and should, if you don't want to run the risk of having your corporate status yanked by the IRS, have its own books, bank accounts, employee benefit plans, annual meetings of shareholders, and employee payroll. It pays taxes a sole proprietorship or partnership would never need to pay.

Part of the confusion over this issue stems from the recent enforcement drive undertaken by the IRS to make partnerships and corporations play by the rules or risk losing their preferential status. Through 1985, it was unheard of for a small partnership or corporation to be audited. The word was that not even the IRS knew enough about these organizations to audit them. Large corporations have always, of course, been subject to audit. Their records are, almost without exception, computerized, and audits focus on their accounting practices and management policies.

Small corporations and partnerships usually have manual accounting systems. Some do not even use a double-entry system. Not schooled as accountants, many small-business owners have improvised as they've kept their books, loaning or borrowing funds from the organization, including questionable expenses, using the corporate or partnership checkbook as a personal account, or having the corporation or partnership pay for expenses on a personal vehicle. The IRS is now treating the small corporation or partnership just like it treats sole proprietorships. Increasing scrutiny of the small-business organization means increasing responsibility for the small-business owner to know the laws and to get those records in shape.

If you can't just walk into a large corporation and take out $500 to get you through the week, why do you think you can do that in your own corporation? That sums up the nub of the compliance argument regarding S-corporations.

● **I'm going to hire my spouse to work in my business so I can have a deduction for his wages but still not have to pay FICA. Is this a good business strategy?**
No. You must pay FICA and withhold taxes for a spouse employed in your business.

● **What is a partnership and how do I set one up?**
A partnership is a working business entity comprised of at least two people. At least one of them must have an active role in running the business. A partnership exists when there is a written or working agreement between at least two people and when that partnership files an informational return (form 1065) with the federal government.

An exception is a business relationship between two or more people in the ownership of residential rental property. This arrangement is not defined as a business partnership, does not require a written business agreement, and is not required to file Form 1065.

A partnership has income and expenses that may result in a profit or loss for the year. The partners share in this profit or loss, via a Form K-1, which is part of Form 1065, to the same degree that they participate in the partnership.

If you establish a partnership, have a written agreement outlining the conditions of working together, including rights and responsibilities. Also identify the length of the partnership agreement, terms under which the partnership agreement can be changed or terminated, and buy-out provisions. This written agreement establishes methods for the reconciliation of future disputes, the addition of other partners, or the sale of the business itself.

Remember that no partnership can adopt a fiscal year different from a calendar year unless more than 25 percent of its revenues are received in the last two months of that fiscal year and have been for all of the past three years.

• Can people invest in my business as a tax shelter?

Yes and no. Your business can serve as a tax shelter if it is a partnership since, in the early years at least, expenses will probably surpass income and the partnership will show a loss. That loss is prorated among the partners and can be deducted by any of them to the extent of their capital investment in your business.

After 1987, their loss on the basis of that partnership is further limited by the amount of passive income they generate from other investments.

If your business is incorporated, an investor can buy stock in it, but this will serve as a tax shelter only if your business fails and the stock becomes worthless. If your business is an S-corporation, any loss or profit will be passed through to the individual owners, much as it is in a partnership, with the same limitations on deductions described above.

If you operate as a sole proprietor, there are no investment write-offs for potential investors.

An important exception to these guidelines is if a family member invests in your business. In such a situation, his write-offs may be further limited by IRS regulations. Consult your tax adviser for specifics on your situation.

• Do I need to have a business plan?

It's a good idea to set annual objectives for your business, mainly because it gives you something to shoot for and something against which to measure your development. A minimal plan would contain financial and personal objectives (such as growth, or the achievement of certain levels of artistry) for one to three years.

Full-blown business plans run as long as 100 pages or more, and describe business philosophy, financial performance history and projections, major actors in the business, and product plans, including the *pro forma* or cash flow scenario for an eighteen-month to three-year period.

A business plan sets down in writing your thoughts about your business at a given time. From that benchmark you can assess your successes and setbacks and gain a better perspective on how you might change your business to accomplish professional or personal objectives.

• What is a net worth statement?

A net worth statement tells a bank or mortgage company how reliable a source of income your business is. It is almost always required if you apply for a personal or a business loan.

The net worth statement details your assets (property, automobile, cash, accounts receivable) and your liabilities (short-term debts, long-term debts, mortgages). Your assets equal your liabilities plus your net worth. Or, net worth equals assets minus liabilities. When you list your assets as of a specified date and follow that with a list of liabilities and net worth, you have created a *balance sheet.*

● **What is the due date for a partnership return?**

Partnership returns (Form 1065) must be filed by April 15 for calendar-year partnerships, or three and one-half months following the close of the fiscal year for fiscal-year partnerships.

Corporate returns (Form 1120, 1120A, or 1120S) are due March 15 for calendar-year corporations, or two and one-half months following the close of the fiscal year for fiscal-year corporations.

Failure to file either return on time may result in a late filing penalty as high as $1,000.

Returns for non-profit corporations (Form 990, 990T) are due May 15 for calendar-year corporations, or four and one-half months following the close of the fiscal year for fiscal-year corporations.

Failure to file Form 990 on time results in a late fee of $10 per day, up to $5,000.

A Quick Guide To Deductibility

Academicians

If you produce art primarily as a professional requirement of your teaching duties, report your art expenses as part of the Miscellaneous deductions on Schedule A. Only that part of your miscellaneous expense total that exceeds 2 percent of your adjusted gross income is deductible.

If you have established marketing channels and an ongoing history of sales of your work, you can instead file as self-employed in addition to your regular employment as a teacher. Use Schedule C to report income and expenses.

Actors

If you are an actor or other public performer who is regularly employed and receives W-2s from two or more employers, you may be able to report expenses connected with your performing (e.g., voice lessons, costumes, makeup, theatre tickets) on Form 2106 and, from there, directly on the front of Form 1040 and thereby escape the 2 percent threshold on deductibility, discussed earlier.

Use Form 2106 to report these professional expenses. If your W-2 income is less than $16,000, you can deduct these expenses without regard to the 2 percent threshold that affects deductibility of miscellaneous expenses. If your W-2 income exceeds $16,000, or if you have only one W-2 employer, these professional expenses are subject to the 2 percent of AGI threshold.

Automobiles

A deduction is allowed for business use of your car. Certain rules apply: 1. you must own the vehicle; 2. you must keep a written record that identifies business use in the context of overall use of the vehicle. Generally this means you must keep a daily log of odometer readings for business use of your car.

The first business trip out each day from your home and the last business trip back each day to your home are considered commuting mileage and cannot be counted in the total number of business miles you drive.

There are two methods of deducting automobile expenses. The first is the standard mileage deduction. For 1989 this is 25.5 cents per mile for the first 15,000 business miles driven (11 cents per mile thereafter). To substantiate this deduction, total business mileage, total personal mileage, and total commuting mileage must be entered on the back of Form 4562. See examples in Part II for proper entries to make on Form 4562 to claim the standard mileage deduction. Without this form, no automobile expense can be claimed on Schedule C.

If you use the standard mileage deduction, you may claim in addition only business parking costs and the business portion of the interest paid on your car loan. All other auto expenses (insurance, repairs, maintenance) are assumed to be covered by the 25.5 cents per mile figure.

Use the 25.5 cents per mile figure until you have deducted 60,000 business miles over the life of the auto. Then the standard mileage rate drops to eleven cents per mile.

The second method of deducting automobile expenses is the actual expense method. This method requires you to keep a daily mileage log plus receipts for all automobile expenditures: gasoline, oil, repairs, maintenance, license plates, and insurance. First you calculate your percentage business use from your mileage log. Then you multiply that percentage business use times the total auto expense. To this expense total can be added business parking fees and interest on an auto loan.

For 1989, all autos are depreciated over a five-year period using the double-declining balance method of depreciation. Luxury cars are subject to special limits on the amount of depreciation allowable each year. See the glossary for more information on depreciation and depreciation of autos.

Once an auto used in business is fully depreciated, only eleven cents per mile driven is allowed as a deduction. Expenses for a leased vehicle are deducted using the actual expense method, with the lease payments replacing the depreciation part of that method.

Bank Charges

Charges on personal accounts are not deductible. Business account charges are deductible on Schedule C if you are self-employed. Charges for mixed accounts (business and personal) are deductible only if the bank charges a per check service fee.

Bankruptcy

Nondeductible. May in some cases lead to taxable income, due to writing off debts. If you are considering filing for bankruptcy, you should consult a tax advisor.

Books

Deductible in year of purchase for self-employed persons (Schedule C) or regularly employed professionals (Miscellaneous section on Schedule A). If you are a photographer and you buy books used in both your regular employment and self-employment, it's more advantageous to deduct the cost of those books on Schedule C. If, however, a particular book deals only with your regular employment, the deduction belongs on Schedule A.

Casualty Losses

Personal itemized deduction on Schedule A only to extent the loss exceeds the insurance reimbursement and 10 percent of adjusted gross income. Use Form 4684.

Business items lost or destroyed through casualty or theft are reported on Form 4684 to determine the loss, and the loss is then transferred to Form 4797 for inclusion on Form 1040. Frequently a casualty loss may turn into a taxable gain due to depreciation taken on an item in prior years.

Child Support Payments

Nondeductible to payer; not income to receiving parent.

Commuting

Defined as the first trip out and the last trip home each day, commuting represents nondeductible mileage for the self-employed and regularly employed alike.

If, however, your business takes you away from the general vicinity of your "tax home" (thirty-five-mile radius) and you do not stay overnight, the mileage you incur is not considered commuting mileage and is, therefore, deductible.

Conferences/ Continuing Education

Deductible if they pertain directly to your business and professional activity. Conference fees are deductible on Schedule C for self-employed people and on Schedule A for regularly employed people.

Travel and lodging costs incurred to attend a professional conference are listed on the "Travel" expense line of Schedule C. Meal costs are only partly deductible, even if the costs are incurred as part of an out-of-town conference.

Conference costs that seem high in the overall context of running your business (e.g., $2,000 in conference fees for a self-employed professional grossing $6,500 in a given year) will invite IRS scrutiny and subject you to questions about whether you are pursuing the activity for profit.

Contributions

Claim a deduction on Schedule A for cash or personal materials given to nonprofit organizations. Contributions of your time and/or artwork are not deductible anywhere, any time. A deductible contribution represents contributions from previously taxed income. If you contribute one of your paintings valued at $500, you never claimed that $500 as income and hence do not have a $500 contribution. You do have a contribution of materials (generally already included on Schedule C) and perhaps some mileage to deliver the donated material to the donee.

Volunteers working in nonprofit organizations can also, on Schedule A, deduct expenses they incur in the act of volunteering. Examples of such costs include airfare to a national conference for board members, or mileage to and from the organization (at the rate of twelve cents per mile).

Costumes

Deductible for actors, musicians, and other public performers. Costumes are defined as clothing that causes you to stand out in a crowd or that is not ordinarily seen otherwise. Furthermore, a costume cannot be converted to standard dress. Hence, tuxedos are not deductible in New York City but are deductible in Des Moines. Corporate suits are not deductible anywhere.

Credit Card Interest

A form of consumer interest only 20 percent deductible in 1989. In 1990, only 10 percent of credit card interest will be deductible; thereafter, no interest deduction is allowed for any kind of consumer credit.

For credit cards used exclusively in business, the interest is fully deductible on Schedule C.

Daycare

Payments made by taxpayers qualify for tax credit. Use Form 2441 to compute. Not deductible as a business expense unless you are the employer who provides the service for your employees' children.

Beginning with the 1989 tax forms, the Federal Employer Identification Number (FEIN) or Social Security number of each daycare provider must be listed on Form 2441 to qualify for the credit. Use Form W-10 to obtain the information you'll need to complete the 1989 Form 2441.

Dependents

Blood relative, relative by marriage, or any other person who lived in your home for a full year whom you support and whose presence does not violate existing law.

Disability Insurance

Not deductible.

Dues and Publications

Dues to professional organizations and associations, and periodicals and publications used in your trade or business are deductible on Schedule C for self-employed people. If you are a regular employee, fees for dues and publications are deductible in the Miscellaneous section of Schedule A only to the extent the total miscellaneous deductions exceed 2 percent of your adjusted gross income.

Education

See Conferences/Continuing Education.

Employees

Wages are deductible, as are amounts paid by employer for FUTA (federal unemployment insurance), FICA (Social Security), Workers' Compensation, health and life insurance, and any pension or disability plans the employer funds. Employees must be sent Form W-2 by January 31 of the following year; the Social Security Administration must receive Form W-3 (as a cover or transmittal document), along with the original (colored) copy of Form W-2 by February 28 of the following year. Other reports required to be filed if you have employees include Form 941 (quarterly report of witholding) and Form 940 (an annual report for FUTA). In addition, state forms for witholding, unemployment insurance, and Workers' Compensation must be completed and filed with the appropriate state agency.

Entertainment

Deductible only if directly related to the production of income and then only 80 percent deductible. Do not include night-clubs, theatre tickets, sports events, cocktail parties, yachts. The IRS has declared that these activities are primarily recreational, regardless of who accompanies you.

You may include the cost of your own meal if there is demonstrable proof of additional cost to you due to the business nature of the outing. You may also include the cost of business gifts (not to exceed $25 per person per year).

Fees

Payments to independent contractors are deductible on Schedule C if payments are made for services incidental to the self-employed person's trade or business.

Fellowship Exemption

Eliminated for 1987 and after.

Foreclosures

See Repossessions/Foreclosures.

Gambling Losses

Deductible only to the extent of winnings on the "other income" line of Form 1040.

Gifts

Not taxable to recipient, not deductible to donor. Current limit is $10,000 per year per person; amounts exceeding $10,000 require donor to file a gift tax return.

Health Insurance

All taxpayers include 100 percent of health care payments on Schedule A. Costs that exceed 7.5 percent of adjusted gross income are deductible. Alternatively, self-employed persons who pay their own health insurance premiums may elect to deduct 25 percent of the premiums on line 26 of Form 1040, with the other 75 percent of the insurance premium cost and other medical costs taken on Schedule A.

Home Mortgage Interest

Reported to the payer on Form 1098 by the bank or mortgage company holding the mortgage to the property. Fully deductible on Schedule A or partly deductible on Schedule C to the extent you claim your office in the home, with the balance deductible on Schedule A.

Home Office

Deductible only to the extent you have a profit. Space must be definable and used exclusively for business. The IRS recognizes two methods of determining the percentage of your home used for business: square footage or number of rooms. Use the square-footage method if rooms in your home are not the same size. Bathrooms do not count in square-foot total or room-number total.

Renters: Deduct a percentage of rent and utilities costs equal to the portion of your residence used for business up to the amount of your net profit prior to the home studio deduction.

Homeowners: Deduct a percentage of mortgage interest, real estate (property) tax, insurance, and utilities costs, plus depreciation, equal to the portion used for business. Don't skip deducting for depreciation to simplify your future tax situation: If you claim home office and deduct a portion of your expenses for everything except depreciation, the IRS will impute that deduction to you at the time you sell your home. Remember that depreciation is an allowed or an allowable expense—take it, or lose it.

Independent Contractors

Persons to whom you pay fees for specific services. Only the fees themselves are deductible by the payer. The payer must issue Form 1099-MISC by January 31 of the following year if payments exceed $600 in a given year to any independent contractor.

Inheritances

Not income to recipient. If property is transferred to beneficiary, value of property listed in estate return becomes beneficiary's basis in property. This is important when the asset is sold because that is when a gain (or loss) may be incurred.

Legal Fees

Deductible to the extent they are related to income-producing activities. Deductible legal fees related to self-employment appear on Schedule C; fees related to regular employment appear on Schedule A as miscellaneous deduction (sum of which is subject to 2 percent of adjusted gross income limit on deductibility).

Local Transportation

Deductible for the self-employed person who uses bus, railway, boat, or auto to travel to work. Not deductible for commuting.

Loans

Not deductible as an expense; not reportable as income.

Loss

There is no tax-deductible loss if a vendor defaults on a payment to you unless you have already counted that payment as income to you. In that case, you are using the accrual system of accounting and have a bad debt. For other information on losses, see the glossary for Capital Gain/Loss.

Medical Expenses

Deductible on Schedule C only if a specific injury occurred in the line of work. Example: An actor who has his teeth punched out while filming a Western could deduct cost of dental repairs and restoration on Schedule C.

Effects of long-term wear and tear, however, are not deductible on Schedule C. Example: Dancers cannot deduct chiropractic fees on Schedule C, or the cost of contact lenses or cosmetic dental work, even though without those services the dancer would be less likely to be employed.

Medical costs (insurance, fees to practitioners, hospital expenses, travel to medical care) are deductible on Schedule A to the extent they exceed 7.5 percent of adjusted gross income. Medical expenses for dependents are deductible. Medical expenses for friends or blood relatives who are not dependents are not deductible.

Moving Expenses

Deductible only if your job moves more than thirty-five miles away, and then deductible only as a miscellaneous deduction on Schedule A. A move for your convenience or preference is not deductible. The move must result in regular employment in 39 of the 52 weeks following the move; for a self-employed person, in 78 of the 104 weeks following the move.

Points

Deductible in year of payment for home purchase if paid by separate check at closing. Not deductible (even if paid by separate check) for home refinancing. Refinancing points must be amortized over the life of the loan. See line 10 of Schedule A. Not deductible at all if rolled over into the mortgage principal.

Political Candidates

Contributions to political candidates and political campaigns are not deductible.

Real Estate Taxes

Also known as property taxes. Deductible on Schedule A.

Repossessions/ Foreclosures

Gain results most frequently from repossession of property or foreclosure on real estate. For a self-employed person using the accrual system of accounting, a repossession will trigger income because a deduction was already taken for the property, even if it was not paid for in full. A gain may also result for a self-employed person who depreciated or expensed the item repossessed.

You must figure your basis at the time of repossession to determine whether you have a gain or loss and how much it is. Foreclosure on real estate also requires calculation of your basis at the time of the foreclosure to determine size of gain.

A loss is possible in the case of a repossession or foreclosure, but it is rare.

Safe-Deposit Box Fees

Deductible on Schedule A only if you keep tax records or income-producing documents in it; deductible on Schedule C only if you use the box to keep your copyrighted work safe from theft or damage.

Sales Tax

A state and/or local tax imposed on sales of goods within a specified political jurisdiction. No longer deductible as a separate item on Schedule A. What is still deductible is the sales tax you pay on supplies used in your business. Deduct this tax as part of the total cost of an item on Schedule C.

Scholarships

Not taxable as income so long as the scholarship pays only for books and tuition. If a scholarship includes a stipend for housing, that portion is taxable income to the recipient. Tuition paid for by scholarships is not deductible as a business or personal expense.

Seminars

See Conferences/Continuing Education.

Start-up Costs

Not deductible in the year of expenditure. Must be amortized over a minimum of five years. Use Part II of Form 4562 for amortization expense calculation. (The annual amortized expense for a sole proprietor is then transferred to the "other expense" line of Part II of Schedule C for inclusion in that year's deductions.)

Tax Preparation Costs   Deductible only as a Miscellaneous deduction on Schedule A, the total of which is deductible to the extent it exceeds 2 percent of adjusted gross income.

Theft   See Casualty Losses.

Travel   Deductible for a sole proprietor on Schedule C only to the extent it pertains to self-employment activities. May be deductible for regular employees whether or not reimbursed by employer. Complete Form 2106 and transfer the allowable deduction to the Miscellaneous section of Schedule A.

Personal travel (recreational or avocational) is not deductible. For travel to be deductible, it must be directly related to an income- producing activity.

To deduct a business trip, you must keep a daily log of your business activities. After the trip is completed, count the number of business days and calculate the percentage of the trip devoted to business. (For trips of seven days or less, only the day you return is automatically counted a business day; for trips of more than seven days, the first and last days are automatically counted as business days.)

The business percentage is multiplied by the cost of the transportation to your destination, then that figure is added to the actual costs you incurred on each of the business days (but nothing for any of the personal days).

Alternatively, you can deduct the business percentage of the travel plus a per diem for meals: fourteen dollars for trips lasting less than thirty days; nine dollars for trips of thirty days or more. Generally, the actual expense method is more advantageous.

Other deductible expenses when you are away from your tax home are cleaning costs, local transportation, tips, and secretarial services.

Examples of deductible travel:
1. Trip to see museums in Chicago as part of required activities of a fellowship you have received.
2. Professional convention.
3. Four scheduled meetings with art gallery directors in New York to set up showings of your works in a three-day period.

Examples of nondeductible travel:
1. Trip to see museums in Chicago (or New York or Rome) for firsthand experience of the art. The IRS will argue, successfully, that you could study it from catalogs or books, or that this is part of your basic education and cannot be deducted as necessary to income-producing activities.

2. Travel to Honolulu in December or January to gather materials for collages. Even if your only sources are in Hawaii, you could order them by mail or pick them up on a family vacation. Not deductible because of absence of specific business schedule and because of overlap with personal vacation.

3. Drop in or casual visit to several galleries while you're in town for your brother's bar mitzvah. Primary purpose for visit is personal.

4. Four scheduled meetings with art gallery directors in a ten-day period. In business, no one hangs around a place ten days because one or two individuals are not available. A tight business trip would accomplish this work in two or three days, maximum.

The primary purpose of travel must be business even to be considered a business expense. Do not try to hook some business function onto a primarily personal trip and expect to deduct it.

The total expenditure on travel is an item watched carefully by the IRS. Your travel deduction is weighed against the normal percentage spent by other professionals in your field. If travel costs you $2,000 and your gross income is only $6,000, the IRS will wonder what prudent business person spends one-third of his total income on travel.

To support your travel deduction, keep a good record of correspondence setting up the agenda for your business trip. This includes copies of letters and notes on telephone conversations. The stronger the documentation, the more successfully you will be able to defend your travel deduction if called upon by the IRS to do so.

Guide To Further Reading

If this book has in any way stimulated your curiosity about taxes and tax law, the following sources can help develop your knowledge of this field.

The IRS publishes two helpful books, available free. The first, Publication 334: *Tax Guide for Small Business*, focuses on the tax issues facing sole proprietors, partnerships, and corporations. Although this book will have more information in it than you can use in your sole proprietorship, it is handy. It contains a variety of completed forms to serve as models as you wade through your own tax return.

The other IRS book is Publication 17: *Your Federal Income Tax*. Like the first publication, this one runs to more than 150 pages and shows how to complete most of the basic tax forms. It is not geared toward self-employment but has useful information about nonbusiness income and deductions.

In addition to these basic booklets, the IRS publishes pamphlets focusing on specific tax issues and taxpayer circumstances. Some of the more popular titles cover depreciation (Publication 534); travel, entertainment, and gift expenses (Publication 463); moving expenses (Publication 521); business expenses (Publication 535); taxable and nontaxable income (Publication 525); business use of your car (Publication 917); and business use of your home (Publication 587). These publications are free.

You can also call the IRS if you have questions on particular points of law or IRS regulations. While the answers will usually conform to the most conservative interpretation of IRS rules and regulations, most service representatives are candid and helpful. Ideally, you will have a tax practitioner or tax accountant who can answer your questions. If not, call the IRS for answers to your specific questions.

On the subject of the business of art, there are a host of books that deal with both basic and sophisticated business issues. The more you read and the more you know about taking care of yourself in business and finance, the better off you'll be.

Index